John Ker

The Victory of Faith

And other Sermons

John Ker

The Victory of Faith
And other Sermons

ISBN/EAN: 9783337160432

Printed in Europe, USA, Canada, Australia, Japan

Cover: Foto ©Lupo / pixelio.de

More available books at **www.hansebooks.com**

THE VICTORY OF FAITH

AND OTHER SERMONS

BY THE
REV. JOHN KER, D. D.

NEW-YORK
ROBERT CARTER & BROTHERS
530 BROADWAY

BY THE REV. JOHN KER, D. D.

1 THE DAY DAWN AND THE RAIN, AND OTHER SERMONS . $2.00
2 THE VICTORY OF FAITH 1.75
3 THE PSALMS IN HISTORY AND BIOGRAPHY . . 1.00
4 SCOTTISH NATIONALITY, ETC. . . 1.00

ROBERT CARTER & BROTHERS.

PREFACE.

THIS volume, now given to the public, cannot be termed posthumous. The sermons were, with only one or two exceptions, selected by the author himself for publication.

It is now fully seventeen years since he published a volume of sermons. It has been a matter of surprise to many, and of regret to still more, that he did not carry out the plan which he was known to have in view, of bringing out a second series. He had abundant and varied stores at command, and had had, besides, every encouragement to do so from the wide circulation and the acknowledged value of the earlier volume. But the reasons for this delay were sufficient to justify it to himself, and to those who knew him most intimately. At the time spoken of, he was beginning slowly to recover strength, after years of forced silence. His pleasure in preaching, always great, increased with returning health, and he could not refrain when he had opportunity from using the living voice for his Master. But strength given forth in this way necessitated rest at intervals, and so the "letter to be written with his own hand" was always delayed.

With all this, however, and with increasing weakness and college work, he rewrote sermons from time to time in the hope of ultimately publishing them; and since his death, which occurred on October 4th, 1886, his friends have thought they would be only carrying out his own intention by issuing a selection from these, adding two or three which had already appeared in print. With one or two exceptions the sermons in this volume have been preached. A peculiar interest is attached to the 17th (The Heavenly Home), as it formed the substance of an address delivered about two months before his death, in a friend's house in the Highlands. It was the last time he was to speak on a theme which, more than most, drew out the powers of his heart and imagination, and it is striking that in this, as in many similar cases, the choice of the last subject for discourse should indicate the growing attractiveness of heaven, and meetness for it.

Those of the sermons which the author had definitely laid aside for publication show that, as in the former series, he aimed at a variety of topics, which would furnish the doubting, the afflicted, the old, the young, the thoughtful and the heedless, with their portion of meat in due season. But if the reader fail to trace the order of arrangement, he will find sufficient unity of thought and feeling in the savour of Christ which pervades the sermons—a unity which at the same time supplies that nutriment by which "all the body by joints and bands having nourishment ministered, and knit together, increaseth with the increase of God."

The proofs have been corrected and carefully revised by the Rev. Joseph Leckie, D.D., of Ibrox U.P. Church, Glasgow, an old and intimate friend of the author, and the Rev. A. R. MacEwen, B.D. Balliol College, of Anderston U.P. Church, Glasgow, a valued friend and attached pupil. To them the relatives of the deceased render sincere and heartfelt thanks for their loving and painstaking labour in this and in other efforts to preserve his memory.

THE HERMITAGE, MURRAYFIELD,
    EDINBURGH, *December* 1886.

CONTENTS.

I.

THE STRUGGLE AND VICTORY OF FAITH.

"And straightway the father of the child cried out, and said with tears, Lord, I believe; help Thou mine unbelief."—MARK IX. 24, **1**

II.

PRAYER FOR A COMPLETE LIFE, AND ITS PLEA.

"I said, O my God, take me not away in the midst of my days: thy years are throughout all generations."—PSALM CII. 24, **18**

III.

THE POWER OF CHRIST'S ENDLESS LIFE.

"Another priest, who is made . . . after the power of an endless life."—HEB. VII. 16, **34**

IV.

INSTABILITY: SOME OF ITS CHARACTERISTICS AND CORRECTIVES.

(FOR YOUNG MEN.)

"Unstable as water, thou shalt not excel."—GEN. XLIX. 4, **49**

V.

BARZILLAI THE GILEADITE.

(FOR THE AGED.)

2 SAM. XIX. 31-40. *Read also* 2 SAM. XVII. 27-29; 1 KINGS II. 7; JER. XLI. 17; EZRA II. 61, ... 67

VI.

TWO MARVELS.

"When Jesus heard it, He marvelled, and said to them that followed, Verily I say unto you, I have not found so great faith, no, not in Israel."—MATT. VIII. 10.
"And He marvelled because of their unbelief."—MARK VI. 6, . . 83

VII.

THE FIRST HOME MISSION.

"Andrew first findeth his own brother Simon, and saith unto him, We have found the Messias, which is, being interpreted, the Christ. And he brought him to Jesus."—JOHN I. 41, 42, . . 100

VIII.

SPIRITUAL JUDGMENT: ITS RANGE, INDEPENDENCE, AND GUIDANCE.

"But he that is spiritual judgeth all things, yet he himself is judged of no man."—1 COR. II. 15, ... 115

IX.

HADAD THE EDOMITE.

(LOVE OF COUNTRY.)

"Then Pharaoh said unto him, But what hast thou lacked with me, that, behold, thou seekest to go to thine own country? And he answered, Nothing: Howbeit let me go in any wise."—1 KINGS XI. 14-22, ... 132

X.

THE CHRISTIAN USES OF LEISURE.

"And He said unto them, Come ye yourselves apart into a desert place, and rest a while."—MARK VI. 31, ... 146

XI.

THE ARK TAKEN AND RETAKEN.

(LESSONS FROM AN OLD DEFEAT AND VICTORY.)

"And the Philistines fought, and Israel was smitten, and they fled every man into his tent; and there was a very great slaughter; for there fell of Israel thirty thousand footmen. And the ark of God was taken; and the two sons of Eli, Hophni and Phinehas, were slain."—1 SAM. IV. 10, 11.

"And when the men of Ashdod saw that it was so, they said, The ark of the God of Israel shall not abide with us: for his hand is sore upon us, and upon Dagon our god."—1 SAM. V. 7.

"So David and all the house of Israel brought up the ark of the LORD with shouting, and with the sound of the trumpet."—2 SAM. VI. 15, ... 162

XII.

THE CRY OF THE ORPHANED HEART.

(FOR A COMMUNION.)

"Doubtless Thou art our Father."—ISAIAH LXIII. 16, . . . 176

XIII.

THE STRUCTURE OF THE BIBLE.

"Thy word is true from the beginning."—PSALM CXIX. 160, . . 186

XIV.

THE WOMAN OF CANAAN.

"Then Jesus answered and said unto her, O woman, great is thy faith: be it unto thee even as thou wilt."—MATT. XV. 28, . 200

XV.

THE LORD'S QUESTION TO MARY.

"Jesus saith unto her, Woman, why weepest thou? whom seekest thou?"—JOHN xx. 15, ... 216

XVI.

THE BEST GIFTS TO BE COVETED.

"But covet earnestly the best gifts."—1 COR. XII. 31, . . . 233

XVII.

THE HEAVENLY HOME.

"In my Father's house are many mansions."—JOHN XIV. 2, . . 247

XVIII.

THE EVENING PRAYER OF CHRIST'S FRIENDS.
(FOR A COMMUNION.)

"Abide with us: for it is toward evening, and the day is far spent."—LUKE XXIV. 29, ... 264

XIX.

CHRIST ABSENT AND PRESENT.
(FOR A COMMUNION.)

"Me ye have not always."—JOHN XII. 8.
"Lo, I am with you alway."—MATT. XXVIII. 20, ... 281

XX.

LIFE ON THE HUMAN SIDE AND THE DIVINE.

"Thou tellest my wanderings: put Thou my tears into thy bottle: are they not in thy book?"—PSALM LVI. 8, ... 290

XXI.

TROUBLE AT THE THOUGHT OF GOD.

"I remembered God, and was troubled."—Psalm LXXVII. 3, . . 305

XXII.

THINGS PASSING AND THINGS PERMANENT.

"And this word, Yet once more, signifieth the removing of those things that are shaken, as of things that are made, that those things which cannot be shaken may remain."—Heb. XII. 27, . 320

XXIII.

THE BETTER RESURRECTION.

"Others were tortured, not accepting deliverance; that they might obtain a better resurrection."—Heb. XI. 35, ... 336

XXIV.

THE COMPLAINT FOR FRUSTRATED AIMS.

"Then I said, I have laboured in vain, I have spent my strength for nought, and in vain: yet surely my judgment is with the Lord, and my work with my God."—Isa. XLIX. 4, ... 353

I.

THE STRUGGLE AND VICTORY OF FAITH.

"*And straightway the father of the child cried out, and said with tears, Lord, I believe; help Thou mine unbelief.*"—MARK IX. 24.

THE greatest of Italian painters has taken this narrative for the subject of the last and greatest of his paintings. It was his dying legacy to his art and to the world. His hand was unable to give it the final touch, and it was carried in procession before him to his grave in the Pantheon at Rome. He has been charged with a violation of the rules of art because the Mount of Transfiguration almost disappears, and he brings the summit with Christ's glory close to the base, where the father is imploring the disciples to heal his child. And this is so far true. He wishes to enclose Christ and man in one scene —Christ in his divine power and mercy, and man in his misery—and so he effaces the distance, and brings them into contact, making the material law yield to the necessities of the spiritual world.

For indeed the Transfiguration gives us a view of the entire mission and work of Christ. We see Him above the world, but not separated from it, surrounded by the prophets of the Old Testament and the apostles of the New, owned by God as his beloved Son, and looking forward to the death which crowns his saving work; while on the earth below there is the demon-stricken child with the anxious father—the tokens of the dreadful power and ravage of sin, where the prince of Evil is, as it were, visibly challenging the Son of God to a contest for the possession of the world. And this history is being repeated all through time till Christ shall come again without sin unto salvation. We have around us human sin and misery in the most varied forms, but we have also the strength and grace of Christ ready to come down, as of old, for help and healing; not as here, first the body and then the soul, but by a more divine order, first the soul and then the body, till at last body and soul are both saved in the day of the Lord Jesus. And we have to add this feature, that we have still within us the same heart of doubt. This man's struggle, is it not a picture of the faith and unbelief which are so often in conflict in our nature? Yet, if we had this man's earnestness, and if we made his prayer our own, we should bring down a grander presence and a mightier power than did the genius of the artist, not the image of Christ but the living Lord himself, to give the victory to faith—" Lord, we believe; help Thou our unbelief." Let us seek to take this prayer as a common human experience, or, at least, an experience of all earnest-minded men.

I. We say, then, that we may learn here, first, that *faith and unbelief are often found in the same heart.* The human heart, small as it is, has a wonderful power of lodging different inhabitants, and lodging them at the same time. It admits fear and hope, jealousy and love, the lowest and most hateful passions and near to them the reproachful thoughts which point us up, in rebuke, to things the most pure and noble. The picture which Milton gives of our first mother sleeping in the garden is true of us. There is the toad-like spirit whispering evil dreams into the heart, and the angel is standing by to keep watch on the tempter. Every day we feel that there is within us what the Bible calls "the multitude of our thoughts." These contrarieties are never more marked than when the heart lodges, as it often does, faith and unbelief. Never probably does unbelief take the whole field to itself at all times. A man can rarely, if ever, reduce himself to a fixed and blank denial of all that lies beyond his senses. The most resolute atheist, who thinks he has reasoned himself into the conviction that matter is the sum and substance of the universe, that the soul is merely a focus of forces cheating itself with a feeling of personality, that God is only man's magnified image in the sky, and eternal life an egotistic fancy, even he has at times his misgivings, or his hopes (which shall we call them?) that there may be more than this. When some exquisite scene in nature makes his heart leap up in answer to a supreme beauty, or when some act of unselfish devotion, pouring out its heart's blood for what is dearer than life, thrills his spirit, he feels for the moment as if the sky held something beyond infinite vacancy, and as if man had something more in him than refined clay. Or take even the man who has not merely said "There is no God," but who has said it with his heart, who has brought his life down to his creed, and wrapped it and steeped it in the world of sense till atheism is his comfort, and eternity his terror; are there not moments in the seasons of the night, and in the awakenings of conscience, when God draws aside the curtain, and looks in with the word, "Thou fool!"—when a past he thought dead starts up and points to judgment, "I will meet thee there"? Atheism, whether it be speculative or practical, can never close the door and windows so fast but that a lightning flash may break through the chinks, and make the man ask, "May there not be something beyond the four walls of this chamber of my thoughts?"

And again, on the other hand, take the man who has the

strongest conviction that there is a soul and a God and a life beyond death, to whom a higher existence is not a thing of reasoning merely, but a thing of experience, who lives as seeing Him who is invisible, who has beheld from a Pisgah summit the spires of the heavenly city, and heard the music of its songs, till the light and harmony have entered his spirit, bringing "joy unspeakable and full of glory"—is he, I ask, always free from doubt? There are moments when the strange portents of evil come to torment him, rising from within, or shot in from without, and the thought is suggested, 'What if all I adore and look for be a vision of the night? what if these glorious hopes are but flashing auroras on the sky, and if no great morning dawn is ever to be spread upon the mountains?' And so the strongest faith may have its moment of doubt. In its clearest and keenest vision a film will pass over it although it is looking at the sun, may we not say *because* it is looking at the sun? The two worlds of faith and unbelief are close to the soul of man. When he is in the dark, gleams from the light will shoot in as if to allure him, and when he is in the light, vapours from the dark will roll in to perplex and tempt him. Every heart knows something of both, and chooses in the end to which of the worlds it will open the abiding entrance. Is it not so?

But it may be that speculative doubts like these are not your particular form of trial. You have no misgivings, or very seldom, about God and the soul and eternity; these things are borne in upon you as sure realities; they come with a weight and pressure from which you cannot escape if you would. But, all the more, painful doubts visit you of another kind, doubts of your personal share in the happiness these truths should bring. There are times when a man is enabled to lay hold with confidence of God as He is made known in Christ, when he can grasp with strong assurance the promise of the forgiveness of sin and life eternal, and when he can look up and say, 'My Father, I know that all things work together for good to them that love Thee, and I feel that Thou hast shed abroad the beginning of this love in my heart.' But then some heavy wave of trial will break over his head, and shake his anchor-hold; or some outbreak of temptation from his own heart will startle him, as if a serpent he thought dead were warmed into life again, till the suggestion comes, What if all my Christian hope be a fancy, and if I have never known in truth the grace of God our Saviour? These are agonising thoughts to some Christians, and there are times of great searching of heart about them. The mountain of their own faith in the Eternal stands strong, but their comfort in it flits across like sunshine and shadow on a changeful day. So, we say, faith and unbelief may be found in some form in every soul of man; there is indeed no Christian out of heaven entirely safe from some seasons of depression, or out of the range of the prayer of this man, " Lord, I believe; help Thou mine unbelief."

II. The second thing we may learn is that *whenever faith and unbelief meet in an earnest heart there will be war.* You see the conflict in the heart of this father. He knew that the life of his child was dependent on his appeal, and his whole nature is stirred by the struggle. And when a man realises what the Bible calls "the powers of the world to come," he finds within himself, as it were, "the company of two armies." There are passions in the human breast which, although wide apart in character, yet may come to terms. A man may reconcile over-vaulting ambition with utter meanness of soul; he may have the avarice of a miser and the vice of a profligate; he may hunger for universal learning, and hold out his hand for a bribe.

"The wisest, brightest, meanest of mankind," is the character given by one of our poets to one of our greatest philosophers. Alexander, Cæsar, Marlborough, Napoleon, are names which remind us that what men call glory may live quietly in the same heart with pettiness, or even baseness. But here are two things, faith and unbelief, which can never come to a settled agreement if men are in earnest, and will seek to understand what the words mean. Let us try to think what the question really is. It is not one of speculative philosophy, or of some scientific theory about stars overhead or strata underfoot, interesting in its own way, but without effect on the life or death, on the hopes or fears of any one of us. The question raised by faith and unbelief not only touches every human being, if he will think of it, but presses upon his whole nature, and penetrates it, and pervades it through and through, with unutterable moment. According as we go to the one side or the other, we shall think differently of ourselves and of every fellow-man, differently of the world and of everything in it, of every child, and what it may become, of every leaf and blossom, and the light in which we are to regard it. It is the question, What purpose does the world aim at? or can we speak of any purpose? Is there an intelligent Maker of the universe, who has an end in view worthy of it and of Himself; or is all that we see a thing of chance or of fate—a ship on a shoreless ocean, drifting no one knows whence or whither, if we can speak of drift where there is no direction, no compass, no star? Is this soul of mine an undying reality, or is it no more than a property of my body, doomed to perish as the atoms fall asunder, a poor *ignis fatuus*, flitting across the night morass which is its birthplace and its grave? The dearest friends with whom soul is knit to soul, are we to bid them an everlasting farewell when death comes? And the most glorious of all concep-

ious, perfect truth and righteousness and purity, are we never to behold their triumph, if triumph they shall ever have? These are questions compared with which all others sink into insignificance, and the struggle in this father's heart is but a token of the war, on a wider and more momentous field, which is waged in the soul of him who realises what is meant by faith and unbelief.

I can imagine, indeed, that in this strange world, where evil has brought in so much bewilderment, there may be earnest men who despair at times of reaching certainty. They become weary of perplexing arguments, and turn the strained thought to smaller but, as they think, surer issues; and they may call this peace, and almost feel, for a time, as if it were so. You have probably seen the picture of a solitary shipwrecked sailor on a raft in mid-ocean, shading his aching eyes with his hand, and searching the horizon for the point of a sail, or for the dim line of land rising above the waste of waters. I can imagine, too, the weary eye, blinded with the glare, or with its own moisture, turning for relief to the little objects round him, to the structure of his raft, to the ripple of the water on its side, or the scream of the sea-bird as it circles overhead. But when his far-off home rises once more to his thought, when the vision of his father or his child flashes on his heart, his eye will once more sweep the wide sea with the question, 'Shall I never see them again, and sink in this gulf alone?'

And so there may come times to a man, and times to the world, when a kind of apathy about these higher questions of God and the soul seems to dull the earnestness of the struggle, when the furniture of the raft on which men are floating appears the chief concernment; but when the soul returns to itself, and feels the need of a Father, the longing for a home, the horror of engulfment in a sea which never restores its dead, then earnestness will revive, and the battle of faith be again renewed. Whatever be the case with some for a time, those who have realised the greatness of the issue will feel that there can be "no discharge in this war."

III. We may learn, further, to foretell *how the war will go, by the side which a man's heart takes.* If you look at the prayer of this man you will see that, though it is very brief, you can judge from it how the conflict is to end. The man puts himself on the side of faith; he throws the weight of his personality into this scale. He says, "Lord, I believe." He does not mean that the unbelief is not his also; no, it belongs to him with its guilt and loss and pain, but he looks on it as a stranger and enemy from which he seeks to be delivered. 'I, myself,' he says, 'am on the side of faith; my deepest nature trusts and hopes and cries to God; Lord, *I* believe; help Thou mine unbelief.' The man who can say this with a true heart is within sight of victory. And in these days of doubt and denial we can almost predict how some men will decide. External reasons and arguments are necessary. They guide us to the place where we make trial of truth in our own experience, and attain to full conviction. We could not reach faith against these reasons; and we could scarcely reach it without them; but after the help of God's Spirit, of which we do not here speak, our faith is determined by the attitude and inmost bent of the soul itself. When a ship is making for the harbour, there is a set in the tide which may carry it straight for the entrance, or to the treacherous quicksands, or to the boiling surf. And there is such a set of the tide in a man's own heart, only that here it is not without but within him; it is acted on by his will, and therefore he is responsible for it. A man cannot use his will directly so as to cause himself to believe or not to believe, but he can use it, in the language of the Bible, in those "things which accompany salvation." We cannot reverse the tide, but we can employ the sails and helm, so as to act upon it. How, then, may we know whether the heart is tending to the side of faith? One token is, that there should be a sense of reverence proportioned to the momentous character of the issues. Easy indifference, light flippancy, superficial glances cast at little incidents and small angles of the subject, can never fit a man for judging the questions of faith and unbelief. The weight of the soul must be felt if we are to decide rightly on its interests. It must be to us what this man's son was to him, an object of deep concern. Another token of this set of the heart is that there should be some sense of need, a feeling that the soul is not sufficient for its own guidance and happiness without help—a pitying, tender care for our soul that should lead us to look out, and up, and cry for aid. And still another token is that there should be some sense of sinfulness, a conviction of the gulf between what we should be and what we are. "They that be whole," the Saviour has said, "need not a physician, but they that are sick." The moral disorder that is around and within us must make itself felt by thoughtful men, and it is not asking too much that we should do for our soul what this man did for his suffering child—that we should seek with earnestness for some means of cure. Reverence, humility, and a sense of sin, these are some of the tokens by which we may discover the bent of the heart toward faith. In these the man is already beginning to say, "Lord, I believe." It may be said that in this we are prejudging the question, and bribing the reason. But the answer is, that while reason has its own part to perform, it must approach it in the right spirit, and it must have before it all the facts of the case.

It advances to science by carefully studying the nature of the external world; and it can advance to faith only by a humble and reverent study of man's inner nature, by listening to the heart and spirit when they give their deepest utterances. The way to God begins in what is most profound in our own souls, and when we have been led by God's own hand to make discoveries of our weakness and want and sin, we learn to say, "Out of the depths have I cried unto Thee, O Lord." When we see a man dealing with the questions of faith and unbelief in this spirit, we can tell how the war will go.

And yet, with all this, we would not forget that there are some who do not find at once the faith which they are seeking. They have been inquiring earnestly and reverently; but they cannot grasp as they would wish the conviction that there is a God and a soul and an eternal world. There must be some path for such to walk in, and I think it is here. If you cannot yet say, 'I believe in God and in eternal life,' yet there are things in which you do believe. There is truth, and righteousness, and lovingkindness. These things you reverence and believe in, else you are dark indeed. You may not be able to say, 'I practise them,' but you can surely say 'I have faith in them.' Begin truly the practice of that in which you believe, and you will grow from faith to faith. Live as if there were a God, and you will come to know that there is a God. "If any man will do his will," even though he may be uncertain for a time that it is his, he shall come "to know the doctrine that it is of God."

But it may be, as already said, that your struggle is not so much to be sure of these primary truths as to be assured of your own individual interest in them. Now, here again we may know how the war will go by the side the heart takes. If men wish with all their heart to be Christians, they have the life of Christianity already begun. It is true they may not see this, and they would be afraid to say it. What is wanted is the power to realise it. Put, then, the desire to be a Christian into the first duty which falls to you, and put it into duty after duty, quietly and perseveringly, with the help of God. This is what the Bible calls "living a life of faith," and it is by living that we feel sure we are in life. We reach the conviction that we are Christians, not indeed by the merit of our Christian life, but by the experience of it. In the degree in which the Spirit of Christ rises up and lives in us, we know that we belong to Him. "Then shall we know if we follow on to know the Lord : his going forth is prepared as the morning."

IV. The last truth, therefore, to be learned from this history is that *the way to be sure of the victory of faith is to call in the help of Christ.* You see what the appeal to Christ did for this man—how it settled the wavering war, and gave him the desire of his heart; and we cannot, perhaps, illustrate this part of the subject better than by looking at his conduct, that we may benefit by his example. We may learn, then, from him to go straight to the Lord Jesus Christ himself. The disciples, no doubt, did their best, and they were of service in their own way. When they could not cast out the evil spirit themselves, they could save the man from sinking into utter despair; they could bid him be patient and hopeful, and could point up the mountain to the Lord, who was about to descend and do what was beyond their power. But when the Lord himself appears, the father must pass through the disciples to their Master—"I spake to thy disciples that they should cast him out; and they could not." Now, it may be that you have been seeking help from others than Christ himself. His disciples first met your view, and you did not see Him; you only heard of Him from them, but you did not come into personal contact with Him. You may have applied to the Church, but it has no salvation in its own hand; at best it could only point you to Christ. You may have had recourse to the law and its precepts. They are "holy and just and good;" but they have no blessing for a sinner, and the law could only be your schoolmaster to bring you to Christ. You may have turned your steps to the doctrines of the Bible. They are excellent; but without Christ himself they are merely words; they are of value only in as far as they present Him. And so from disciple to disciple you may go, to find that you must press into the presence of the Lord Jesus—"Lord, to whom shall we go? Thou hast the words of eternal life." Christ is saying to churches, to precepts, to doctrines, to all ordinances and means of grace, "Bring him unto Me;" and we shall find full deliverance and rest only when we come to the Saviour himself, and feel ourselves in personal contact with his person and his life.

But what is there in Christ to attract us? We may discover it also, I believe, in this narrative. We cannot say that this man knew it all as we may know it, but the heavenly forces of Christ's nature were there, meeting him and making themselves felt. If the brightness of his transfiguration was no longer visible, as that of Moses' face when he came down from the mount, there was a power in his words and look which amazed the people, and which gave confidence to the father of the child that Christ had help for him in his hand. And there was a pity in his tones and bearing, which drew the heart of this man to Him with a hopeful trust. This majesty and this mercy of Christ were brought home, we cannot doubt, by his own secret impulse. Though He had not yet begun to draw all men by his cross and by his Spirit, He was beginning the work on one and another, to show what He was about to do. Now, these are the two things in Christ which are to attract us still. We cannot read his words, and look on his face, as they are presented to us in the Gospels, without being struck with the superhuman purity and dignity of the Son of God; and we cannot help feeling at the same time the tender sympathy of the Son of Man, who " takes our infirmities and bears our sicknesses." Not in all the histories of mankind has such a portrait of divine purity and love ever been offered to the world as in the recorded life and death of Jesus Christ; and even those who will not bare their feet before it, as holy ground, have turned aside to look on it as a great sight. But if He guides us by his Holy Spirit we can see more. We can ascend the Mount of Transfiguration, and behold his glory as of the only-begotten of the Father, and we can hear the subject of the discourse when "He spake of his decease which He should accomplish at Jerusalem;" we can go further still, and stand before his cross with the words, " Truly this was the Son of God "—and, " He bare our sins in his own body on the tree." To come to a Saviour who is almighty in power and all-merciful in heart, to whom the throne belongs of right, but who chose the cross that He might make his throne the seat of pardon and eternal life—this is the way to the Rock of security, where we can at last say, " We have the witness in ourselves; God hath given to us eternal life, and this life is in his Son." As the life rises in the soul, we become assured that this could proceed only from God in the most divine manifestation of Himself, and we can part with our doubts when we come, like Thomas, to the crucified and risen Saviour, " My Lord, and my God!"

Yet how are we to be drawn to the fulness of this life of faith in Christ, so as to realise it? We do not speak here of God's part directly in the work of his Spirit, but of the part He assigns to us in our conduct and character. Here also we may learn from this man. He came burdened and bowed down with care about his child, thinking little at first of his own spiritual need. But Christ did not reject his natural affection, He made it the step to a higher possession; He did not bid him forget his son, but He taught him to look in upon his soul. And you must have remarked in most of the cures Christ wrought that He began with the relief of some outward affliction, and, having guided the faith of the sufferer to Himself, He then taught it to look to Him for a greater deliverance. He employed his sympathy with what is human to lead men up to the divine. It was for this that He was "God manifest in the flesh." And if there be any who are pressed down by the weight of some trouble for which they can find no cure within or around them, let them know that they are invited to bring this at once into the presence of Him who is the God of the spirits of all flesh, and who sent his Son in our nature to assure us that "He knows our frame, and remembers that we are dust." Confidence in God is not to be learned apart from life, but in it, by taking our first care, whatever it may be, and committing it to Him as a faithful Creator, and as we have been led to Him through Christ. He may not at once remove the burden, but He will give you strength to bear it; and if He keeps it for a while resting on you, it is to lead your heart inward that you may ask of Him strength of soul, as this man did. It is in this way that Christ conducts us from faith to faith. He is a living, personal Saviour, and we must go to Him in living, personal acts. We get to know and trust Him not in some abstract, theoretical way, but in the duties and trials of our daily life. If we have reason to believe that we have carried to Him not only our sorrows but our souls, this is still the means by which our faith is to grow up into a sense of surer reality. Whatever, then, be thy trouble, whether of body or mind, of family or estate, something which man can see and estimate, or something known only to thyself and the Searcher of hearts, or something which thou thyself canst feel but canst not fathom, bring it to Him, and seek to bring also thy soul with all its sins and shortcomings. He makes thee welcome to come as thou art, and when thou dost feel the comfort and strength which He provides, thy faith shall gain a growing power. The way to be sure there is a God is to admit Him into the soul; the way to be persuaded there is a Saviour is to accept his help.

But still, with all this, some one may be saying, 'When I turn my eye in this way within, the first thing that meets me is this weak and wavering faith of mine. I wish I could strengthen it, that it might have power to lift my sins and sorrows into the presence of Christ. Can you tell me of any means by which I may acquire the faith which shall carry my soul to Him?' Now, if we look to the example of this man, we shall again be helped. For, see, he does not continue fighting out the question in his own heart, answering reasons with reasons. He brings not only his trial to Christ, but his faith, or rather his want of faith. He seems to have no more of faith than suffices to cry out and pray against his unbelief. It is like the ship when the disciples were contending with adverse waves, ready to sink, and there was only light enough to look to Christ—

> "Watcher in the night!
> When the billows' might
> O'er the heart's frail bark is sweeping,
> Let my faith be in thy keeping;
> Lose me not from sight,
> Watcher in the night!"

Now, what the Church of Christ wants, and what all of us individually want, is to bring the reasonings and doubts of the heart into the presence of Christ himself. When we turn our back on Him, we are toward darkness; when we look to Him, we are lightened. God means that sunshine should remove mists, and that Christ should take away doubts. There is an endless depth of meaning in the saying of the Psalmist, "With Thee is the fountain of life: in thy light shall we see light;" and it has been applied by the Evangelist to Christ, "In Him was life; and the life was the light of men." If, with all the reasonings we employ, the Church of Christ were to cry more earnestly to Him for the life He gives, she would confirm herself, and she would do much to convince the world. It is ordained that the strongest life should conquer, and the strongest life is surely the Divine. And if there are men who have lost their faith, or fear they are losing it, while they deplore the loss, let them cry toward that quarter of the heavens where they once felt as if light were shining for them, and an answer will in due time come. Christ is there whether they see Him or not, and He will hear their prayer though it has a sore battle with doubts. Let a man only say, 'If there be a God, it must be his wish that I should know Him and love Him, if not for his own sake, yet for mine; if there be a Christ, it must be in his heart to hear me and help me, for I do deeply need his help; and so I will make this man's prayer my own, and I will press it as if I saw Christ himself. If Thou canst do anything, have compassion on me and help me.' All that we can read or think of Christ shows that He must be willing to give final victory to faith. It is for man's truest good and God's highest glory that we should come to God believing that He is, and that He is a rewarder of them that diligently seek Him. He has an eye for it in its deepest weakness, "If ye have faith as a grain of mustard seed." He encourages it even when He rebukes its faintness, "O thou of little faith, wherefore didst thou doubt?" He prays for it when it can scarcely pray for itself, "Satan hath desired to have you, that he may sift you as wheat; but I have prayed for thee, that thy faith fail not." Therefore let us make this prayer more than ever ours, since Christ himself is praying with us. There are many short prayers in the Gospels put there for those who have weak hearts and short memories, or who may need a brief, strong word to send up to God in the press of life and the thick of battle. For the man who is ready to sink, "Lord, save me, I perish!"—for the man who is struggling with darkness, "Lord, that mine eyes may be opened!"—for him who longs for purity, "Lord, if Thou wilt, Thou canst make me clean!"—for him who is looking death in the face, "Lord, remember me when Thou comest into thy kingdom!" But here is one which is needed for them all, and suited to every heart, "Lord, I believe; help Thou mine unbelief." It comes far down like the Lord Jesus Christ himself, stretches out a hand of help to the feeblest, and secures at last an answer to all the other prayers of the Word of God. If men will use it truly, it will give power to the faint, and to them that have no might it will increase strength, till it issues in the full confidence, "I know whom I have believed, and am persuaded that He is able to keep that which I have committed unto Him against that day."

II.

PRAYER FOR A COMPLETE LIFE, AND ITS PLEA.

"I said, O my God, take me not away in the midst of my days: thy years are throughout all generations."—PSALM CII. 24.

This is a prayer which springs from the bosom of the Old Testament, and it bears the impress of its time. Life and immortality had not yet been brought to light; and long life in the land which the Lord their God had given them was a special promise made to these ancient saints. The prayer looks to that promise. The man asks that he may not be cut off prematurely from the work and enjoyment of life in this world. It is thus the request for a complete life. But he is a believing man who submits his wish to the will of God, and who is ready to accept life in the form in which God orders it. He feels that there can be no real life without God, but that with Him it is certain to have a perfect and happy issue. In such a prayer, then, a future and eternal life is implied. The desire for it is struggling in the man's soul, though the full vision of it has not yet opened before him. When the Gospel comes, and shows us eternal life in Jesus Christ, it merely unfolds into flower and fruit the germ which is already contained there. We shall avail ourselves of the light of the Gospel to explain what the meaning of this prayer is, and on what ground it is urged. Our subject briefly stated, then, is—a Complete Life, and the Plea for it.

I. WHEN IS IT THAT A LIFE MAY BE SAID TO BE COMPLETE?

And here we may observe, that while length of life in this world is not the chief blessing of the New Testament, there is nothing wrong in desiring it, and that, when well used, it may have on it special marks of God's wisdom and kindness. The love of life is natural, for God has given us a strong attachment to the world where our eyes have first opened on this beautiful earth and pleasant sunlight. He has surrounded us with families and friends, whose love makes existence sweet. There are duties to be performed in which we feel we are needed, and spiritual interests to be fixed and promoted before we enter with full acquiescence on the great and untried scenes that lie beyond. Length of days, like every other possession, like power or wealth or intellect, is a gift to be employed in God's service—the woof on which a good man may weave valuable material, and many rich and fair colours. And yet we must remember that long life has not always been granted to some of God's truest friends. Even in the Old Testament there is the lesson that a complete life does not need to be a prolonged one; the very first death recorded, that of Abel the righteous, was sudden and premature. Enoch lived but a short time on earth compared with his contemporaries, and Elijah was called away before his natural powers had failed. It is enough to mention Abijah the son of Jeroboam, and the good Josiah, and to remind you, above all, that our Lord and Master, the central life of God's entire Word, was cut off long ere He had reached the midtime of his days. It is necessary, then, in speaking of a complete life, to find those elements that will suit either him who has come to his grave in a full age, or the young who have been taken away in the beginning of their days. We thank God that in his Word we can find a goal, where the old and the young may meet in a complete and perfect life.

1. The first thing needed to gain this is that a man should have lived *long enough to secure God's favour.* Until he has found this he has not attained the great end for which life has been given to an intelligent and responsible creature. Whatever else a man may possess in this world—its power, its fame, its riches, its learning—if he has not entered into the favour of God, if he is not living in his fellowship, he has not seen life. Its palace gate has not been opened to him, its light has not visited his eye, its pulse has not begun to beat in his heart. He is less the possessor of what he calls his own than Belshazzar was of his kingdom when his dethronement was being written on his palace wall; as little as a dead Pharaoh in his pyramid was lord of the treasures of Egypt. The favour of God alone can make anything on earth truly ours, and truly good; can give permanence to what is good, and render it a foretaste of things infinitely better. Whensoever a man dies without this, he is taken away in the midst of his days, hurried out of existence before he has secured its one grand prize. Death draws the curtain at midnight and breaks his dream: "Thou fool, this night thy soul shall be required of thee; then whose shall those things be which thou hast provided?" But if God's favour has been gained, we can rejoice in the blessed equality of all who reach it. "The child dies an hundred years old;" the youth comes to his grave "in a full age, like as a shock of corn cometh in, in his season." We lament early Christian deaths as untimely, but in that favour of God which is life every term attains maturity. Some find the gate of heaven by a short path, while others enter after long years of toil and travel. While some of us continue careful and cumbered about many things—an honourable work if we do not complain of it—there are those who go in and sit down at once at the feet of Christ, when they

have found "the one thing needful, the good part which shall not be taken away." Let me ask myself, Can I say that death shall find my life thus complete? There is but one way of assurance. It is through laying hold of that Saviour of whom it is said, "Ye are complete in Him;" who offers Himself freely to our acceptance with the words, "He that findeth Me findeth life, and shall obtain favour of the Lord."

2. A complete life has this in it still further, that *it has done God and his world some service*. We are here not merely to find God's favour, but to do God's work, to be followers of Christ, who said, "I must work the works of Him who sent Me, while it is day." His was the one great, perfect life, which never spared a labour, never missed an opportunity, and looking back on which He could say so calmly, "It is finished." How far we are from filling up that model! How ready, while the bridegroom tarries, to slumber and sleep, and awake with a start because we have let the supreme moment take us unawares! And, therefore, there are degrees of completeness even in Christian lives. They all reach the haven, but some of them with fuller sail and richer freight. The salvation in the great day will be to all God's people of free grace, and yet we must believe that its rest will be sweeter to the wearied labourer, and the enjoyment greater to him who brings home sheaves which are the fruit of tears and toil. "They joy before Him according to the joy of harvest." But withal, and in view of those who have reaped long and largely, it is a comfort to think that no true Christian life is passed in vain. God will not terminate it till it can appear before Him in Christ's own spirit, "Behold, I and the children whom Thou hast given Me." Stephen's Christian life was short, and yet what ends it gained! The dying thief's was still shorter, but how many sermons

his words have preached to dying men! The child that Christ takes into his arms, through death, from its mother's bosom, can be made to draw the heart to the heavenly kingdom, and when we can do no work, but only lie passive in his keeping, we may be fulfilling purposes of far-reaching wisdom and mercy. It is a view of the coming judgment, as wonderfully tender as sublime, that what Christians forget Christ remembers and reckons up, as done to Himself—the cup of cold water given in his name. It may stir us up, if we are indolent, to be active; it may persuade us, if we are weak and helpless, to lie resignedly still; it may encourage us to cast over our imperfect past his perfect righteousness, and to dedicate our feeble all to his service, when we have the assurance that whether the life be long or short, He will make it "neither barren nor unfruitful in the day of the Lord Jesus."

3. The next thing we mention in a complete life is that *it should close with submission to the call of God.* Even a good man may not always be ready for this. Warm hearts and active natures are sometimes so interested in the friends and work around them, that it is hard to find an open place for parting. The speaker in this psalm felt it so, and Hezekiah likewise when he wept sore against the door of death. Yet God has his own way of making such as these resigned, and He doubtless does it in the secret of his presence, when we cannot hear their words of consent. But it is more pleasant to us when we hear from the lips, or see from the bearing, the act of self-surrender. Joseph reached it when he said so simply and quietly, "I die, and God will surely visit you;" and Moses when, leaving his great labour and wish unfinished, he looked up and touched completeness in that word, "Thou art a Rock, thy work is perfect." We have lived long enough when we can tranquilly give up the problem

we have been working at to God, that He may complete it, when we can rest assured that He will still be a God to us, and to our friends, though He makes death for a while divide our paths; and that his way to the triumph of his cause can be over the graves of his servants, with a banner that never droops though the hands of all of us relax their hold. This submission may be gained through the long experience of the Christian life; it may be witnessed in the quiet peace with which the setting sun falls aslant on the softened look and silver hair, but it is granted often to those who close their eyes on a beautiful dawn, or bright noonday, as unrepiningly as if they had seen all God's goodness in the land of the living. There is a dew of youth that exhales in sunlight, as there is a dew of nightfall that waits for the morning. It comes, like God's dew, always from a clear sky, and tells of his completed work. The man is not torn from life, but loosed. He signs his own name beneath God's discharge, and goes to other work which is ready for him. The great Roman general gathered his robes round him under the strokes of his enemies, covered his face, and sank like a conqueror rather than a victim. But in that same Rome there was a nobler farewell to life when the apostle said, "I am now ready to be offered, and the time of my departure is at hand;" and when he invited all to share in it "who love Christ's appearing." For still, when any one has learned at God's call to gather in human desires and hopes, and to put them in his hand, and has been seen, not with covered but open face, to meet the last enemy, his life is complete, for he is ready and willing to die.

4. The last thing we mention in a complete life is that *it should look forward to a continued life with God.* Without this, all we have spoken of would be incomplete. What

estimate can I set on God's favour if it lifts me up to the view of Divine loving-kindness, only to let me fall into nothingness? What deep interest can I be taking in the cause of truth and righteousness, if I have no care about seeing its progress and triumph? And how can I be ready to give up my earthly life at God's call, if I am bidding an eternal farewell to God himself? Would it not be of all things the most imperfect and unnatural that a man should be a friend of God, and take delight in approaching to Him, and conversing with his thoughts as they speak to us in his Word and in his works, and that the man should feel, at every moment, that all this can be broken off for ever? that he should have a view of a universe of truth and beauty and goodness, opening up through parting clouds—of a divine purpose working to a far-off end which he knows and feels must come, and that he should lay down his head in the dust of utter forgetfulness, and be willing to have it so? Then, the higher the form of life the more miserable its issue. There are many bitter farewells in our world, but we can bear them all if we do not need to bid farewell to God; for to live with Him is to preserve the hope which shall restore all we meanwhile lose. But the thought of such a farewell has in it the proof that its reality is impossible. Where God shows his face, opens his heart, to a man, it is the seal of eternal life. This gift and calling of God is without repentance. And herein we have the assurance of the final completeness of a life. There is room here for rectifying all that is wrong, for supplying all that is wanting, for doing to us above all that we ask or think. It meets the longest life and the shortest with the same promise of perfection. Our night taper lasts long enough if it lets in the eternal day. "He asked life of Thee, and Thou gavest it him, even length of days for ever and ever."

II. We come now to consider THE PLEA FOR A COMPLETE LIFE WHICH THIS PRAYER CONTAINS.

The Psalmist contrasts his days with God's years, his being cut off in the midst of his days with those years that are throughout all generations. There is deep pathos in it, a sense of his own utter frailty and evanescence. And yet in the heart of it there is faith and hope. It is an appeal to God as the possessor of a complete life in the most absolute sense, the inhabitant and owner of eternity. 'Thou hast thine own perfect and everlasting existence; give to thy creature a share in it, according to his nature. He thirsts for life and comes to the fountain of it. Here in thy world, or elsewhere, if it may be, let him live in thy universe and look up to Thyself.' In putting this plea beside the prayer, we do not in any way strain the meaning of the passage. Let any one read this psalm attentively, and he will feel that this is its entire bearing. We have a man to whom life, as he sees it behind and around him, is broken and disappointing. His body, his spirit, his earthly relationships, the cause of God so dear to his heart, are falling to decay. What can he do but turn to God himself? What but hold fast by his eternity and unchanging purpose? In the mind of an ancient believer the prayer had reference, first and most clearly, to this present world; in our view it has widened to the full expectation of a world to come. But, by whomsoever presented, it expresses the instinctive aversion of man to give up a conscious and personal existence. It is a cry from the profoundest depths of the soul to be preserved from extinction, and it is a cry to its Maker founded on his nature as the living, everlasting God. Let us look at some thoughts implied in this plea.

1. The eternal life of God suggests the thought of his *power to grant this request*. He is the possessor of indepen-

dent and everlasting existence, and can share it with his creatures as seems good to Him. "He only hath immortality," that is, He only, as no one else. It belongs to Him, underived, unconditioned, held by no will, ruled by no law out of Himself. But, as we see, He is a generous giver; it is his nature to be not only living, but life-giving. In his hand is the breath of all that lives, and the soul of all mankind. And they take from Him not so much as the showers of the earth do from the waters of the ocean, or the rays of the sun from the brightness of his orb; for these draw from the substance of their source, but the creatures of God derive being from his will, and leave Him unchanged and unchangeable. No one can rise to this view of God, without feeling that it is in his power to bestow life in higher and more enduring forms than any that are seen around us. Would it not be a most unnatural and irrational limitation of the Eternal Source of being, to affirm that He can give origin only to kinds and measures of life such as appear in this world, that He can be the parent merely of creatures that die? If this world shows us the extent of his ability to be the Giver of life, it may be said that death more than life is the sign of his workmanship. The graves have long since far outnumbered the living inhabitants; and existence, in the highest modes in which we are acquainted with it, is so brief, so troubled, so occupied with thoughts of its own preservation, and fears of its extinction, that life can scarcely be enjoyed in the anticipation of the loss of it. An eternal and conscious Author of the world must surely have ability to pass beyond the limits of our narrow experience, and must have some means of answering the cry of his intelligent creatures, that "they may have life, and that they may have it more abundantly." This cry, so deep, so constant, whence does it come if it is not of his own prompting, and shall not the everlasting God be able to satisfy the desires He suggests? When we think of it thus, the tokens of his quickening and preserving power in nature come to sustain us. We can look not at the side of death but of life in them, at sunrises and springs and perpetual renewals, and we can reason that He who gives life in such wonderful profusion can bestow it in still more glorious and permanent forms. "O Lord, Thou preservest man and beast. Therefore the children of men put their trust under the shadow of thy wings. For with Thee is the fountain of life; in thy light shall we see light."

2. The eternal being of God suggests the thought of his *immutability to secure the request*. The unchangeableness of God in the midst of all the changes of our life is a deep source of comfort. Those ancient saints dwelt upon it more than we seem to do, and they were made very strong by it. It consoled them in the absence of the clear view of their own immortality; it was the soil in which the seed of it lay, and to which we should still seek to carry down the roots of our faith. Beneath this shifting face of things, where we look on endless change, there is a great Life that is not only the source but the sustenance of ours, a Life that is not blind and purposeless, but conscious and wise. It is not merely a Life, but an ever-living One, and it is in his bosom that we are born and live and die. We have many deaths before we come to the last—some of them which seem sorer than even the last can be—deaths of desires, deaths of hopes, deaths of friends. And yet, if we have carried them to God, there has come, from these deaths, a life, some new and higher hope, some deeper and richer possession of the soul. Amid these changes we have felt that we were taking in something unchanging, felt, at least, that there was something unchanging which could be taken in. And this may give

us the hope that the last change will have a like result, the last death a corresponding life to us. We may have the confidence of this, if we realise the thought of an ever-living God, who not only gave being to our souls, but holds them in his hand, and puts into them desires after Himself. All the changes, whether of life or death, cannot affect our relation to Him, except in bringing us nearer. Without an eternal God, what refuge would there be for troubled souls? When the sea is tempest-tossed, we flee to land; when the land quakes, we look to heaven; when all things are dissolved, then to Him who says, "I am the Lord, I change not." We may lie quietly down in our little earthly homes when we have the overarching sky of God's hand above us, the shadow of the Almighty; and we may lie down hopefully in our graves when we commit ourselves to an unchanging God. "The eternal God is thy refuge, and underneath are the everlasting arms."

3. Still further, the thought of God's eternal being suggests his *Divine consistency as an encouragement to this request*. He has done so much, that we may infer He will, if we ask Him, do still more. Man's wish for immortality does not, as some say, spring from a mere animal craving, from the love of living on, but from his being made able to conceive of an endless existence. The lower creatures have no such desire, because they have no such conception. But man can conceive of endless existence as in the possession of one great, personal Being, and may plead for it on the ground that he has been made capable of looking forward to it. It could not be his Maker's design to tantalise him with a vision of what is for ever unattainable, to show him the glory of an endless life, and then to say to him, 'This shall never be thine—no more of life for thee than this drop with which I now touch thy lips, and which awakens in thee the thirst to live on.' What a universe

would such a thought present to us! a God who drinks of the golden cup of immortality all alone, in full view of creatures whom He tempts with its sparkle, to whom He shakes some scattered drops from the brim, while they beg for more that they may not die, and beg in vain! For, let it be considered that the life they ask, if it be a true request, is not a mere life of animal existence. There are ties formed here between soul and soul that cry out for an eternity to be renewed in, and better never to have known hearts so tender and true than to feel that we have bidden them an everlasting farewell. There are questions raised about the problems of being, the wisdom, the justice, the goodness of the arrangements of this universe, which our little life cannot answer, and which knock with an imperious demand at the eternal gate. Above all, there are the aspirations of the spirit after the infinite Friend and Father, for which we thank Him most, if He has stirred them within us, and which we know to be deep realities, longings that draw down divine bequests, communings which find an answer from a Spirit higher than our own. Are these never to close upon their object, and become something more than glimpses and foretastes?

Let us think, then, with ourselves in this way: I feel when I am in my best moments that these things are to be the perfection of my nature, if I ever reach it. But I cannot reach it without an immortality. Will not the Being who presents me with this aim, and has formed me capable of conceiving of an immortality, grant me the immortality without which the aim can never be reached? When I contemplate Him, I see that his eternity is the enclosing zone, the compact and mighty girdle of all his attributes, without which they would be scattered, conflicting forces, aimless and chaotic and fruitless. And what eternity is to God, immortality is to man. It is the indispensable requisite to the unity and completeness of his being. If, then, God has made Himself my highest standard, his unalterable truth and righteousness and goodness the goal towards which I should press, may I not expect that the course will be opened which leads to the goal? Without this, his attributes would be, for his children, the perpetual object of their despairing gaze. We may plead surely that He who has given us such a Divine plan of life should, in his consistency, make the term of our life commensurate with it. "O my God, take me not away in the midst of my days: thy years are throughout all generations."

4. Last of all, let us say that God's eternal being is a plea for this request, because *it suggests his Divine compassion for us.* Those men who think they exalt God by making Him indifferent to humanity are as far wrong in their philosophy as in their divinity. They speak of Him as so high above us in his infinite nature that He regards us no more than we do the short-lived insects of a summer evening, or the drifting leaves on the autumn winds. But the greatest natures are the most sensitively tender, and a true man has a feeling akin to sympathy for the insect of a day, a touch of pity when he sees the yellow leaf; if not for itself, yet for what it signifies. Great natures are made not more limited by their greatness, but more comprehensive; and the eternity of God does not shut out the thoughts and trials of human lives, but brings them more within his merciful regard. It is thus the Bible puts it, and it finds an echo in our hearts: "He knoweth our frame; He remembereth that we are dust." Frail man! "He remembered that they were but flesh, a wind that passeth away, and cometh not again." When we feel a touch of tenderness to the feeble creatures round us, to the bird or butterfly that sings its song, and flutters its hour, and

dies, let us not imagine we are more compassionate than God. Every spark of mercy is from his hearth. And when He has put into our souls a sense of a higher life, and a cry for its fulness in Himself, let us not believe He will treat us worse than the beasts that perish, that He will meet their wants in his great liberality, and leave ours in endless disappointment.

When we converse with such thoughts as these, when we feel that, short-lived and imperfect as we are, we can conceive of God's eternity, comprehend something of his consistency and compassion, our future life becomes not so much a thing of doubt. It is when we dwell only in dust that dust seems all. As we let the spirit waken and rise to God, it feels its kinship with his eternal nature, till we can say with the prophet, "Art not Thou from everlasting, O Lord my God, my Holy One? we shall not die." It is not always that we can realise these truths, but, in the proportion in which we do, we feel them to be the power and blessedness of life. If we have not learned them at all, the shadow of the solemn words of Scripture falls from this world upon eternity, "Without God, without hope." "He is light, and in Him is no darkness at all;" but without Him, the future is "a land of darkness, as darkness itself." The only way to have the hope of a blessed immortality is to have something in our souls which we can reasonably wish to be made immortal, something that is worthy to survive death and earth and time; that is, something of God within us now. As we live with Him here, we have the assurance of living with Him for ever. Where He gives Himself, He gives a share in that eternity which is his home.

We have thus tried to show what a complete life is, and the plea that is here presented for it. It is complete when it secures God's favour, when it does Him and his world some service, when it yields itself up with submission to his call, and when it looks forward to a continued life with God. For this last, we have sought to examine the plea contained in God's own eternal life, suggesting his power to grant this request, his immutability to secure it, his consistency since He has given us the conception of it, and his Divine compassion when, from his eternity, He has regard to our short and troubled life.

Yet we would not leave the subject without saying a word about the full answer to this request. We have been dealing with a question which to some extent involves the answer; and it is well that it should be put in every point of view, in order that, when the answer is finally given, it may be felt to be sufficient. This, indeed, may be one reason why God left the wise men of the old heathen world to deal with this problem on a mere human basis, and why He put it in such different ways into the hearts of his ancient saints by his Holy Spirit—" If a man die, shall he live again?"

It was, no doubt, to fix attention on the great answer, and on Him who has given it. It will require time for this answer to work its way into the world's heart, as it required time to mature the question. But we who profess to be Christians should feel already how it meets the case. Our Saviour Jesus Christ has appeared " to abolish death, and bring life and immortality to light through the Gospel." His earthly history shows us what a complete life is, a life led in no imaginary sphere, but amid the duties and temptations, the pains and sorrows, which daily press upon us. And it was followed by a death which puts us in a position to aim at his life. When we receive it in its divine meaning, " the Lord our Righteousness," it covers all the sinful past which paralyses our endeavour, offers us a free pardon that we may serve God as his reconciled children, and secures that Holy Spirit who is the Giver of life, and who works all our works in us. And, what is most wonderful, while He was accomplishing all this, it was in a way that never removes Him out of the reach of our experience and sympathy. He was performing a work beyond our power, and yet walking the path we have to tread. The cry of frail, dying man in these psalms passed through his heart and lips. He met death in the midst of his days, felt, as truly as we feel, its forebodings and bitterness, " offered up prayers and supplications with strong crying and tears unto Him that was able to save Him from death, and was heard in that He feared." We may say that the struggles of his people in past ages crying for eternal life were breathed into them by Christ's own Spirit, and that then He entered man's world to gather these prayers into his own heart, and secure their answer. The Old Testament is man feeling after God, the New is God finding man, and He who is the Leader in both, who breathes the question into man's heart, and then answers it, is that Eternal Son, " whose goings forth have been from of old, from everlasting." And now the sharer of our dying nature, the sympathiser with its cries, the bearer of its sins, has become the Lord of eternal life. " Lord, to whom shall we go ? " Let a man, let any man, come in humble faith and cast on Him the burden of guilt, and he will receive a divine power from Christ himself that will make his present life the beginning and the pledge of an everlasting one. Though the beginning be small, the latter end shall greatly increase; and when death comes, the prayer, " O my God, take me not away in the midst of my days," will be changed into, " Lord, now lettest Thou thy servant depart in peace, for mine eyes have seen thy salvation." " Lord Jesus, receive my spirit."

III.

THE POWER OF CHRIST'S ENDLESS LIFE.

"*Another priest, who is made . . . after the power of an endless life.*"—HEB. VII. 16.

ONE of the chief objects of this Epistle is to compare the priesthood of Christ with that of Aaron and his sons. The points of difference are mainly three. The first is in the dignity of the persons invested with the office. Under the Old Testament they were men who had infirmity; now it is the Son of God, the brightness of the Father's glory. The second is in the duration of the office. The Old Testament priests lose their office when they die; to Christ belongs "the power of an endless life." The third difference is in the nature of the sacrifice. In the Old Testament the priests made atonement only in figure; Christ's atonement is real and efficacious. We wish to direct attention to the second of these, to what is said of the duration of the office of Christ. When we speak of his office, we do not confine it to his work of atonement. That is the beginning and the foundation; but the Epistle looks at it as rising up into all his work as Mediator, when "He is entered into heaven, now to appear in the presence of God for us." His atonement is connected with his work as a Prophet and a King, as the Dispenser of divine knowledge and strength; and all this belongs to Him, "after the power of an endless life." This endless life is not the eternity He had with the Father before worlds began; it is his endless life as Mediator. The word means an *indissoluble* or *indestructible* life, safe against the assault of all enemies, and secure from all decay, or possibility of diminution. It may be said, But is not this, after all, the same, for none but the eternal Son of God could become the endless Mediator? Yet, granting this, it leads us to a different point of view for contemplating the work of Christ. Do we not feel that in his incarnation, as God manifest in the flesh, we can have thoughts about God which we could never have gained from the study of the divine nature in its absolute essence? And so, in considering the endless life of Christ, we may rise to conceptions and feelings about the world to come, and our share in it, which we could not receive from any attempt to grasp the idea of Christ's original and eternal nature. In his own inherent eternity He comes forth from the Father on his saving errand, enters into the limits of the finite, takes our nature, dies our death, rises from the grave, gathers to Him the sons whom He conducts to glory, and presents Himself before God with the words, "Behold, I and the children whom God hath given me." When we seek to look back to his unbeginning eternity, we are lost in its depths, for we have no such existence of our own, and we have not the bond of his human nature to aid us in our thinking; but as we return again to God, and advance into an eternity to come, we can follow Him in thought as the Son of Man, and we can conceive of a continued existence of our nature, which in some faint way resembles his. Since God has been pleased thus to help our thoughts as they "wander through eternity," let us humbly avail ourselves of his aid, and try to see in what way there is a power for our help in the endless life of Christ. In so vast a subject, we can select only a few points.

The first thought is the power which this endless life has of *communicating itself.* The very idea of such a life brings with it an inspiration of hope. Even if it were said that the idea is only the offspring of the soul of man, is it not a ground of hope, that his soul has the power of forming such ideas? To conceive of eternity is so far to be partaker of eternity. We share what we see. That we should be able to think of a life like our own, but free from all the impurity which attaches to us, going forward, age after age, without a break and without a check, rising and widening, a joy to itself, and a source of joy to others: is this not something to make us hopeful about the soul of man? There is no creature around us that has such a power, and may we not then cherish the expectation of something corresponding to it in reality? But if, moreover, we can come to the reasonable conclusion that such a life really exists; that One of the race has risen above the power of death; that He gave such evidence of it to those who were about Him as made them willing to endure any extremity, even to death, for this conviction; if He has been giving proofs of it since, by new spiritual life in the men, and new moral life in the nations, that have come into contact with Him, must there not be power in the faith of such an endless life? Let us suppose that it had been otherwise; that there had been nothing visible in this world but the triumph of death, no sign of any backward current in the perpetual and overwhelming flood which sweeps everything to one gloomy gulf; that there had been nothing in human history, as far as we could trace it, which gave the assurance, or even the hope, of a retrieval; could we have stood in the face of this pauseless defeat? The thought of God's eternal life, if we could have formed it, might have given us some gleams of expectation; but they would have been too faint to have been a guide for action, too cold to have inspired us with abiding courage. They would have crossed our sky like meteors, brief, fleeting, scattering themselves in dust, when in the black night our hearts were longing for a day-star. And so we can say to any of those who are hoping for an endless life, but who do not yet believe in Christ, Do you not think it a probable thing, that, if God meant us to have a hope of immortality, He would give us some such help as this to sustain it? Is there not a mighty power in the thought of the endless life of a member of our race? There is one grand reversal, the force of which all men may feel—one standard of hope lifted up in front of the enemy to which all eyes may look; where the faintest hearts may revive, and find fortitude for the last struggle. I think that if it were meant we should be immortal, some such aid as this would be granted to us.

But the power of Christ's endless life does more than communicate the hope of it to others, it gives the possession. When the original well of life had been tainted and poisoned by sin, He came to open up a new and pure fountain. All the figures of the water of life proceeding from the throne of God and of the Lamb, of the tree of life, of the bread of life, are presented to us in truths which reveal themselves to our souls when we come to the history and work of Jesus Christ. He secures for us a pardon consistent with righteousness, without which it could have brought no real life. He begins a new life in the soul, which has hard and manifold struggles with the fierce reluctances of the old nature. He encourages, strengthens, renews it, and at last makes it victorious. All this He does, not merely by presenting knowledge—" This is life eternal, that they might know Thee the only true God, and Jesus Christ, whom Thou hast sent,"—but by an act of creation through the Holy Spirit. He gives, not the perception or hope, but the possession of it. " I give unto them eternal life, and they shall never perish."

Now we may begin to see what power there is in

the endless life of Christ. It belongs to Him, not to reserve it for Himself, but to bestow it on all who will take it from his hand, who do not shut their eyes and steel their hearts against the gracious influences that are visiting the world through his death on earth and his life in heaven. But in order to this He must have a continued life. Had it been merely an example, a system of doctrine, He might have died and left it to itself, but for a power He must live, and live onward. Men are being born who need Him, and they will be born while this world exists, men who have sins, sorrows, temptations, death; nothing can help them—none but Christ himself, and so He must have the power of an endless life. And even when all are gathered in from earth, when time in its present form is closed, and another kind of time, an eternal time, begins, He will be needed. He will be the Mediator between the unseen God and man for ever, through whom they see God, and know Him, and have fellowship with Him. It is He who with his one hand, in his divine nature, lays hold of the infinite, and with the other, through his human nature, makes it the growing possession of finite beings. God does not bestow eternal life, here or hereafter, from his own absolute and unbroken eternity; He puts it into a separate and accessible channel. He causes his own infinite existence to flow out into the endless life of Christ, as if the ocean should spring up amid the earth into a fountain, and be "a well of life to all them that find it." But, for this, the great High Priest of humanity, and may we not suppose, in some way others besides, must have the power of an endless life.

This thought, which we have been trying to express, contains the germ of all we can say, but we may attempt to unfold it in some of its applications. Let us think then of the power Christ has in his endless life of *conveying knowledge and experience.* Death is the one great barrier between man and growth. He begins to cast his eyes about him, wonders at the strange features of things, at the stranger problems they raise ; collects some facts, forms or half-forms some conclusions, and when they seem pointing to a definite end, death is on him, and he has to drop the thread which seemed leading him into some open ground. The wonder is, that with this life men have learned so much, and it fills us with regret when the life which has gathered all this disappears in mid-sea, like a ship laden with gems and gold. It is true there is a continuous life of humanity, of which some speak much. The lower creatures have no power, at least no direct power, of transmitting their experience. But we have speech, and books, and history, by which we become the heirs of the ages, the owners of the thoughts and lives of the mighty dead. Past humanity may live in us. Yet consider how little our short life can reap from that growing past. As the harvests grow, our life seems to shorten. The fields of knowledge are so wide, that they fill our dwindling years with despair. "Life how short," we say with the old sage, " knowledge how long," or with the speaker in the Book of Job, " We are but of yesterday, and know nothing, because our days on earth are as a shadow." What secrets might the man of science wring from the bosom of nature, if he had countless years in which to put his questions, and mark the answers ! What wisdom might philosophers gain if they could watch for ages the course of thought and the currents of emotion ! But what wrecks lie scattered around us of plans scarcely begun, and what noble thoughts have passed away without an utterance ! We do not say that there are no compensations for these short earthly lives, and no sufficient reasons for this sad check to our fallen nature in the pursuit of knowledge.

Sometimes, when we are disappointed and weary, we get reconciled to the pause, and are glad to think of rest. But when the soul is strong and wisdom sweet, the conception of endless progress in knowledge answers to something very profound in human nature. We recoil from death, not merely as the animal recoils, but because it cuts us off from answers to the greatest questions the spirit can raise. How fitting it would be that beside the tree of knowledge there should be the tree of life! And this want is met when we think of One in our nature with the power of an endless life, who can be our Leader in all the paths of nature and providence and grace, by which souls can advance in the wisdom of God.

There is a great mystery about the union of the divine and human natures in the Lord Jesus Christ. But the Scripture makes two things certain, that the divine nature was there in its endless essence, irradiating the human, and that the human nature was there in its reality, becoming more and more filled with the divine. He grew in wisdom on earth, and yet his knowledge never had error in it; and we cannot think of this growth as ceasing, else we should lose in Him that true humanity which makes Him the Mediator our hearts need. It is not a growth outside the divine, but enclosed in it, like a channel embraced by an ocean, and ever enlarging to convey its infinite fulness. Our short human lives thus come under the conduct of that endless life of Christ. All the experience which He gained in his own earthly life is carried up into the higher life, and with it all the experience of all the ages since, in his contact, through the Holy Spirit, with doubt and struggle and grief in the lives of men. Thus Christ is full of endless, fresh life in his word, so that we find it deeper and higher, and need to grow up to it. And when we pass in thought from this side of death to those who have entered into the immediate presence of Christ, we can see that the endless life of Christ has its relations to them. What we have in the word of God, they have in the living Christ. We may apply to Him the words, "The lips of this priest keep knowledge, and they shall seek the law at his mouth, for He is the messenger of the Lord of Hosts." But to be their teacher, their guide, their example, He must move for ever before them, the divine-human ever ascending as the Son of Man to loftier heights, which command grander visions, and penetrating into deeper fountains of godlike joy, and realising the ancient description of Wisdom which foreshadowed Him, "when He was with God as one brought up with Him, daily his delight, rejoicing always before Him," but also, "rejoicing in the habitable part of his earth, and having his delights with the sons of men." Thus He comes forth from eternity without losing it, and returns again by his endless life, making his brethren joint-heirs of his wisdom and experience, and fulfilling the promise, "The Lamb which is in the midst of the throne shall feed them, and lead them unto living fountains of waters."

We may think, next, of the *sense of unity in Christ's plan*, which we may derive from the "power of his endless life." Men are often afraid to plan extensively, because those who follow them may be unable or unwilling to carry out their purposes. The prospect of death narrows their scope, and forces them to snatch at near results. But God has been pleased that the greatest enterprise the world contains should not be passed from hand to hand; it is not to flicker to and fro amid the gusts of grave-vaults, but to be in the power of an endless life. There are two things secured for the unity of Christians by Christ's unending life. The first is a oneness of *heart and sympathy*. He becomes the centre of a common affection, not as a dead abstraction, but as a living person who draws them all to Himself, and infuses into them common feelings, not at one time or in one place, but through all time, and in all places; and so the apostle, speaking of the unity of the Spirit, puts first the one Lord, and then the one God and Father. They are scattered through many generations and many lands, but the thought of an abiding, living Christ makes them brethren of the same family, puts into their heart the same life-blood, and prepares them for dwelling at last in the same house. It is by the life of Christ that we may have kindred affections with Paul, and John, and Isaiah, and David—may understand them, and hope and rejoice with them. So powerful is it, that it goes back before his visible coming, and like the shadow of the apostle, has its quickening effect on all upon whom it falls. Looking forward to his life, they shared it, and so it is said, " They did all drink the same spiritual drink ; for they drank of that spiritual Rock that followed them ; and that Rock was Christ." In this way the endless life of Christ fits all who come under its power for being " fellow-citizens with the saints, and of the household of God."

The other unity secured by this endless life of Christ is that of *action*. The Christian Church grows up under the hands of innumerable labourers. They come and go, and " are not suffered to continue by reason of death;" they have their own views and temperaments, and portions of the building bear the marks of it. There are chasms in the walls, raising and removing of scaffolding in dust and noise, to the perplexing of our brief lives. In the midst of all this there are minds eager for unity, and ready to take whatever seems to promise it. It is not to be found in any ecclesiastical despotism, nor even in the outward gathering of faithful men under one discipline, good though this may be in its place. It is to be sought in the one heart of which we have spoken, going toward Christ, and then in the overruling plan which He carries out through all their work. We might have had confidence in the future, from the conviction that God knows the end from the beginning, that the universe is not an experiment trying all ways and paths, if it may at last wander into the right; but now it is brought closer to us, and as it were put into our hand when we can think of the infinite, divine wisdom presiding over it through Christ, "who is the same yesterday, to-day, and for ever," "putting all things under his feet, and giving Him to be head over all things to the Church, which is his body." Now we may be sure of the unity of the plan, and sure that we can have a part in it, however short-lived and short-sighted we are; if we have any share in his life, and any desire to promote it, our hand will be guided to lay a stone in its place, which shall enter into the final building. What lofty trustfulness should this give us to go forward in hope! We have over us the promise of the power of his endless life —" Lo, I am with you alway, even unto the end of the world," and we can present the prayer with confidence, " Let thy hand be upon the man of thy right hand, upon the Son of man, whom Thou madest strong for thyself. So will not we go back from Thee." Whatever our part in the work, if it be true, the plan accepts it, " both he that soweth and he that reapeth shall rejoice together, and gather fruit unto life eternal."

Think, moreover, how the power of Christ's endless life may fill us with *the spirit of patience*. One of the most difficult things in the Christian life, or in any life, is to work energetically and yet wait patiently. It is so hard to keep to the watchword "without haste, without rest." Many of the evil schemes of the world come from the impatience that belongs to short lives. Men make fevered efforts to build up empires or fortunes in blood or fraud. Their race for success is a race with death; the grave is near, and they must have it now. Even good men take ill-advised ways, because they are anxious for speedy results. They wish for something they can see, "Let thy work appear unto thy servants." But he who has the power of an endless life will not only choose no ways that are unrighteous, he will not be hurried into any that are premature. A subject that causes doubt with many is the slow progress of justice and mercy in the world. See how sanguinary wars, iniquitous acts of oppression, great national vices and follies, run the weary round. There is progress; yes, there is progress; Christianity is slowly forming a moral opinion which compels men to have some pretext of right for war, and it is sending its messengers of healing to help friend and foe alike. But how tardy in its approach is the reign of righteousness and peace! The endless life of Christ is a source of comfort to us. He could very soon check the symptoms, but the disease would remain. Have you considered that war between man and man is the result of the war between man and God? All these outbursts are the insurrections of the evil human heart. The great problem is to put down sin not merely because it is opposed to the will of God, but because it is also opposed to the happiness of his universe; it is not simply a contention of power, but of goodness, and this needs time. The endless life of Christ gives Him patience in working for it, bringing his moral and spiritual motives to bear, and using his power at last for those whom no motives could persuade.

Within Christ's kingdom of the church we need the same help for the use of patience. Materialistic indifference comes with a chilling breath, and we cannot help feeling it in the atmosphere It is painful to have our life cast in one of these periods of reaction, for our fears sometimes mistake the backward ripple for the outset of a tide, or the outset of a tide for the exhaustion of the ocean. If our lives were long enough we might be re-assured. These reactions have their term, they yield to something higher, and the night swings round to a brighter morning. It is well at such depressing seasons to remember what the Psalmist calls "the years of the right hand of the Most High"—the lengthened time which God takes for his greatest works. He is patient in his earthly life, because He endured the cross. He looks behind and before, and not only sees the coming tides, but is prepared to send them.

It was hope not only for his own life, but for that of Christ's cause when it was hard pressed, that made Stephen say, "Behold, I see the heavens opened."

> "For proof look up
> And see thy lot in yon celestial sign."

Or perhaps death is busy among us. Men engaged in Christian work, and apparently indispensable, are suddenly called away, or terrible catastrophes happen which make us wonder that God should permit them, or that Christ does not interpose to prevent them. It is not the want of compassion, it is the wide and far vision which his position gives Him. He sees, when soldiers are falling in the front of the battle, that there are reserves at hand whom He has summoned. And in the sorest trials He looks beyond the narrow verge of the suffering to the enduring peace. If we could look up to Him, patient amid relapses and losses, not from want of feeling, but because "He himself knows what He will do," it would calm our fears. "He that believeth shall not make haste."

The last remark we make is that the power of Christ's endless life opens *the prospect of abiding joy*. There is a philosophy of the present day called Pessimism, which holds that life is so entirely wretched, and the universe so tainted with misery, that the only resource possible is utter extinction. It proposes in various ways the question,—Is life worth living?—and after weighing its short pleasures against its long suffering, it concludes that non-existence for men, and, if it could be, for the universe, is the desirable goal. There is no likelihood that such a theory will ever make much way among healthy-minded, active men. Even in that great religion of the East, which sets up annihilation as the last aim of life, it is remarkable how far forward it puts it, and how it clings to various forms of existence before it resigns itself to sink into nothingness.

Nevertheless, this theory of despair is a token of an atmosphere around. It is on the one side the result of a materialistic philosophy in which "earth to earth" is the end of all, and it is on the other side the outcome of self-indulgence, when it has become wearied of superficial and unsatisfying things. The question—Is life worth living? must be answered by another—What life? There are lives which are not worth living once, and the one token of wisdom in these theoretic lives is that they seem to feel they are not worth being continued. If those who put such questions would only be led to widen their inquiry, they might find that there are other balances than theirs in which the pains and pleasures of life are to be weighed. When we come to the emotions of the soul, the measure is not by quantity but by quality. There are moments of joy which outbalance years of toil and pain. The first glimpse of the New World to Columbus, the tremulous delight which seized Newton when he was in sight of the new law of gravitation, and which made him unable to finish the last figures of the calculation—these led them to forget as nothing sleepless nights and long anxieties and depressing fears. And there are greater things than these.

The joy of self-sacrifice for the cause of truth and righteousness has been to some men more to be chosen than crowns and palaces, and has made flames unfelt as if He who walked in the furnace of Nebuchadnezzar were with them in the fire. This is the joy of souls, and Jesus Christ is the Lord of that Kingdom where its home is fixed. He could make men sing in perfect calmness, " And not only so, but we glory in tribulations also ; " and He gave them this gladness out of his own heart, when for the joy set before Him—the joy of saving men—He endured the cross, despising the shame. It is not necessary that a man should rise to the height of martyrs and apostles to be convinced that such a joy exists ; let him but forget himself in Christ's spirit, in doing good, and he will discover that there is a life in life, that what he surrenders comes back to him in gold from God's own treasure-house of love to which Christ has opened the door. The power of his endless life is still engaged in works like those which occupied Him on earth, but in grander measure and in wider fields ; and what He offers to all who will accept it is a joy not like his, but a joy the very same : " that they might have my joy fulfilled in themselves." It is the joy of knowledge, of purity, of holy, happy service in doing God's will—in self-sacrifice itself continued in self-forgetfulness, for without this the joy of heaven would be less than the joy of earth.

Will you turn away from this, and refuse Him who is speaking to you from heaven? It is the choice between life and death. He who has the power of an endless life can make you blessed only by your receiving that life into your heart. He cannot make it yours except by your having it within you. God can make no man happy save in Himself, and it is to bring you to Him that this High Priest is exalted a Prince and a Saviour. How sorrowfully He said on earth, " And ye will not come to Me that ye might have life!" How touching his words still! Will you suffer them to be parting words? "He that sinneth against Me wrongeth his own soul: all they that hate Me love death!"

How should our hearts leap up in gratitude to Him who has opened such a way to life eternal, and who comes to us now and says, "I am the way," who, having the life of eternity, quitted it, that through death He might have the power of an endless life for men; and how should our souls bend forward more than ever at such a prospect, to make sure that we are in the road! "Thou wilt show me the path of life; in thy presence is fulness of joy!" And should we not bless the great God who has not left us face to face with the infinite and eternal, unaided and uncovered, but has given to us this life, kindred to our own, which leads us, in experience and patience and blessedness, nearer to Himself as we are able to bear it? He has put his hand over us—over us in the sky—as the poet says,—

> " On all his children fatherly,
> To save them from the dread and doubt
> Which would be, if from this low place,
> All opened straight up to his face
> Into the grand eternity."

But He covers us here, more safely and tenderly, and yet makes a way open through the heavens into the holiest of all.

IV.

INSTABILITY: SOME OF ITS CHARACTERISTICS AND CORRECTIVES.

(FOR YOUNG MEN.)

"*Unstable as water, thou shalt not excel.*"—GEN. XLIX. 4.

WHEN we speak of this as addressed to young men, we wish to take the word men in that larger and truer sense which includes humanity. There is much being done in our day for the education of women; and man, in the limited sense, will never be fully educated till we care with equal justice for man in the larger sense. With equal justice does not mean, however, with the very same apparatus, and towards identical ends. God has given to man and woman a common nature with diversities, in which we cannot speak of higher and lower, for both are equally necessary to an entire humanity, and to the health of the family, the State, and the Church. In regard to what is common in their nature, they should have the same education, and, in regard to what is different, the same impartial provision for their peculiar faculties, remembering that all faculties are given, not for mere ornament or pastime, but for service in the cause of God and man. If woman's education received its just rights, she would become not less woman but more, and men would have the benefit of it in being made more manly, and in the mother, the wife, the sister, the daughter, infusing a higher tone into all the relations of life. Let it be understood, then, that when we speak of man, we wish to keep in view the larger sense of our entire humanity.

The aim set before us here is *excellence*, by which we do not mean a rivalry for superiority over our fellow-men, or, indeed, an endeavour at distinction in any way. We do not stop to consider whether this is good or bad; we shall try to think rather of something more practical and Christian, of taking up that position and doing that work which God designs for us, and which He has a right to require. This is the noblest of all ambitions, and here every man may be alike successful. There need be no jealousy, for the victory of each is the gain of all. Nor are we deprived, in this aim, of the stimulus of rivalry. We have a twofold consciousness within us, one of something achieved and past, another of a goal to be reached in the future. It is the ability to hold these up before our thought which marks us out from all other creatures, and it is Christianity which, above all, gives the power of making an advance to the highest ideal, "leaving those things which are behind, and reaching forth unto those which are before." It is towards this excellence, the most unselfish and noble, we wish to urge endeavour. There is, however, one fatal enemy to this excellence; it is *instability*. A sorrowful father spoke of it to his first-born son, in the hope that it might still rouse him: "Unstable as water, thou shalt not excel." There are few of us who have not seen more than one friend fail in life through this defect. Some young men have begun the voyage with apparently everything which could make it successful: talent, amiability, opportunity, troops of friends; but through want of a fixed point to steer to, or a steady hand on the helm, they have drifted aimlessly about, or made utter shipwreck. And, on the other hand, some poor, friendless youth has advanced to eminence and honour, not through help from others, nor by commanding ability, but through quiet, persistent purpose. There is a secret power in steady, resolute purpose which develops faculties before unknown, which seems sometimes to supply the place of genius, and almost to create it; genius itself without it is maimed and helpless. It is a subject, then, of very great importance, especially for the young who have habits to form; and we shall take the figure employed here to illustrate it. It has been variously rendered by translators, and we shall not try to settle which of the renderings may have been in the mind of the speaker; we shall rather take different aspects of it, most, if not all, of which are to be found in other parts of the Bible, used in a similar way.

I. The first thing which strikes us in the instability of water is that it has *no cohesive shape of its own.* It takes the form of the vessel into which you pour it; it changes one form for another without resistance; and water spilt on the ground falls asunder and vanishes. Wood and stone keep their place in the world, and may rise into enduring structures, but what can be built out of water? This suggests the first defect of instability, that it prevents a man gaining an *independent position in life.* There is, indeed, a great deal of false talk about position, as if the one end of life were to be rich and distinguished. It is impossible for the great mass of men to succeed in this, and therefore God has not made our happiness or usefulness dependent on it. But there is a true position in the world which we should all aim at, a place where we may stand on our own feet, fill our own sphere, and meet all the just claims which come upon us in the family, in friendship, and in society. He who reaches this in any honest walk in life " excels; " however humble his position, he may stand with erect head among the highest. But it cannot be gained without some measure of stability, though that measure is not always the same. Some men have a nature of granite which holds its own shape anywhere, the cohesion of the quartz crystal which can be crushed but not changed; others, like the common stone which may be moulded by the chisel but can keep the form it takes. Both of these have their uses, but the lamentable case is when a man's nature is entirely fluid, when it will take any shape, and keep none. When a man is constantly leaving one kind of occupation for another, he cannot acquire power for any one; and, next to immorality, the cause of failure in life may be found in some feeble hesitancy in the first start, or want of steadiness in following it up. These two are generally connected. Vacillation in the start makes itself felt in the course, and brings that perplexity of parents and misery of young men—change upon change. Hence the supreme importance in the guides of the young not pushing them unduly to what is not their bent, and in young men themselves not yielding to first difficulties when they have made their choice. If, indeed, there is entire instability in the ground of the character, it is very difficult to deal with, and if men were under fixed laws of nature, the case might be incurable. But nature has its emblems of hope even for this indecision; there is a possibility of crystallising water.

II. Another thing in the instability of water is the *changefulness of its reflection.* It is like the glass of which James speaks, where a man sees his face and straightway forgets it. Look at the water in an outspread lake. It takes sun and moon and stars and changing seasons into the depths of its confidence, and its seeming depths are only a surface. It is enamoured of every passing cloud, waves back a recognition to every tree and flower which bends to it, and, when they withdraw, drops all remembrance of them to take up the next impression, or to fall into vacancy. This is very beautiful in nature, but very unhappy in men, and we may see in it an illustration of how instability unfits us for gaining either true culture or character.

Let us think of *culture*. It is regarded sometimes as the chief end of man, and in the shape of literature or science or art, it is the religion of many. Whenever the living God is put out of sight, and humanity takes his place, culture is the worship offered to the idol. Man is never so vain as when he falls down at the shrine of his own intellect. But true culture can never be gained when we make it our end. We must seek something out of and above self, in the service of God, and the good of his world; and then culture gains an unconsciousness which is its greatest beauty. When we have given God his place we may safely seek a knowledge of his works, an acquaintance with whatever is true and good and beautiful in the thoughts and actions of man; and we may wish to add something of our own, in our own way, for the world's benefit. The humblest mind may take its own shape and colour, so as to grow up into a distinct personality, and to yield its contribution to the family or friendly circle of which it is a part. But, for this, stability is indispensable. If a man flits from one branch of reading to another, without concentration or discrimination, his mind will become a succession of dissolving views, or a collection of curiosities without plan and index. There are men of universal knowledge, Macaulays and Sir William Hamiltons, but they are so rare, and we are so unlikely to be among them, that it is better to leave them out of count. Even these, if examined, might be found to have gathered their multitudinous learning round one strong centre; and therefore, in reading, we should advise a man that, while he makes excursions on many sides to escape narrowness, he ought to have one branch to which he gives himself more thoroughly for the sake of exactness and strength. It is of great importance to have a home to the mind, some one thing which we feel we are sure about; it gives the mind a power to judge of other things as they come before it. In these days of journals and magazines and incessant talk on passing topics, it requires nerve to push through the daily tide, and get out into the depth. But we should be impressed with the truth that reading is nothing unless it lead to fixed knowledge, and knowledge little, unless it helps culture—personal growth—and culture little, unless it is given to the service of God and the good of man. Let us urge, then, on young men, and on young women too, that, while they do not neglect the movements of the day, they should always have on hand some one book which demands thought and repays it. We must try to deliver society from the superficial desultoriness which is the epidemic of the age, and we must try to rear a generation, not of echoes and talkers, but of men and thinkers. Each of us may help, with some little grain of resolve and self-denial, and we shall reach a far higher pleasure in such bracing exercise, than in the lax feebleness which begs only for amusement, and looks on thought as torture.

But, besides the help which stability gives to true culture, there is the question of *character*. By character we do not mean outward repute among our fellow-men, but the stamp on our nature that marks us as having individuality; this is the proper meaning of the word. A man should have something by which he is known, and differentiated from others, besides his name and his address. Character is something more than culture; it is wider and deeper; it takes in a man's ways of feeling and acting as well as thinking, apart from the spiritual side, of which we do not here speak. In this sense we should all aim at character, for this means that we should bring out the special nature God has given us, that we should be ourselves, and not lost like a blade of grass in a field. We were not made, as hundreds seem to think, to be dreary transcripts of the fashion round us, leaves in children's copy-books, written over and over with the same dull commonplaces. It is a wonderful relief to escape from society of this kind, and to get among people who have their own natural, independent way of looking at things. Even a crotchet or a quaintness, if it has no sting in it, gives us pleasure in a man, because it creates an interesting personality, as a straw gathers amber round it. It is a poor enough affectation, and soon wearies us, when it is consciously cultivated; but personal character founded on some firm, intelligent principle is necessary to our having any place in the world's estimate, or to our doing any great good in it. There has always been danger of gregarious or mob life—the mob of the drawing-room as well as the mob of the street—and from certain causes it is increased in our time. Thousands who believe that "the customs of the people are vain" give in to them because they are afraid of losing the countenance of their class. It is one of the difficulties about man's immortality, when we see multitudes in whom there appears to be no personality to be continued, and who pass their life in the crowd of beetles burrowing in the earth, or of butterflies beating the air. To build up in this world a true, fixed character is to contribute a proof for another world. If you wish to form such a character, there are two things to be remembered. The one is common sense, which will let you see the great landmarks of the true and good, and save you from being drifted into a one-sided eccentricity, under the name of independence. The other is conscience, which will bring you under the light of the higher law, and give you firmness to follow it. With these two a man may steer his course between the opposite shores of eccentricity and fashion, and unfold his own nature. And, as we spoke of studying some one book in order to mental culture, we may say that there is pre-eminently one book for the formation of a strong, independent character. We speak of the Bible at present merely as a book among others; but we dare to say that not all others, if used without it, will give the individuality and power which it will give alone. Take the populations in centuries and countries where it has been a sealed book, and compare them with those among whom the Bible has been the people's counsellor and charter, and mark the difference. It has given to its readers the marrow of lions and the intelligence of men, indomitable love of liberty with regard for the rights and liberties of others; and history has so far shown that freedom and order are not long possible in a country where the Bible has lost its creative, and, at the same time, its controlling power. What it is to a nation, it must be to a man. It gives the firmness to conscience which is at the basis of all true character, and it educates the common sense which is referred to in its own saying, "A good understanding have all they that do his commandments." Whatever other books you read for breadth and height of culture, remember, for your character, to be 'men of the one Book.'

III. A third thing we mention in the instability of water is that it *inspires distrust*. We may take here for our example water in the sea, "the troubled sea," as the prophet names it, "which cannot rest." You know how calm the sea may look, like a sleeping child, and to what rage and havoc it can be roused. Its very calm has danger; there are hidden rocks under the smoothness, and treacherous currents which wind like serpents round those who trust them. Before we are aware, it ruffles to the breeze, and swells into the storm; and the Bible, to picture the perfect security of heaven, says, "There shall be no more sea."

This illustration reminds us that instability *destroys our power for influence.* What men cannot reckon on they will not trust; they must know where they will find a man to-morrow, if they are to walk and work with him to-day. And so nothing isolates a man more for action than unsteadiness of purpose; no talents, nor amiability, nor even purity of intention can make amends. There is a kind of respect for the man who goes on resolutely in a mistaken course, but only contempt for him who is always wavering in the right. If we would have influence, we should bear in mind that the world is governed not so much by men of talent as by men of will. Some may think very little of the importance of influence; but, in whatever sphere we are, our influence is the measure of our power for good. It is the accumulated capital of a good man, impalpable but real, and often more precious than gold. We have seen it growing, as a shadow grows with a tree, longer, broader, deeper, till it becomes a shelter and solace to all about it. The very look, the thought of these men gives a sense of confidence to people in perplexity. They are to be found in all ranks and classes, and society could not exist without them. They are the binding stones in its walls, and our homes are more indebted to them than to the carved top-stones which the multitude admire; or, to borrow from the present illustration, they are the steadfast lighthouses on the shore of the unstable sea, doing more for the world's good than the flashing meteors which burn themselves out in the higher air. It is a just ambition to be a quiet, fixed light for some few souls around us; and when excellence is weighed by Him who holds the balance, it will receive its due, "Thou hast been faithful over a few things, I will make thee ruler over many things."

But this word influence will be better understood by some if we connect it with friendship. There are men who pass through life and never have more than acquaintances. They touch other men only on the outside—speak to them at the door. We do not mean to say that acquaintances are of no use in life. One sometimes gains glimpses of things which are happening, and handles them in an easy way as he could not do through friends. But this we say, that to any complete nature acquaintances can never supply the want of friends—of those to whom we can unbosom ourselves and speak in confidence. Books speak to us, but we cannot speak to books. We can speak to God, but there are times when we need help to do it. In seasons when we are disappointed by the emptiness or shaken by the falseness of the world, we feel as if we lost our hold even on God. A true heart in a fellow-man is an anchorage at such a time, for we ask ourselves—Where could this heart come from? Could there be brethren if there were no Father? There are some who have said that the New Testament discourages friendship, or at least passes it by. But can we forget that the Son of God, when He was on earth, drew men close to his heart and said, "Henceforth I call you not servants, but I have called you friends;" that He carried them with Him into his last struggle, and felt strengthened by their affection—"Tarry ye here and watch with Me"? To have true friends is to have the greatest help in the world, out of God; and to be a friend is to have the greatest influence for good to the heart which trusts us. Every young man would wish to have true friends; but here is one indispensable requisite, stability. The penalty of fickleness is that it can never have friends.

We should aim at steadfastness of character, for this reason if for no other, and when we have found it in another we should forgive many faults for its sake. "Thine own friend and thy father's friend forsake not." Do not lightly break ties which cannot perhaps be formed again in all the days and years to come; and value them as a divine gift, when you feel that they have some union in a divine principle. This is the way to find the help of which the wise man speaks: "There is a friend that sticketh closer than a brother."

IV. The last thing we mention in the instability of water is that *it is ready to move any way but upward*. Take, for this, water in a river. It flows on, sparkling and pleasant, plays with the nodding flowers, meets a rock and turns from it to a rippling eddy, finds some opening in its bank and wanders through a meadow. But it may happen that the eddy plunges into a gulf or the meadow stagnates into a marsh, and the river makes no choice. It descends, but it cannot rise to its source; and it illustrates this most serious defect of instability, that it *unfits a man for a successful endeavour after the higher life*. We see, every day, such natures, open and amiable but ruled entirely by the world of circumstances, allured by pleasant opportunity, repelled by the need of self-denial, and incapable of a decided choice. They follow the prevalent course, and the prevalent course, unhappily, is downward. There are more ruined by this fatal weakness of will than by a positive bad purpose, at least in the beginning. But then let it be remembered that failure to decide for God is more than a man's misfortune; it is his sin. When rebels have risen against the rightful King, it is treason to stand neutral. There was a time when simple indecision did not commit a man—the time when the first temptation offered; though even then a bold Get thee behind me, Satan, would have been the best answer to the seducer; but that time is long gone by, and he who does not resist is in the power of the tempter. If any one thinks this is hard, let him reflect that it is the rule in other things. The sailor does not complain that, if he sits still, the tide will carry his ship on the rocks, or the farmer that weeds will be his only harvest, or the merchant that his balance will be on the side of ruin. It is the law of life, and how should it be otherwise in the concerns of the soul? There is only this difference, that the issues are more momentous; and in a world fallen, and flooded with evil, the choice should be more intense. And so, when we read the Bible, we find that its supreme object is to press decision. It does not occupy itself with speculation, it leaves curious questions aside and places itself right across our road with its challenge, "Choose ye this day whom ye will serve." Pass your finger down the Old Testament, and you meet "thou shalt" and "thou shalt not" at every turn. And in the New Testament the fervid rush of compassion never rises to such power, or melts to such pathos, as when the Son of God wrestles with the will of man. What an earnestness in his words, "Strive to enter in at the strait gate!" "The kingdom of heaven suffereth violence, and the violent take it by force." And what grief at failure when He looked with love on the young man who hesitated in the great choice, and missed it! This is the strangest thing about man's will, that it should have power to refuse God; and this is the saddest, that its indecision can bring on itself such infinite loss.

It would be wrong if, after speaking of the evils of

instability, we were to close without saying something about its correctives, and, if possible, its cure. There are some, among whom John Foster may be reckoned, who seem to look on indecision as incurable. If it were so, it would be one of the most melancholy things in human life, that the power of will should be all-important, and that multitudes should be shut out from acquiring it. But can this be true? There are many things which nature, or, to speak more correctly, God has put beyond our reach. No amount of resolve or endeavour, with the age of an antediluvian, could make a man a Raphael, or a Beethoven—could enable him to discover the law of gravitation, or write the *Paradise Lost*. The sooner we realise this truth the better for the cure of a feeble will, and the more cordially we acquiesce in God's gifts to others, the happier we shall be. But the things essential to our life, not as artists or poets but as men, are within our power, and growth in decision is one of them. It is true there is an original force of concentration possessed by some which is like genius, and a man who starts with an unstable will can never overtake it; it is true also that the cure of instability must, in general, be indirect and gradual, must be reached rather by sap and mine than by assault; but with these deductions there is almost no faculty in which it is more possible to make advance. Let this be settled first, then, that indecision has not written above it, Leave hope behind.

We shall ask this, next, that there be a sincere desire to escape from this defect where it is felt. We are surely not asking too much; for God has made man reasonable that he may learn his wants and wish for a remedy. The understanding can turn round and examine the will, and act upon it. Something has been gained already if, while we have been reviewing the miseries of instability, any one has been convinced and convicted, and brought to reflect on the remorse which will be felt when the emptiness of a useless day has been carried on to the end of all the days in a useless life. Should any one have reflected on it thus far, he may be induced to begin "on reason to build resolve, the column of true dignity in man." To *build* resolve is not to *create* it; to build is a gradual, often a painful process; but let a man say, 'I shall spare no pains for such a work, it carries in it the meaning and end of my life; I shall begin by laying a stone this day, a determined *I will*, and I shall seek, day by day, to add another!' If this is sincerely done, there is something gained; if it is deferred, there is so much lost.

The next thing to be said is that, in arriving at decision, a man should seek to ascertain what he is capable of; and this he may do by some reflection, by counsel well taken, and by trial; if he despises all these, he is in a bad way. Many grow into instability by undertaking things impossible to them, or by grasping too quickly at things which are possible. They take two steps where they should take one, and are thrown back and discouraged, till their life is a history of great conceptions and weak endeavours. The secret of success is, as far as may be, to succeed at first—to measure our strength with our enterprise, and to leave behind a sense of thoroughness. Though it be small, it gives us courage, and carries us on; if there is ease in idleness, there is an impulsive pleasure in every successful effort. At the same time, it should be said that failure ought not to be taken as defeat. It is a reason not for giving up, but for trying it in another way, or at least by a better measurement of means to end. The Lord has said that we should forgive our brother "until seventy times seven." We do not say that we should be so ready to forgive ourselves, but we should be determined in God's strength not to despair of ourselves.

There are helps in this struggle with indecision which it may be good to mention. One of the first is *method* or *system*. There are some who, having heard of the wonderful power of method, begin by reducing their whole life to a plan, and mark out work for every day and hour. They generally fail for a reason already stated : they attempt too much. Such a rigid division of life can scarcely be a good rule for any man, and certainly it is not the best for beginning the cure of instability. Rather let there be some one thing resolved on, with room for freedom round it, and this one thing will give its character to the rest. A particular time set apart for mental and spiritual improvement, and maintained against all lower claims, will have a wonderful effect in steadying the whole character. It throws its influence back and forward, and, like the little leaven, leavens the whole lump. Try method at first in this simpler way, bearing on some one thing which you feel will be a gain to you in your walk in life, and you will soon feel the benefit of it. Acts pass over into habits, habits become pleasures, and as soon as we have pleasure in self-control, the victory is won. Another help is found in our *associations*. It sometimes happens that the sight of some miserable case of indecision is a corrective to a witness of it, but he will not gain much by keeping its company. The strength of the weak is in the society of the strong, or of those at least who are seeking strength. We can allow ourselves liberties with our own rules, which we should be ashamed of when we are under obligation to others. The necessity of taking a share in the common work, and of punctually meeting engagements, will have an effect on every young man who has a sense of self-respect. It is what discipline and the presence of his comrades are to a soldier, enabling him and them " to breathe united force "—a picture which the apostle has before him when he says, " Joying and beholding your order (tactical array), and the steadfastness of your faith in Christ " (Col. ii. 5). The Christian Church was intended by its author to give this aid to the weakness of the single will; and every congregation in it should have its associations suited for different temperaments and wants, for personal improvement and quickening, for common action in doing good, where the feeble would find a place of shelter, and the solitary a home and friends. There is no society in the world, none even that can be conceived of, which has the motives, the influences, and the opportunities for strengthening the young, like to a Christian Church, if it is rightly organised,—for carrying out the mission " of healing that which is sick, binding up that which is broken, bringing again that which is driven away, and seeking that which is lost." How weak we are, nay sinful, that, with such a power, we make so little use of it; and therefore every Christian Church should be more active in opening doors of shelter all round. Wherever they exist, let young men join them, and, where they do not, let them create them, though they begin with two; " for if they fall, the one will lift up his fellow: but woe to him that is alone when he falleth; for he hath not another to help him " (Eccles. iv. 10). We do not contradict this when we say, besides, that a young man may gain strength of will among adversaries, the strength which comes from an *early and manly stand*. There is sometimes a single test which decides his future. Should he from self-interest, or fear of a sneer, belie his convictions, he is at a double disadvantage; he has weakened his own moral nature, and given a weapon to his tempters—has, so to speak, lost his own shield, and sharpened their swords. But if he stand firm, he has a double help; he is stronger within, and covered by his consistency. Duty and interest alike advise a young man, in the workshop or counting-house or any company, to take his stand, quietly but firmly, at first. If, like Daniel, he find himself, for his fear of God, in a den of lions, their mouths may not be shut, but he will have their secret homage, and they will not only be kept from hurting him, but be made to help his character to higher power: "The righteous also shall hold on his way, and he that hath clean hands shall be stronger and stronger" (Job xvii. 9).

We should like, in closing, to say that, besides the young, this question appeals specially to parents. It was a father who made this sorrowful complaint over his first-born son, more sorrowful, perhaps, because he saw in him some of the features of his own early inconsistency. Parents can do much to give stability to their children by their own firm resolve: "I will walk within my house with a perfect heart;" and, next, by their wise and tender treatment of them, not forcing them to that for which they are unfitted, and so bringing a recoil; watching where the character is weak, that they may strengthen it, and urging the most touching of all motives from their own experience: "My son, know thou the God of thy father, and serve Him with a perfect heart, and with a willing mind."

But the last word of all must be to those who are growing up to manhood and womanhood. It is on the character formed at this stage that the happiness and usefulness of life, as a rule, depend. In all that we have said, the thought has been present that successful endeavour must be made in the strength of God. It must begin and go forward in the spirit of Augustine, "Command what Thou wilt, but give what Thou commandest;"

and this came to him from a higher speaker, "Thy God hath commanded thy strength. Strengthen, O God, that which Thou hast wrought for us." No stability can be assured until the one decision has been made: "Lord, I will follow Thee!" What sluggish natures have been quickened, what wavering wills confirmed, what noble aims attained, under the power of this one resolve! What companies of the weak have been turned into victorious armies, in the track of this Leader, who endured the cross and despised its shame! "Let thy hand be upon the Man of thy right hand, upon the Son of man whom Thou madest strong for Thyself. So will not we go back from Thee." But choose Him for his own sake; and choose Him now for "righteousness and strength"—for the sinful past, for the anxious future. Beware of the miserable "Go thy way for this time," which, like all delays, leads down. "Let us give earnest heed to the things which we have heard, lest we let them slip,"—lest we "be floated past them"—this is the figure. Thou art on a stream which will carry thee with it, if thou dost not seize his offered hand. Thine may be paralysed, but He will renew the old miracle if thou wilt look to Him: "Then saith He to the man, Stretch forth thine hand. And he stretched it forth."

V.

BARZILLAI THE GILEADITE.

(FOR THE AGED.)

2 Sam. xix. 31-40. *Read also* 2 Sam. xvii. 27-29 ; 1 Kings ii. 7 ; Jer. xli. 17 ; Ezra ii. 61.

Some of the most interesting spots in our Scottish landscapes are hidden from the hasty traveller. He passes through a beautiful valley, sees the clear rushing river, the green fields fringed by the dark woods which climb the skirts of the hills, the mountain tops with their massive swell or rocky precipice indenting the sky, and he thinks he knows the whole. But there are exquisite spots of beauty hidden among the hills, shady pools in the streams, quiet retreats so fresh and far away from the world's eye, that when he sees them he feels as if the foot of man had never been there before. It is so in the Bible. We read the great roll of the heroes of faith in the eleventh chapter of the Hebrews, and it seems as if we had traversed the history of the ancient Church of God. But when we pass through the first ranks and the grander scenes, we light upon spots of tranquil beauty and characters of transparent faith and truthfulness which fill us with the gladness of surprise.

The story of Barzillai is one of these. We shall not attempt to rehearse what is told so naturally in the words of Scripture itself, but shall rather ask you to read it over for yourselves with the different references to it, and meditate on it, till it becomes filled with detail and colour, and lives and glows before your mind's eye. There are some thoughts about it which strike us at the first. There is the true-hearted loyalty of the old subject for the old king. He had much to lose, but he came out openly in the time of danger. He was faithful, you may be sure, not from any blind belief in the " divine right of kings to govern wrong," but because he knew on which side justice and freedom and the fear of God were to be found; and it is such men, never heard of before, nor known about court, who are the true support of rightful governments. You will observe, also, what a large generosity and fine delicacy of feeling may lie hidden in the quiet ways of life till opportunity calls them out. Barzillai has the nobility and courtesy which were seen long before in his father Abraham, and long afterwards in the apostle Paul, to which one must first be born in the natural way and then, to give them their finest grace, born of the Spirit.

David, king though he be, and kingly in his words and acts, takes the lower place. He is not ungrateful, as monarchs too often have been to those who stood by them in their time of peril. But there is more than gratitude; there is an insight into the sincerity and magnanimity of the old man which fills him with admiration and love, and makes him wish to have him always with him, as if his presence would be a benediction. May we not suppose that his own shepherd life, when he kept his father's flocks in Bethlehem, rises before him with fond remembrance, and when he cannot return to it he would fain carry a memory of it with him to his palace in Jerusalem? Kings are so little sure of personal affection, they are so surrounded by hollow conventionalism, and sometimes, as David had experienced, by treachery, that they are drawn by strong attraction to those who are bound to them for more than their rank and riches. Perhaps, also, he felt that he would be a wiser and better man, more safe from the temptations of vanity and luxury, if he had Barzillai beside him. A good man always in view may become to us like a second conscience. When the king could not persuade the father, he gladly accepts the charge of his son. He seems to feel as if the care of this young man would bring comfort to his heart, which was still bleeding for the loss of Absalom. It was not in lightness that David made the request. When on his deathbed, he remembered it, and charged Solomon to show kindness to the son for the sake of what his father Barzillai had done for him when he fled from the face of Absalom. In the book of Jeremiah, many generations afterwards, we learn that the habitation of Chimham's family was in Bethlehem, by the house of David; and, in the days of the return from the captivity, the daughters of Barzillai the Gileadite are named as having a place among the tribes of Israel. If we read the Bible carefully we shall find such miniatures as these scattered among its great historic paintings, bearing marks of the same designing hand in God's providential care and in the living likenesses fashioned by his grace. At present we shall select only a portion of the story. Let that portion be the words of Barzillai on parting with David.

I. We have a man *who knows that he is old, but who is not distressed by the thought of it.* There are old men who do not know that they are old, or who seek to suppress the knowledge. "Grey hairs," the prophet says, "are here and there on him, yet he knoweth not." They do all they can to hide their growing age from others, and from themselves; and when multiplying infirmities compel them to confess it, it is with melancholy, if not with bitterness. Now here is an old man who has no difficulty in owning that he is old. He has no reticence, no shame, and, so far as we can see, he has no regret. He numbers up his weaknesses indeed, but it is much in the way a soldier counts the scars he has brought from his battle-fields. "So long have I served my king and country, and here are the marks of the wounds." 'Look,' Barzillai says, 'at what eighty years of life-work have brought me; dim eyes, dull ears, grey hairs, feeble hands, and tottering limbs; this world is fading from my soul's vision; I cannot be far from my bed in the grave.' And he says this not to ask for pity, and vex others with the care of his infirmities, but to save them from trouble: "Wherefore should thy servant be yet a burden unto my lord the king?" A brave-hearted, unselfish old man this is, bearing up when the strong men bow themselves, and sustained, no doubt, by a deep hope within. We feel that if he had lived in the time of the New Testament he would have been such an one as Paul the aged, and that he would have expressed himself in such words as these: "I have fought a good fight, I have finished my course, I have kept the faith." "Now is our salvation nearer than when we believed." Few things in the world are so pleasant as the sight of such a conscious, cheerful, hopeful old age, certain that it has not long to stay, but interested to the last in the best things of life, in the cause of God and man, and country and church. This is the hoary head which is so beautiful when it is found in the way of righteousness. We should aim at this even from youth, for, if we live, we shall grow old; yes, if we live, we shall grow old. It is a truism which most people forget. They think often of life, they think sometimes of death, they seldom think of old age.

But how are we to prepare for this? First, surely, by taking God with us early in the journey of life, that we may be able to press the plea: "O God, Thou hast taught me from my youth; and now, when I am old and grey-headed, O God, forsake me not." God is willing to receive a man whenever he turns to Him; but the later he turns, the more shall be his regrets. Next, by providing beforehand the compensations which God is willing to give for everything that may be taken away by the changes of life. If the eye is to become dim, we may be preparing an inner vision more open and clear for divine and eternal realities; if the ear is to be dulled to earthly music, and hard of access to the voice of friends, we can ask that friend to say to it, " Ephphatha, Be opened!" who will enter our solitude with his words—" To old age I am He, to hoar hairs I will carry you;" if the feet and hands become powerless for their accustomed work, we may exercise ourselves in the faith and hope which make the feet more than youthful and change the hands to wings, so that we shall mount up like eagles, and run and not be weary, and walk and not faint. And, if we reach old age, we can make it happy by seeking to make it unselfish. If, as we advance in life, we make our growing infirmities a discomfort to all about us, if we dwell upon them with needless and peevish rehearsal, if we use them for taxing our friends to do what we can perform for ourselves, we shall make our load heavier, by having it always in our thoughts, and we shall lose the sympathy which would have made it lighter. But if, while we are conscious of increasing weaknesses, we strive to save others from suffering by them, we shall more than half forget them in forgetting ourselves; and we shall commend old age by showing the young that every period of life has its resources for being happy, and for doing good. This is the true way of rejuvenescence, of renewing our youth like the eagle's, and of bringing forth fruit in old age. Some one has said that it would be a melancholy world without children, and an inhuman world without the aged; and the world is never better than when these two can meet and give and receive gladness.

Now, it is quite true that the great majority of men, and even many good Christians, cannot attain to the thought of a happy old age without a hard struggle. We have a natural reluctance to the feeling that we are growing old; we put it away, and when something at last forces it upon us, it is like the rush of an armed man from an ambush, or the flake of the first snow to tell us that the long summer days are gone, and that winter is at hand. And yet, as you may have seen, it is the transition which is the most painful. When the first days of brown October show us the fresh green leaves of summer, now sere and yellow, dropping from the boughs under the wind that wails through the thin woods, we cannot help a feeling of sadness creeping over the heart. But when winter has come it has its own enjoyments; there is the long, quiet evening, the cheerful gleam of the hearth, the closer bosom of the family and of friendship, the pleasant memories of summer, and the hopes of its return—these give to winter its gladness, and even its glow. If we are in this transition, or nearing it, we should seek to realise it, and to rise above it by looking forward. Every time of life to a true man is only a transition to something better. 'I am growing old; yes, I am growing old; Lord, teach me to count my days, and to look not so much wistfully back as hopefully forward, forward to the quiet peace and happy thoughts which God can give in winter, and, still further, to the day when winter shall be past, and the rains over and gone, and the time of the singing of birds shall again have come.' The experience of an aged Christian woman [1] was, that "at eighty-five she felt old age to be the happiest period of human life, because the most free from cares and worldly anxieties, and the nearest to its happy destination." We would not forget, however, that there are those to whom old

---

[1] Mary Hill. See *Autobiography of Mrs. Fletcher.*

age comes not free from cares. The poet has spoken of "age and want as an ill-matched pair," and Richter says, "Welcome poverty, provided it comes not too late in life!" Barzillai's character is an example to us here. It is the part of all to help old age in want; but it seems specially fitting that the old who have the power should help the old. To see an aged man overburdened with wealth, and clinging to it, when he could relieve the wants of those with whom he most of all should sympathise, is a pitiable thing. It seems to have taken the weight of years from Barzillai's head when he could unload himself of his substance for the help of David. We have still our way of reaching a higher King, and of receiving his blessing—"Inasmuch as ye have done it unto one of the least of these my brethren, ye have done it unto Me."

II. We have a man *who is rich, but who is satisfied with his natural position*. No doubt, the remark will readily be made by some, 'It is easy for a rich man to be satisfied; let us have his wealth, and we shall blame ourselves if we ask for anything more.' But if you look round on the world, you will perceive that it is at the stage of prosperity that the dissatisfaction of many men begins. They are ambitious of quitting their old society and habits, their tastes and even their temperament, and of taking a flight into an untried region for which they have frequently no aptitude and no training. A poor man may be dissatisfied with his poverty; a rich man is often dissatisfied with all his old circle, and with his former self. If Barzillai had been of the mind of many, he would have made his wealth buy wings for his vanity, and, old as he was, would have tried to flutter in the sunshine of the court. Here was his opportunity for getting a ribbon or a star, or whatever might then be the name for it, for being pointed out in the streets of Jerusalem, and having a splendid mausoleum in the king's dale. But he was a wiser man, and a happier, and stands in higher honour this day than if he had wronged his nature, and finished his life with an act of folly.

It is quite true that the Bible forbids no man to seek the improvement of his worldly circumstances, or to use that improvement in a wise and generous way. It has no malediction on wealth itself, and no canonising of poverty. When our Saviour bade the young man sell all he had, and give to the poor, it was a test of character, not a condition of discipleship. Wealth gives a man many advantages; it enables him to ward off evils which flesh and blood find it hard to bear; it opens up the way to fair fields of knowledge; it puts it in his power to relieve the sufferings of others, and to help causes dear to God and to every good man. But there are two things against which a man who has risen to wealth should carefully watch— becoming the slave of sensual gratification: 'What more can I eat and drink?' or the servant of vanity and love of display: 'How can I shine in the social circle?' We have much of both in our time, and, perhaps, the last more than the first. How many do we see who would have been happy, useful, and honoured if they had considered the laws of natural fitness, but who make themselves contemptible and miserable by aiming at a kind of life for which they were never made! They imitate the style and talk, and perhaps the religion, of what they think and call the upper class, and all the while they have as little perception and enjoyment of the fashion they affect, as old Barzillai would have had of the music of the singers in Jerusalem. One evil of this is that it prevents many people who have wealth being listened to, when they protest against the sensualism and intemperance which would ruin our country. The froth cannot, with any consistency, rebuke the dregs. Another evil is that many in this foolish chase are injuring their own best nature. If they have been brought up in a reasonable way, they cannot, in their inmost heart, approve of this unnatural change, and if they persist in it, it will destroy the reality of their character in more important things. For the greatest evil of all is that the grace of God in the heart finds it hard to live with pretentious struggle and unreality. Those who are to the manner born may be humble in royal circles, if they are God's children; and those who have duty to perform are steadied by it, and may stand safe in high places; but if we covet the company for the mere repute and fashion of it, we are on slippery ground. David might be able to pray in his palace in Jerusalem as fervently as in the wilderness of Judah, but it would not have been so easy for Barzillai. A man who is diligent in business may stand before kings, but he will not thrust himself in, he will wait to be summoned, and when he stands before them he will not turn his back on his own true nature, on tried friendships in any walk of life, or on the religion which has commended itself to him as in accordance with God's Word, though it may be lightly esteemed in the fashionable world. He is a very small man and a very feeble Christian who forgets his old friends, or forsakes his old faith, because he cannot own them in some circle he would fondly enter; he can never reach the highest honour or feel the deepest happiness. In the midst of empty ambitions, and vain contests for pre-eminence, our wisdom is to prefer the position which agrees with what is deepest in our nature, and which is most helpful to our spiritual life. It was the choice of Barzillai, and of the wise woman of Shunem: "What is to be done for thee? wouldest thou be spoken for to the king, or to the captain of the host? And she answered, I dwell among mine own people."

III. We have a man *of long experience, who has kept up his love of simple pleasures.* We can infer this from the tone in which he speaks. He had reached an age when the love of sensational things fails, in all but the most frivolous; yet the way in which he speaks of them puts them quietly aside, as not to his taste, and never likely to have been so. He had been brought up among the hills of Gilead, a land of flocks and herds and grassy pastures and clear streams, with the sights and sounds of free nature around him. And where he has lived, he wishes to die and " be buried by the grave of his father and his mother." The old man of fourscore is a child again, back in his heart in the home of his youth, where he felt a mother's love and a father's care, and he cannot leave the spot where they lie. We feel that there is a fresh, tender heart in him which has not grown old with his years, with pensive memories of the past, but full power of enjoying all that is natural and true around him. "A right man," it has been said, " should carry all the past stages of his life within him, as a tree carries the circles of its growth." Such a man evidently was Barzillai.

In these times of tumult and change, we think with envy of the quiet, primitive days, when men grew up in their place with leisure for spreading out their thoughts like branches, and sending down their affections like roots. We have no wish to depreciate that kind of life which occupies itself with the activities of the world, which presses into the highways of cities, and the throng of business, and which has its pleasure in breasting and battling with the great waves of public movement in social and intellectual and political progress. There are faculties in man's nature which find their proper exercise in this; the world could not advance or even live without it, and the calm recesses, which seem shut out from the great sea of life, would stagnate if they were not stirred by its tides. But we should take care that the whirl of public life does not unfit us for enjoying private life. A man must judge for himself how far he can go in the work of the world, or even the work of the Church, without losing the essence of his personal life; and his safety lies in remembering that, after the friendship of God, his happiness is found in never losing the power of being pleased with simple things, things which can be easily reached, which do not pall with the possession, nor create a craving for fresh excitement. What is needed for young and old is to preserve a love for home and its affections, and an open eye for interest in the most common things which God has scattered round us in his world.

We may turn aside to touch, for a moment, a question often discussed, and of importance for our time—the comparative advantage of country or of city. We have Barzillai's choice here, and we all know the poet's saying, " God made the country, but man made the town." The country has its calm, its opportunity for reflection, its freedom from some temptations; but it has its dangers, its tendency to stagnation and narrowness and selfishness. The town has its stimulus of society, its energetic pulse of life, its spirit of progress, but it has its evil sights and sounds, which wake up sleeping demons, its false ambitions, its fevered unrest. The one may become a marsh, the other a whirlpool. The happy case, if we could reach it, would be some union of the two. The Son of Man laid his hand on both when He taught on the shores of the Lake of Galilee, and the hilly slopes around it, and when He mingled with men in the streets of Jerusalem. Eden begins the world with man almost lost in nature; the new Jerusalem closes it with the city which God has built for man, and nature scattered through it. And in these things there is this truth, that in the throng of human life we should keep within sight of the works of God. If, in our artificial society, the masses are shut out from this, it is unhealthy both for body and soul. It is for the good of a nation that the balance should be kept up, that the country should become more, if the city does not become less; or that the cities should, in some way, disperse themselves and "go forth into the fields, and lodge in the villages." The opportunity to raise, with his own hands, a few flowers, makes a man more human, and brings him more within reach of God and of his grace. It may seem a dream to hope for this to any large extent, but even now the thoughts of men are being turned to it, and if we had man more in contact with nature, we might have God more seen in them both, and might bring back that fellowship of Eden when the Lord God came down "to walk with man in the garden, in the cool of the day."

But meanwhile, this is not a dream, that a man can keep the love of natural things in his heart, and can call them up in fancy, as he reads. We feel as if one could not peruse this simple story of Barzillai the Gileadite, without a pleasure stealing unconsciously over him, and helping him, though he is tied for the time to the mart or to the mill, to "scorn the multitude of the city, and regard not the crying of the driver." Next to the value we set on the Bible for its great truths of redeeming grace—for Christ and the salvation of the soul—we should love it for this, that it takes us to nature and to the home affections, and that it was an earlier guide than Wordsworth to the thoughts which are shut up in flowers and clouds and stars. If a man will but read his Bible with a fresh heart, he may walk with patriarchs in the world when it was young and green, may rest with Abraham under the shade of the oak of Mamre, and see the upspringing of the well to which the princes of Israel sang. It will place him beside Job in that wonderful procession of God's works and creatures which give him such humility and confidence. He may sit on the mountain-top with Christ among the lilies and the birds, to understand what they say and sing, and he may listen till he hears far off the final hymn, which shall be a concert of nature round regenerated men, when "the wilderness and the solitary place shall be glad for them; and the desert shall rejoice and blossom as the rose."

IV. We have a man *who is attached to the past, but who does not distrust the future.* There was evidently a great change coming over the land of Israel at this time. The old patriarchal ways were losing their hold. The capital was growing, and men and gold and silver flowing into it. New views were prevailing which looked on the past as antiquated, and pressed forward, often recklessly, into unknown futures. The young men of revolution who gathered round Absalom were a sign of it, and after the splendour of Solomon's reign it came out more distinctly under his successor. In the parting of Barzillai and David we seem to have the two tendencies, the recoil of the old, the advance of the new. But the recoil is only one of personal feeling. For himself he has grown up in the old way, and cannot change—he loves its simplicity, its naturalness, its antique virtues. But he is not one of those who think that the world is to stand still at their grave, that all the good is behind, and all the evil before. He says for himself, 'I am too old to transplant, I shall die as I have lived, contented among my fields and flocks, and I shall lie down in my father's grave. But the new has its rights and the world will be on. My son is here; the future is beaming in his face, and beating in his heart; I give him into hands I can trust for leading him in the way of truth and righteousness. Do with him what seemeth good unto thee.' The training of his family had no doubt been that of faithful Abraham, "commanding his household after him to keep the way of the Lord," and under David's care the counsel would be that which he gave to his own son: "And thou, my son, know thou the God of thy father, and serve Him with a perfect heart, and with a willing mind." If the old can thus pass over into the new, there is security amid all changes.

We are in the midst of one of these transitions now, when many are fearing, and some are predicting, only evil. The quiet old life of our country is retiring evermore into the background, and the towns with their rush of life, their battles of thought and action, their impulses for good and evil are in the front. The sons and daughters are flocking to them, the fathers and mothers, with less choice than Barzillai, are often compelled to follow. We cannot help regretting it, and wishing to retain as much as we can of what was so good. When we think of the old life of Scotland among its hills and cottage homes, of its men and women so intelligent and God-fearing, so independent in spirit, yet so kindly and courteous, it is hard to believe that its departure can be a blessing. The land can scarcely anywhere rear a nobler people than those who, on a Sabbath morning, gathered like streams from the valleys to the house of God, to sing the psalms which had been the strength of their fathers when they were outcasts among the mountains.

There is another view of the time which may make us still more anxious. Insurrections of self-will and lawlessness are breaking out which threaten all things human and divine. Men are setting their mouths against the heavens, and laying bitter and persistent siege to the citadels in which faith has felt itself secure for ages. These things sadden and startle us when we think of the future. The world looks like a ship descending the rapids, and some surge of the stream may dash and shatter it on the black reefs of atheism and anarchy which shoot their heads above the foam. We may be quietly sleeping by the grave of our father and mother, beyond the shock and terror, but what of the poor children growing up around us, who have to meet this crisis ? We cannot help, even now, pitying them when we think of the doubts and evil suggestions cast in on hearts which should be opening trustfully to a heavenly Father's care. Let us have faith in God. Changes there have been, threatening destruction all along the march of the kingdom of God, but each one of them has led to something higher and better. God is in the future as He has been in the past, and his path is that of the Just One, shining more and more unto the perfect day. Only, let us do with the children what this aged Israelite did with his son. Let us commit them, with faith and prayer and Christian training, into the keeping of the wiser and mightier King under whose rule the world is placed. "Let them go over with my Lord the King, and let Him do to them what shall seem good unto Him." "He shall save the children of the needy, and shall redeem their soul from deceit and violence." He cannot be dethroned, till men find a purity and love which are holier and more compassionate than the heart of the Lord Jesus Christ. There are times when men may think He has lost his throne, when Ahitophels betray, and Shimeis cast dust and insult; but He will come back again to a larger dominion; "judgment shall return unto righteousness, and all the upright in heart shall follow it."

We would not forget that there may be some who have no anxiety about living children, but whose hearts have a life-long sorrow for the dead. They have parted with them like Barzillai on the bank of Jordan, and lost sight of them as they moved away to that great world which is gathering all to itself. But if they have been given over into his care who has said, "Suffer them to come unto Me," "they have been brought with gladness and rejoicing; they have entered into the King's palace." Nothing is lost that is surrendered into his keeping; and when He gives it back it shall be a portion of that good part which shall not be taken away. Let us, then, confirm our hold of Him to whom all these ancient believers, with knowledge less or more, were moving forward, but who has been made manifest to us, the guardian of childhood, the joy and strength of youth and manhood, the hope of darkening years, who can make the light shine in at eventide, and change the shadow of death into the morning.

VI.

TWO MARVELS.

"*When Jesus heard it, He marvelled, and said to them that followed, Verily I say unto you, I have not found so great faith, no, not in Israel.*"—MATT. VIII. 10.

"*And He marvelled because of their unbelief.*"—MARK VI. 6.

OUR Lord Jesus Christ had the sinless feelings of our human nature, and there are two cases recorded here in which He was struck with wonder. The first was at the faith of the heathen soldier who asked Him to heal his servant, and who felt sure that He needed only to speak the word and the cure would come. He looked on Christ as a captain of salvation who had all delivering powers at his command, and who could send them on his errands at any time and to any place. "When Jesus heard it, He marvelled." The other case was when He came to his own country, and found the faith of the people so weak that his works of healing were hindered. It should have been otherwise with men who possessed so much light and privilege, "and He marvelled because of their unbelief." There are two sides to almost everything, according to the way in which we regard it, and there are two sides to faith and unbelief. Sometimes faith looks wonderful—we are surprised when we see men believe; and sometimes unbelief looks wonderful—we are surprised that men do not believe. This is the subject on which we intend to speak; the marvels of both faith and unbelief. In doing this, we shall leave the special instances in these two histories aside, and deal with the subject in a general way. There is a world in which we live that lies open to our senses, with its objects and laws—the world of matter which we look on with our eyes, handle with our hands, and examine by our natural reason; and in regard to the existence of this material world, men, except in metaphysical abstractions, have no doubt. But there is another class of thoughts, which passes beyond the world of sense, which men can conceive and speak of, and which numbers of men in all ages and in all countries have held to belong also to a real world. It is apprehended by that power in man's nature which we call faith; and to this world belong God and our own souls, Christ and the great doctrines taught by Him, and presented to us in his life and death and resurrection. It is of this unseen world that we intend to speak as the object of faith, and we shall, first, give some illustrations of the twofold marvel—it is wonderful that men should believe in such a world, it is wonderful that they should not believe in it; and, next, we shall give some principles that may help us to a decision.

I. Let us look at SOME OF THE THINGS WHICH MAY LEAD US TO MARVEL BOTH AT FAITH AND AT UNBELIEF.

Take first *our own nature*. When we think of it we may sometimes wonder that any one believes in more than dead matter. The world with which we are connected all through our life has so much of the presence and power of matter in it, that it seems at times as if there were room for nothing else. Our senses make us acquainted with nothing but qualities of matter. We see, we touch, and we taste, and we never pass beyond material things; and when we refine and analyse, we reach only matter in more subtle forms. The laws which govern the universe around us are material forces. Light, heat, electricity are regulated by laws which can be measured with fixed certainty, and men never reach, or expect to reach, in their researches any higher than a material agency. We never arrive at a point where a hand comes in from above, and where we can say, 'There material law ends, and the spiritual begins.' The writer in Ecclesiastes had this same feeling: "The wind goeth toward the south, and turneth about unto the north; it returneth again according to his circuits."

And the end of these laws, to our perception, is death. Change, ending in decay and dissolution, is written on the face of everything around us. Man dies, the body returns to dust, graves are heaped up age after age and lie unbroken, and the old question returns, "Man dieth and wasteth away; yea, man giveth up the ghost, and where is he?" These things are pressing upon us day after day, from our cradle to our grave, and they proclaim the apparently invincible power of matter and material law. Yet there are men who, in the face of all this, believe in something more than matter. They have the conviction that there is something in them which will survive this change and decay; that there are other laws which, if they do not contradict the material, will escape and rise above and conquer them. Yet they have not seen this other world, they cannot prove by any demonstration the existence of these supernatural laws, and still they firmly believe in them. May we not marvel at their faith?

But, on the other hand, if we continue to think of our nature, is there not something which makes us wonder at unbelief? There is a world within us entirely different from all this world of sense and matter. A physiologist can show how the light affects the eye, enters the nerves of the brain, makes them move and thrill; he can explain how the waves of sound fall on the ear, and prolong their undulations into the furthest caverns. But does this explain the feelings of beauty and tenderness which visit us from a sweet landscape, or the visions that flit before the imagination as we listen to strains of music? Will any analysis of the spectrum make us understand how we are moved by the glory of the stars, or are led out by them into an idea of the infinite? By what transposition or transmutation of particles of matter could Milton's view of Paradise arise? or how, as our eye lights on some black characters in a book, can that view become ours?

Or think of the power of a moral law in our nature. There is something in us which says, "Thou shalt," and "Thou shalt not," as a fixed and eternal law in the face of all desire and advantage. The philosopher Kant said there were in the universe two sublime things, the starry heavens and the moral law. Attempts may be made to show that the moral sense is a growth of development in our nature, on the ground of utility, but the fact remains that the moral sense exists, that it asserts itself against all motives of utility as unchangeable and universal, and that we cannot think of conscience approving us when we do what we believe to be wrong, without destroying the foundation of our nature. Since our planet existed, it has rolled from west to east; we can imagine this reversed, but it is impossible to imagine a reversal of the golden rule as a principle of right. Is there not something in our nature older and deeper than material law?

Or think of the existence of an ideal in our nature. We have a conception of the true and beautiful and pure, and to any one who can think about them they are as real as any sight or sound can be. It may be said that there is no real object corresponding to them, that they are only creations of the human mind; but it cannot be denied that they are real thoughts. Man has the power of creating ideas of spiritual perfection, and they have been so real to him that he has struggled toward them in all ages, and has made every sacrifice, even to death, to maintain them. Even if one should say, 'there is no God, there never has been a Christ such as the Gospels present,' yet there is the thought of a God, there is the vision of the character of Christ. Whence did these come? And can we think that the nature in which such visions arise, where they persistently remain, which they impel to such disinterested and self-renouncing efforts and sufferings, has no more in it than matter and material force? It is quite possible, on Christian or on merely philosophical principles, to account for the existence of unbelief in men. We can account for it on the ground of moral freedom, the opportunity for probation, the permission of evil in a world of responsible action, the entrance of sin into the world; but if there were nothing save matter and its laws, how can we ever account for faith? Whence came all this universe of thought in man's nature, so deep, so high, so powerful, that it has shown itself again and again able to set at nought every motive which the world of matter can draw from the weight of its profit or the fascination of its pleasures? When we think of these things in man's nature, may we not wonder at persistent unbelief?

But, again, if we would see another instance of this opposition of faith and unbelief, let us look at *the Bible*. There are many things about the Bible which try our faith. There is this, first of all, that the Bible professes to be a book which has come from God as man's guide for time and for eternity; and yet its evidence of divinity is open to dispute. Since the proof of its origin is so important, should not God have made it so certain that no man could doubt it—as clear as the sun in the sky, or the great laws which govern our physical life? What guide who cannot show undoubted credentials will inspire confidence in those who need his guidance? Does it not shake our faith to think that so much argument is needed to repel the objections that have been made to the Bible? When we come to the contents of the Bible, they look so scattered and disjointed; many of the parts seem to have found a place in it by accident, and are questioned, not only by those whom we call its enemies, but by men whom we esteem its friends. There are what seem so many trifling details, irrelevant circumstances in the book, and difficulties which we cannot solve to others or to ourselves. Could not the Author of the Bible, if it be a divine book, have removed these stumbling-blocks from the way of our faith? Then there is in the centre of the book, and pervading it, this one point, this marvellous declaration, that the Maker of the universe became man, a suffering man, and died, and was laid in the grave, and took on Him the sins of men, to secure pardon and purity for them. Is it easy to believe this? And with this central marvel, there are all those wonderful works which are told of Him and of others, that surpass all the powers of nature, and bring in a new world and new laws, of which there are no outward, supernatural traces remaining among us. Then there is the declaration that the dead who have slept in the grave for untold ages shall rise, and that there is a world beyond death utterly unlike this, where decay and sin and sorrow have no existence. So strange and unearthly do these things seem to us, that we at times put the question to ourselves, 'Do I really believe them, and do I receive the book which speaks of them as the most certain Word of God?' And yet these things have been believed, and are believed, by numberless multitudes of men and women, of all ages and classes and ranks of intelligence. In the face of the most wonderful features that could belong to any book, faith in the Bible has been maintained. Men have gone cheerfully into exile and prison, and have mounted the fiery pile, clasping the Bible to their heart, and at this day, after all has been said against it that the learning and wit of man can discover, there is no book that has gathered so many hearts to it, that has moulded so many lives, that could summon round it so many deaths in ready sacrifice. May we not marvel at faith?

But if we look at the Bible in another way, we shall think unbelief wonderful. For, beneath its fragmentary form, and amid all its difficulties of detail, it has a unique and consistent character. It has this strange peculiarity, that, though it has come from widely different men and times and circumstances, it is one book; it has one pervading thought and purpose—to bring man and God together. It has something of the freedom of external nature, with one life struggling up through it to an ever more perfect expression. It tells of a fall from God which has brought terrible consequences within and around us, in sin and suffering, and, if we accept this, it becomes a key to the contradictions and miseries of the world, on which Pessimism dwells without being able to give a cause or a cure. It presents a plan of recovery which centres in one great Person, whose character rises above all others, as the sun rises over mists and marshes; and if his words and his work be received they open the prospect of a remedy to the deep moral disorder of the world. The name of Christ becomes to those who dwell on it the name above every name, which reveals us to ourselves, meets the yearnings of our hearts, satisfies the wants of our nature, and points the way to the ideal of perfect truth and purity and blessedness. Instead of never-ending death and eternal sepulchres, it opens the way to everlasting life and progress. And it has not only promised this, but shown its power of fulfilment. It has breathed into multitudes of men a new life, and has bestowed on their character a courage in action, a calmness in suffering, a loftiness and purity, which have been the admiration of those who did not join them in their faith. Thousands have visited its secret springs of revival, and have left them with the beams of a new gladness on their face, like Stephen's when he looked up to Christ. It has had much to contend with, in the persecution of enemies, the taunts of scoffers, the faithlessness of professed friends, the inconsistency of true Christians; but it has held its place against them all. In the proportion in which its principles have penetrated social and national life, kingdoms and commonwealths have become strong, and vice and misery have disappeared. Whatever objections may be made to parts of the Bible may be answered by its effect on the life of the man or the society that receives it in the entireness of its spirit. If it has not cured the evils of human nature, it is because it has not been truly and fully used; but even in its partial working it has shown a power of transformation greater and wider than the world has yet witnessed; and if a moral purpose be sought for the individual life, or for the history of the world, there is none comparable to what is found in the spirit of the Bible, and in the person of its great subject, Jesus Christ. When some men, then, assert that the book is the product of some imposture, or the result of some accident, may we not marvel at their unbelief?

There is still another instance of this opposition when

we turn to *the course of life and its events.* There are many things in the course of life which shake men's faith in what may be called the providence of history. The government of the world does not appear to be regulated on any principles of justice, and when men look up they cannot see the face of a Lawgiver. There are periods when greater apparent confusion enters human affairs, and, besides this, there are times when the defect is in the spirit of the onlookers. In an age of materialism doubts come up thick and heavy, like fungous growths in dark recesses. At such seasons the suggestions of Epicurus find many listeners, that the gods, if there be any, have gone up above the clouds, and ceased to concern themselves with the order of the world. The poets sing their festive songs, and the essayists write their easy, pastime papers to magnify the present hour, and put judgment out of sight. But as the wind blows on the aspen leaf it may turn to the other side from light to dark, and for the thoughtless laugh there may be the bitter groan. We know how these meet in the same age and in the same heart, and how " in the midst of laughter there is heaviness,"— a philosophy of despair under a surface of levity. At such a time, when the clouds are dense and far down and the stars are gone out, even good men do not escape the pressure. Then Job and his friends feel the difficulty, and the Preacher imagines that " all things happen alike to all." Jeremiah asks the question, "Wherefore doth the way of the wicked prosper?" And the shadows seem to project themselves up over the souls beneath the altar, till they cry, "How long, O Lord, holy and true?" These are sore seasons to pass through, when the heavens are brass and the earth iron, and the spiritual breath seems to have quitted the world's frame, and matter and force are proclaimed supreme rulers. It needs more strenuous effort then to keep hold of a living God, "working salvation in the midst of the earth." This difficulty on the divine side is increased by symptoms which often appear on the human. There come outbreaks of lawlessness on the part of some, and of meanness and selfishness on the part of others, which make men appear like "the flies of latter spring," which "sting and sing, and weave their petty cells and die." Christian churches become unfaithful to truth and purity, raise any sail which will catch the breeze of popularity, and make success, not principle, the star which guides them. The successors of Judas and Peter make their appearance to betray Christ, or weakly deny Him, and the world's finger of scorn is pointed to them with a justice which makes the reproach go very deep. It is hard, when these times come, to believe that they will pass away, and that days of firm faith and high-toned integrity will return. And yet there are men who fasten their hands on God's throne in the greatest tumults of the world, and so stand firm not only in their character, but in their hope, —who believe in God's sunshine above the thickest clouds of doubt, and see assured victory beyond all disasters and desertions. Should we not say, 'Servants of God, well done!' and marvel at their faith?

And they are right, for there is another way of looking at life than on its present surface. The awards even now may be found in the peace which goes deep down into the heart of the man who holds fast to his integrity, and has an anchor within the veil. In the darkest times and places there are those who stand fast in truth and uprightness. Judas falls, but Peter returns, and there are the faithful few who never waver—John at the cross, the faithful women at the sepulchre. When darkness visited the world in that great eclipse, the meteors fell to earth, but the quiet stars shone out till light came again. And in the many nights of unbelief which have obscured the world since, God has never left Himself without witnesses. There have never been persecutions without the uprising of martyrs, or seasons of apostasy from truth and righteousness without men who would die, but not deceive. We should rejoice greatly when we find them still, those who in the mart of business maintain principle against all the seducements of interest, those who are resolute in hard duty, patient in tribulation, cheerful in humble walks and sunless sick-rooms, because they grasp the higher law and discern the unchanging light. They are the martyrs of our time, and let us thank God they are not few. One such is a witness to a living God, and to the truth that man is made of more than earth. It is only a spirit within him which can respond to a spiritual attraction. And if we look through time, may we not discover that there is a power working in the world which is causing this testimony to grow? Slowly and with many a turning, but certainly and onward, we may perceive the advance of a kingdom of righteousness. If it cannot be measured by years it can by centuries, in a higher standard of rectitude, and a more disinterested regard for human welfare. The secular mind itself has its prophecies of a brighter future for the world, its dreams in the clouds though they do not rise to heaven, and though there is no divine ladder. Even this is a witness to a law of progression and a hope of its kind. Only, it seems strange that these men fail to see that but for Christianity this power would want its mainspring. There is no such movement among the worshippers of Brahma, the disciples of Buddha, or the followers of Mohammed; they stand still or recede. Art, science, and philosophy themselves are strong only in Christian centres, and yet many of these men turn their back on the light that has given them the power of knowledge and the hopes of progress, amid which they live. May we not marvel at unbelief?

II. Having looked at the two contrasted sides, we shall now present briefly SOME PRINCIPLES BY WHICH WE MAY BE HELPED TO A DECISION.

The first thing to be realised is that *God's plan of impressing spiritual truths is not by demonstration.* There are many who object to Christianity, and to religion of any kind, on the ground that it cannot be proved irresistibly to their reason. There is something to be said, they tell us, both for and against the Bible, and they remain agnostics, with this feeling, that if the matter were so important it would be surrounded with evidence which would leave no room for questioning. Now, let us frankly admit that Christianity has no irresistible proof. If it had, there would be neither unbelievers nor Christians, for in such a case there would be no such thing as faith, but only knowledge, and a Christian is a man who has knowledge but who also lives by faith. Religion would be pursued and practised as mathematics are, or as science is when mathematics are applied to it. But observe under what system we should then be placed. Man would not be capable of moral freedom in conducting his life and forming his character. He would think of God and of his soul and its interests in the way in which a man builds up the propositions of geometry; his convictions would be the theorems, and his actions the problems which were fastened to one another by iron links. Man would be a creature of mind, but where would there be room for his heart and its loving surrender to God, for his will and its resolve to listen to the divine voice and obey it? These can only exist where man has power to give himself away, that is, where he has moral freedom. And if we take away freedom and love and will in man's relation to God, there would be no meaning in them as between man and man. If we destroy the source there can be no streams, and sympathy and love and gratitude, the feelings which unite men in families and friendships, cease to exist; these have their life, not in necessary chains of reasoning, but in the free exchange of the soul. In such a world God might be a supreme architect and mechanician, building up a universe by fixed physical laws; He might even be an author of scientific thought leading forth intellects into higher and wider investigations in the track of his own creations; but He could not be a Father and Friend, drawing to Him the love of children for the glimpses they have of the supreme beauty of his purity, and the pulsations that come throbbing from the love of his heart. The universe might be a temple, but where would be the worshippers with songs of love and joy and self-devotion? The interest which men of science find in their researches has, no doubt, something of the pleasure of intellectual power in exercise, of pursuit and attainment and surprise, but much also of the half-conscious feeling that the world they are studying is not one of dead atoms or hard theoretic thought, but of life, with secret springs of feeling in it which freshen them when they are not well aware. Were it a universe of mere rigid thinking and demonstration, it is difficult to see why there should be a world of immortality beyond it. It would be a world where the growth would be that of calculating pieces of mechanism, a surface growth without depth or height, no deepening of the nature in reverence and affection to the Father of spirits, no ascent step by step in approach to the infinite fulness of his holiness and love. Let us seek to understand this well, and we shall not be surprised and perplexed by the fact that God does not make spiritual truths subject to the laws of mental demonstration. He could not do it without making them no more spiritual—without depriving man of his freedom, and leaving him no room for his heart and conscience and spirit. If there are to be ties of sympathy between man and God, and an immortality which has in its bosom an eternal life, man must be dealt with as capable, not only of knowledge, but of the choice of love. God has made man capable of faith, but therefore also of unbelief; the kind of proof He gives him may persuade, but it will not constrain. God does not force his own existence upon men. He gives them reasons to seek and discover Him, "if haply we might feel after Him and find Him, though He be not far from every one of us." Christ, who loves man so much, will not force the door of his will. There would be no love if He did. He is very careful of the mysterious power He has bestowed on man; very courteous, we may say it with all reverence, when He asks an entrance. "Behold, I stand at the door and knock, if any man open, I will come in"—O how gladly! and then in the fellowship there shall follow full conviction.

The next remark we make is that to reach a decision in faith, *we should look at things in their full breadth and in their practical bearing.* From the view we have been taking of unbelief and faith, we may perceive that unbelief in spiritual things proceeds often from the too exclusive study of details, from analysis without reconstruction, and that faith is helped by the wider view. There may be a man of vast learning and acuteness, a master of science and criticism, who cannot judge rightly of the life of any subject because he studies it in parts, and does not regard it as a whole. The more minute the parts, the further are they from life; and the soul is not in any one part, but in the union of them all. The eye of an inquirer may become so microscopic that he can detect the smallest differences, but if he looks only at them, he may lose the power of adjusting his vision to the compass of their agreement. The dust of details may blind a man, and he becomes like the fly of which Addison speaks, which creeps up the pillar of St. Paul's and measures with its foot the smallest inequalities, but has no perception of their span and of the overarching dome. We may dissect God's universe till God himself, who is the life of it, disappears; and we may anatomise the Bible till Christ is not seen in it, and we have nothing left but words and phrases and shades of speech. We can never have too much of careful and close study, but to see the full truth we must draw back our view, and look at things not merely with the close inspection of students, but with the eyes and feelings of men. Then the details of the world become a universe again, and God's face looks out from it; the books of the canon become a Bible, and Christ moves through it to give it meaning and soul. We only carry out this view when we say that we must look at things not merely in their breadth but in their practical bearing. What man needs both for body and soul is the nourishment of his life, and whatever makes his life strongest, most real and vivid, attests thereby its truth. What cannot live and move, or in some way help life and movement, is not made for this world. That view of the universe will prevail which gives man the noblest prospects, and puts him on the way to reach them; and that conception of Christianity will conquer which makes men most just and pure and benevolent, that is, most like Christ. The true spiritual medicine is that which cures the diseases of the soul; the bread of life is that which gives most strength for suffering evil in the day of adversity, and for doing good to all as we have opportunity. It may be said, this is a utilitarian test, and so it is, for utility is a true test if we put into it the true things—not those which concern time and secular advantage merely, but those which give to the spirit life and power. The way to approach this question, then, is to apply to it our reason, for God gives us sufficient grounds to lead us to count true the testimony He has given us of Christ, and to take, besides, our whole nature and bring it into contact with the remedy He has provided. From the very nature of the case we can reach full conviction only by experience. As the heart is renewed, as the conscience is enlightened, as the will is strengthened, as the life of the spirit is elevated, we increase our certainty, and unbelief gives place to faith.

We remark therefore, finally, that *to have faith raised to certainty we must find it in the life.* We are assured of our existence in the physical world by the fact of our life in it. There is no way of demonstrating it either to ourselves or others. It may be asserted to me that I dream when I am waking, or that my view of the world itself is but a waking dream. But the one answer is, 'I know that I live.' And we must endeavour to advance to this consciousness in the spiritual world; we must seek its life till we know it and are sure of it. The difference between the two is this, that our conviction of the life of the physical world is instantaneous, and is forced on us whether we will or not; but conviction of spiritual life comes gradually, and is gained by choice and effort. In some cases it may come more quickly than in others, but in every case it must enter by our free will. And the reason of the difference is that spiritual life can be reached in no other way. It cannot be forced upon us by the impression of the senses or by the demonstration of the intellect; it must enter by the attraction of the heart. We may be brought to the conviction that there is an architecture of the universe by the study of its physical laws, but to believe firmly in an Architect requires some personal contact with Him, and to have faith in Him as a Father and a Friend requires the surrender of ourselves. There is no other way ; to live a spiritual life we must choose to live, and in the choice of the life comes the conviction of its reality and of its divine excellence. When God by his Holy Spirit acts on our nature, He deals by a mighty power of persuasion. He makes us willing; and when Christ gives the reason of our exclusion from this divine realm, He says, " Ye will not come unto Me that ye might have life." There must be room therefore left in the spiritual world for unbelief as there is room for faith. The world is so made that it admits of both, or rather men do so make themselves that they turn to the one side or the other, and find reasons by which they sustain their conclusions. In whatever way the world might have been made, this state of the case could not be altered. Souls, whether of men or angels, could become God's children only by having the child-like heart, and if this is rejected any conviction about God is no door to true faith in Him; it could only make them believe and tremble. Their faith, if we may so call it, would be their punishment and loss.

There are two struggles in men's nature : the one to end ignorance by knowledge, the other to end doubt by certainty; light and life, the mind and the spirit. God's will is that the soul should rest by life, by life alone ; so it grows by faith, by reverence, by love, by the very life of God received into the soul. " With Thee is the fountain of life, in thy light we shall see light."

VII.

THE FIRST HOME MISSION.

"Andrew first findeth his own brother Simon, and saith unto him, We have found the Messias, which is, being interpreted, the Christ. And he brought him to Jesus."—JOHN I. 41, 42.

THE history in the beginning of John's Gospel may teach us many lessons; for the Bible is like a gem with different facets, each one of which sparkles with its own light.

We cannot help, for example, being struck with the clearness and graphic reality of the narrative. It is the commencement of the greatest movement that has ever taken place in the world, the Christian Church; and here, as from a transparent little well, we can see the first gush and overflow—the well of life which is in Christ running over to begin the long course and windings of that river which makes glad the city of God.

We have here, too, the beginning of one of the most beautiful human characters, that of the apostle John. It is he who tells the story, and we can see his warmth of heart and retiring modesty in the way in which he tells it. "One of the two disciples," he says, "was Andrew, Simon Peter's brother." He was the other, but he keeps himself unnamed. He remains in the shade that he may let us look on others, and, above all, look on Christ. And we have a view not only of what we can call his natural, but of what we can call his Christian spirit.

This was the day of his first acquaintance with Jesus Christ. He was the disciple whom Jesus loved, in whom there was, perhaps beyond all others, the purest, deepest affection to Christ—at the last supper, at his cross, at his grave. Many years have come and gone since this first meeting, years filled with strange and absorbing events; but every little incident comes up fresh as if it had happened yesterday. He speaks of it day by day and hour by hour—of Jesus as He walked, of his words as He asked the two friends to his dwelling; all is imprinted on his heart, and will be to death and through eternity.

And from all these things we may infer the truth of the history, that it is from the hand of an eye-witness, and the eye-witness the same disciple who elsewhere says, "What we have seen and heard declare we unto you, that ye also may have fellowship with us." But, besides all these views, there is another well worthy of our attention. We have here the first Home Mission in the Christian Church. We cannot tell certainly who was the first foreign missionary. The greatest who ever lived or laboured was probably the apostle Paul. But we can scarcely say he was the first. Peter was before him when he preached to Cornelius the centurion, and Philip the evangelist when he brought the Ethiopian eunuch to the faith of Christ, and sent him with the tidings into the heart of dark and oppressed Africa. But we know who was the first home missionary. It was Andrew, when he first got to know Christ, and then went to his brother Simon, and said to him, "We have found the Christ. And he brought him to Jesus." Now, no doubt, this is written for our instruction, and we shall mention some things about this first home mission in the Christian Church for our guidance and encouragement.

1. We have here the *spring* of all true home mission work. Andrew had himself made acquaintance with the Lord Jesus Christ. He had been in the house with Him for hours on that first evening when they met in close and earnest conversation, and the result of it was the discovery, " We have found the Christ." There is no record of that conversation left to us. We know what formed the subject of another, years afterwards, with the two disciples who journeyed to Emmaus. It was, "Ought not Christ to have suffered these things, and to enter into his glory ?" when, " beginning at Moses and all the prophets, He expounded unto them in all the Scriptures the things concerning Himself," when " He went in to tarry with them, and was made known in the breaking of bread." He could not make Himself so clearly known to Andrew and John, for they were not yet prepared ; but the conversation was about the same things, the things concerning Himself. The Baptist had pointed Him out as the Son of God and the Lamb of God, and these are the two great truths which fill the Bible from beginning to end. They dawn gradually on the hearts of those who look for Him, but the light, whether it be that of the faint sunrise or the full mid-day, is of the same saving and gladdening kind. It left these two disciples convinced that all the deep desires of their heart, and all the promises of the Word of God, were fulfilled in Him who spoke to them ; and so they were ready to go from the house with the message, " We have found the Christ."

This must still be the spring of all true mission work. We must come into personal contact with Christ, we must be in the house with Him, we must learn to know Him as the Son of God and the Lamb of God—as that One who came from his Father to be our Brother, to share our nature and to bear our sins and to take us back to

God as his Father and our Father, his God and our God —a Friend in sickness and sorrow and death, who points us through death to life eternal. " In my Father's house are many mansions: if it were not so, I would have told you. I go to prepare a place for you. And if I go and prepare a place for you, I will come again, and receive you unto Myself; that where I am, there ye may be also." This is the one great discovery, compared with which all other inventions are shortlived opiates of an hour—a little ease on the road to death. If there are those who have given up all hope of finding such a friend, no wonder they put the question, Is life worth living? Is a man better than a beast? Nay, is he not worse, for the beasts have no such desires, and cannot be disappointed? But those who by God's grace can say, "We have found"— yes, we have found " the Christ," a Saviour from sin and death, an almighty and all-merciful Brother and Friend— these know that life is worth living, for " in his favour is life, and his loving-kindness is better than life." In the degree in which churches or men have been in the house with Christ, and have learned to know Him, will they be ready to go out with the message to others. It is the depth and fulness of this discovery which blesses ourselves, and makes us anxious to carry the blessing to our fellow-men.

> " Now, methinks, I hear him praising,
> Publishing to all around :
> Friends, is not my case amazing ?
> What a Saviour I have found! "

2. The next thing we would have you to remark is the *object* of the first home mission. " And he brought him to Jesus." It was not enough for Andrew to speak to his brother about Christ, and tell him some things he had heard and felt; his aim is to bring him as close to Christ

as he himself had been, into the house to listen for himself, and look upon and learn to love his person. And in any mission work we undertake we should be satisfied with nothing less than this. We may use every persuasion in our power, but the end of it all is to bring men into personal contact with Christ. It is not instruction which will suffice, not emotions or impressions, not convictions of sin, not laying aside some evil habits, not coming to church, not sitting down at the Lord's Table; all these have their place, but they will not avail without coming to Christ himself. Christ does not say, 'Come to a better mind, come to reformation, come to church, come to the Communion,' but "Come unto Me." There is no real life in all the rest, no security, no endurance, unless we bring men to Christ himself. Here is a lesson for parents with their children, for a teacher with his scholars, for a missionary or minister with his hearers. We must neither begin nor end with ourselves, but point from first to last to Christ. It is not 'Come to our station, our school, our church,' but 'Come with us to the Lord Jesus Christ.' Christ has said, "Go into the highways and hedges, and compel them to come in, that *my* house may be filled,"—not your house, but mine; and the best thing that can be said about our house is that it is a door to the house of the Lord Jesus Christ. So let us make Andrew's object ours: "And he brought him to Jesus."

In this object of Andrew there are some things worthy of notice. He was perfectly sure that Christ was willing to receive his brother, just as willing as He was to receive himself. It does not appear that Christ had said anything about this; he left it, in the first place, to the feeling of Andrew's own heart. And Andrew does not seem to have thought it needful to ask Christ whether He would make his brother welcome. He knew it from the way in which He had welcomed him, and conversed with him—from the opening of his heart in the words of truth and grace He had spoken. If Peter had been disposed to object that his coming might be looked on as an intrusion on the privacy and leisure of the great Teacher, Andrew would have said, ' Why, brother, if I could come and be welcome, why not you ? He saw me following and bade me enter. He has an open door and an open heart for all who wish to speak to Him about these things. I am sure He never would refuse any : come and see '—" and he brought him to Jesus."

And you may see, also, that in this object of bringing his brother to Christ Andrew is sure that he himself can have his own share in no way diminished. There would not be less of truth and love falling to his lot when Peter came to have his part. If a man covets land or wealth or power, the more he gives away the less he possesses.

"If I possess riches or lands, I may
Bestow them, till they are consumed away."

But let a man bring others to the treasures of the Lord Jesus Christ, and his own share will be increased, " his bliss still growing when with millions shared." I think if there be any shade of regret in heaven, it will be that we did not bring more to that house of many mansions to swell its songs and share its joys ; and so let us make Andrew's aim ours when he found his brother and " brought him to Jesus."

3. The next thing we would have you observe is the *place* of this mission. It was in the most emphatic sense a *home* mission ; and this has its lesson for us. There are some who say we should have nothing but home missions —no foreign missions till our own country is redeemed from sin and ignorance. 'Why think of Caffreland and

China until you have Christianised your own wynds and villages?' But these people forget that when Christ said, "Preach the Gospel among all nations, beginning at Jerusalem," He did not say *stopping* at Jerusalem. They forget that if the apostles had acted on their principle we should have been heathen still. They forget, moreover, that it was only when the Church of Christ began to think seriously of the foreign heathen that she had her thoughts turned to the home heathen. We generally find that those who are always talking of confining our attention to the home heathen are those who do least for them. But let us see a man who, like the apostle Paul, burns with zeal for the salvation of the whole world, and we shall have one who is ready to say like him, "I have great heaviness and continual sorrow in my heart for my brethren, my kinsmen according to the flesh." This is one of the cases in which we may hear our Lord saying, "These ought ye to have done, and not to leave the other undone."

But this surely we may say, that in our zeal for the foreign heathen we are not to forget our own kinsfolk; and here are some reasons. They have not the only claim upon us, but they have the first claim. We are to begin with them as Andrew did. "Go home to thy friends," the Lord said, "and tell them what great things the Lord hath done for thee." And even when we move forth to the foreign heathen, to prove the all-embracing love of the Gospel, we are to abide and labour among the home heathen, that we may prove its long-suffering mercy and patient continuance in well-doing. The Gospel has a voice, like its Master, for him that is far off and for him that is nigh.

And even for our own sakes we must think of home. We cannot let masses of ignorance and sin and wretchedness fester and grow, without bringing a blight on our own Christianity. It is like having an unwholesome marsh beside our house; it spreads malaria and fever and ague. Think of your children living in this atmosphere, and of the danger to them in the sights and sounds and associations around them. To keep our families and our churches in health, or even in life, we must work to counteract the evil about us. So God seeks to compel us not to hide our face from our own flesh. If we will not do them good we shall share in their evil. We must rise or fall together. Think of this, moreover, that in the home mission field there is opportunity for every one of us to do something personally. Few of us can go to the foreign field. We cannot cross the seas and learn a new and difficult language. But there is always a sphere not far from our own door, where we can use our own tongue and employ whatever influence we may have for good. It seems to be part of the divine plan that this opportunity should be given to Christians for the benefit it brings to themselves to obey the divine command, "Son, daughter, go work to-day in my vineyard." It is thus we are to be like our Master, "going about doing good," and to grow always more like Him in the work of doing it. It is quite true that we Christians shall need to live higher and more consistent lives if we are to do this with success, but would not this be a happy necessity? As the Church labours for the world around her, she would feel the duty of arising and shaking herself from the dust and putting on her beautiful garments, that she may become Jerusalem, the holy city. We should, each one, ask ourselves, What place lies nearest to me, nearest in opportunity and hope of influence? To what friend, to what neighbour, can I speak a word or do an act that shall help to bring him into contact with Christ? Sure we are that the world will never be put right by ministers and missionaries, as no battle will ever be gained by captains and officers. There is room for all here, and need for all; there is no discharge in this war. If we could but see this spirit of personal responsibility spreading, it would be a happy presage for the world, and for the Church herself, for growth in number and growth in character. It would be a return to the first fountain of influence, personal contact with Christ, when Andrew went out from Him and found his brother and brought him to Jesus.

4. Look at the *time* chosen for this first home mission. Andrew did not wait to speak to his brother till he had been made an apostle, or even till he had become one of Christ's regular disciples. He began at once. And there is a lesson here for ministers. If we never think about doing good to the souls of men till we are licensed by the Presbytery, we should think seriously if we ought to be licensed at all; and if, when we are licensed or ordained, we look upon our work as a task, and measure carefully what we have to do and what we have not to do, we should ask ourselves, Is this not the place of a hireling? Christ sent out some who should devote themselves exclusively to such work, but they must feel first that they have a call from Him; they must have answered it, "Here am I, send me;" and they must devote themselves to it, "in season and out of season," with their strength as the only measure of their service. It is this which makes the Christian ministry not a profession but a work of love, and the ministers not hirelings but the servants of Christ for the good of men. They must begin and continue in the spirit of Andrew, not counting hours, but watching opportunities and forgetting self in love to the souls of men and zeal for the glory of Christ.

And the same lesson comes home to all. A man may never think of being a minister or missionary; he may have other ways of serving God in the world, which he feels to be more suitable for him; but he is not thereby freed from the duty of beginning at once to speak a word to his brother about the Gospel of Christ. Some may object that the apostle has said, "not a novice, lest he be lifted up with pride;" but you will observe that the apostle is speaking of those who are to be full teachers of Christian truth. Our Lord kept his disciples three years under his eye and teaching before He commissioned them to the world; but He approved every one who did work for Him up to his knowledge. And it is not necessary to wait for a great deal of knowledge; let us use the knowledge we have, not pretending to more. If we have five talents, let us lay out the five; if two, let us deal with the two; if one, let us not hide it in the earth. The way to have it increased and to get the approbation of our Master is to say, 'I have only one, but I will do what I can with the one.' All cannot speak in public, all cannot teach in the Sabbath-school, all cannot go from house to house and influence strangers, but what one is there who has not some friend, some acquaintance, some neighbour, by whom his word will be regarded? Let him speak to him, and let him live so that his life will let him speak. This is the greatest thing of all, that a Christian man should have his life behind his word; then the word tells. So it was with Christ: "in Him was life, and the life was the light." The life sometimes speaks for itself, like the sunlight which shines and never says a word; but generally the word is needed to guide men to where the light comes from. It may be a brief word like that of the Samaritan woman: "Come, see a man which told me all things that ever I did: is not this the Christ?" Or it may be briefer still, like that of Andrew: "We have found the Christ." But it will serve the purpose if it leads the man to where he will learn more. This is, indeed, all that any of us can do. We may use more words, but, if we are true speakers, all we say is, 'We have found the Christ; He has met our need, answered our desire. He will meet yours; will you not come and see?' Let us aim at this so soon as we have found Christ, whether our words be many or few, and bring men to Jesus.

5. The next thing we say is, Let us learn from the *spirit* of the first home mission. Andrew went to his brother; he did so from his interest in him; and, no doubt, all that a brother's heart could feel was put into his manner and words. He did this naturally, not from calculation, but because he had it in his heart. It is in this spirit we must go to our fellow-men, whether they be closely related or not. They are our brethren, with the same nature, the same needs, the same sins and sorrows, the same eternal destinies. We should stir up our hearts with the thought of these things, and then it will find its way into our words and bearing and very looks. It is love to Christ and love to men that are the secret of power in Christian persuasion. We shall never have great success otherwise. There is a story told of a young man who had fallen through the ice, and was holding on to the edge in the agony of a death-struggle. They pushed a plank towards him, but the end of it was covered with ice, and again and again his fingers slipped. "For mercy's sake," he cried, "don't give me the frozen side." We must not give men the frozen side. God does not give the frozen side to us when He so loved the world as to send his Son; Christ does not give the frozen side when He is not ashamed to call us brethren; the Holy Spirit does not give the frozen

side when He strives and suffers long. And we must go to men as those who have felt all this, and who wish them to feel it also. There is a sympathetic bond in these things stronger than the touch of nature which makes the whole world kin. It is the new nature seeking to build up the new and blessed family. And in carrying it out we may learn a lesson here. Andrew did not say to his brother, 'Go:' he took him by the hand and led him. There is a way of urging men to Christ as if we stood on higher ground, and did not need Him for ourselves, or did not need Him so much. But we must feel that in this we all stand on one level, that we all need one cure. Do we not all require to go back to Christ to learn more from Him, to be again forgiven, to receive grace upon grace? And can we go better than in the company of one whom we lead for the first time to that Saviour whom we need every day and every hour? Let us think of this, and it will give us something of the spirit of this first home mission.

6. The last thing we would say is, Look at the *success* of this first home mission. Andrew gained his brother. Simon yielded and went, and the first interview must have gladdened Andrew's heart. When Jesus beheld him He said: "Thou art Simon the son of Jona: thou shalt be called Cephas, which is, by interpretation, A stone." We cannot now tell all that Peter did; how his boldness and open confession of Christ confirmed the hearts of Andrew and his fellow-disciples; how, though he fell, he received this charge: "Strengthen thy brethren;" how thousands were converted in a day by his preaching; and how, in the epistles he has left, he has been made such an instrument for comforting and building up the people of God in all ages. We hear very little afterwards of Andrew; no

doubt he continued to work in the spirit of his first mission effort, and, no doubt also, he had his continued success; yet he had not the ability and energy of Peter, and he retires into the shade. But we cannot forget that it is to Andrew we owe Simon Peter, and all that he did.

Often afterwards, we may well believe, when Andrew saw Peter's character unfolding, when he beheld him opening the door of faith on the day of Pentecost, and standing forth as one of the pillars of the Christian Church, he must have thanked Christ that He not only touched his own heart, but put it into his heart to bring his brother. And now in heaven, where they see the full result, these two brothers must admire the wisdom and grace of God which has brought out such fruits from the seed planted by the hand of the first home missionary of the Christian Church. Let us take this, then, for a great encouragement to do our part, whatever it may be; to begin and do it now, and to do it with all our might. Perhaps we may see fruit from it, and much fruit, even here. In any case, if our work be sincere and loving and prayerful, if we go out from Christ to men that we may bring men to Christ, the work will not be in vain. We may touch one who will touch many more. A humble soldier may draw in some young recruit who may become a leader among thousands and subdue kingdoms. In the great day of account, those who sow and those who reap shall rejoice together, and an obscure hand may find itself connected with the fruit that shakes like Lebanon. God has a place for the dust of his people, and a day of resurrection for it, but He has a place also for their efforts and their prayers, and these too shall be remembered and raised with all their results. Wherefore, "in the morning sow thy seed, and in the evening withhold not thine hand, for thou knowest not whether shall prosper, either this or that, or whether they both shall be alike good."

There is one remark that may be needed to help any good resolve to an issue, and it is this—that if the work is to be well and perseveringly done, there should be common counsel and co-operation. Many good resolutions are made by Christian people that they will do more by personal effort for the cause of Christ; but they are afraid to commit themselves, and the effort is either never begun, or it dies away after a few endeavours. Now, it is certain that we should be, each one alone and personally, doing our part in our daily life, shining as lights in the world; but to form ourselves into union for special efforts is also needed for our mutual quickening and guidance. It will give us courage, it will pledge us to perseverance, and it will put purpose into all the rest of our conduct.

Andrew, indeed, went alone with the first instinct of the Christian life—he could do nothing else; but, when he was joined by others, co-operation at once commenced. Our Lord sent them out two and two, and brought them together again to speak and hear about their work. Even in a Christian church such arrangements are needed, if work is to be done with order and efficiency. If some diffident young Christian, wishful to work but not knowing how, were to ask—What am I to do? I should say, Join such a union, the one which you feel is most suited to your power and opportunity. A Christian church ought to be able to give every one his and her place, for, when the Master of the household left, He appointed to every one his work, and commanded the porter to watch—Occupy till I come.

But there is one last difficulty. Some one is saying, I think I could go to my brother if I were sure that I had been at Christ for myself. I have been at his house, but I do not know that I have closed with his offer in my own heart. And what then am I to do to work the works of God? What answer can we give but that of Christ himself?—"This is the work of God, that ye believe in Him whom He hath sent." Christ himself is at the door of your house this day. He has often been there before, and He comes now, earnest as ever: "Behold, I stand at the door and knock; if any man open I will come in." Will you not open the door? Will you not even ask Him to help you to put to hand and let Him enter? "Come in, Thou blessed, wherefore standest Thou without?" He is waiting—do not keep Him waiting—do not send Him away with "At a more convenient season I will call for Thee." Give Him the heart, and then it will help you to realise the decision, if you go to your brother with a message of good. To take the side of Christ and help his cause is to help yourself, and thereby "thou shalt both save thyself and them that hear thee."

VIII.

SPIRITUAL JUDGMENT: ITS RANGE, INDEPENDENCE, AND GUIDANCE.

" But he that is spiritual judgeth all things, yet he himself is judged of no man."—1 Cor. ii. 15.

THIS declaration looks at first sight a very startling one, and has been charged with having the essence of fanaticism and self-will. The spiritual man an infallible judge of everything, and he amenable to none! In what way can ordinary human beings meet such a claim save by passing it by without answer? He above us in everything, and we able to approach him in nothing! But before condemning the declaration so summarily we should examine it, and before examining it we must ask who the spiritual man is. The apostle Paul does not use the name with any kind of supercilious pride, but simply in the way of explaining a certain state of things. In his view the Gospel of Christ meets with two kinds of men. There are those who approach it with their natural reason, and who ask no other help, because they believe no other help is needed. To these men the Gospel in its essence is foolishness, as far as they can understand it. There are things about it, its precepts, the life of its Founder, its elevated and ideal tone, which many of them admit to be very beautiful and, to some extent, very useful; but what is called the essential Gospel, that sin is so terrible an evil that it needed the cure which the Bible describes, that God's nature should be moved, that He should send his Son into the world to suffer and die, that this miracle of miracles, of which all the others are only sparks leaping from a central fire, should break up through the surface order of nature, and begin a new and supernatural state of things, appears to them irrational and extravagant. This is what the apostle means by "The natural man receiveth not the things of the Spirit of God: for they are foolishness unto him." But there are men who form their judgment in another way, called the spiritual. They get this name not because they judge from a deeper part of human nature—the spirit. It is quite true that there is such a deeper part, and that it enters into their view of things; but it would never be used by them, and it would never be able to guide them truly, but for the Spirit of God. It is not the spirit of man which rises up by some native strength, and forces its way to God and the spiritual world; it is God's Holy Spirit which reaches forth to man, renews, enlightens, guides his spirit to see and realise things which otherwise would have been to him unreal and unintelligible. That this is the view of the apostle in this chapter can scarcely, we think, be denied by any one who reads it in its plain meaning. We may agree with him or not, but we can scarcely misunderstand him. The man who comes under the quickening life and teaching of God's Holy Spirit, and who enters into the world of truth and feeling and action disclosed by Him, is called "the spiritual man." We are now prepared for considering what is here said about his manner of judgment.

I. Consider, first, *its Range.*— "He that is spiritual judgeth all things." The claim that is put in is for universality; but to see what this universality refers to, we must weigh the words and their accompaniment. It is not said that he judges all men, or any man; he has his opinion as to their views, but in regard to their persons, "to their own Master they stand or fall." God alone can judge their history and surroundings, their opportunities and temptations, and we have no right to say where they shall stand in the great day of decision. A Christian man, if he is earnest, cannot help exposing what he believes to be false, and impressing what he feels to be true; he could not love his neighbour as himself if he did not do this; but God is the only judge of the heart and of the final award, and the more deeply spiritual a man is the more he will act on the Lord's precept—" Judge not, that ye be not judged."

Spiritual judgment, then, has to do not with persons, but with things. Still, it may be asked, Does it absolutely judge all things? It is clear that there are many things in which spiritual judgment will give us no help. It will not make a man acquainted with the truths of astronomy or geology, or the facts of history, or any of the great branches of secular knowledge which occupy the human mind. It will not of itself enable him to conduct successfully the business of the world. Many a great statesman and prosperous merchant has had very little spiritual judgment. "The children of this world are in their generation wiser than the children of light." It will not make a man a skilful critic of the canon of Scripture, of the time and circumstances in which the books were written; nor will it, by its own law, fashion a man into a profound theologian acquainted with all the intricacies of doctrine. The spiritual judgment certainly has its value in these matters, but, without a great deal of knowledge outside itself, it cannot judge them. What meaning then are we to attach to these words, "The spiritual man judgeth all things"? The apostle speaks of those things which come within the sphere of, or which touch, the spiritual nature. The Spirit of God reveals to the soul a world of which we can say that it lies both within the present and outside it. It is in a hidden chamber whose existence we dimly felt, but which God's Spirit makes known to us; and this chamber has in it a window which looks out on a new and infinite universe. The Spirit of God not only reveals it, but introduces to it, and gives the possession of things in it which are felt to be the very truth and reality of our soul's life. We do not know ourselves for what we really are, our depth and height, our wants and wishes, our fall and possible rise, our sin and what is meant by salvation, until we are taken in there, spoken to in our most secret thoughts by Him who makes us feel that He is greater than our hearts and knows all things; and makes us feel also that He has in his hand the very things which our heart needs, though it could not have expressed its need. This world may seem to those who have not been in it a narrow and poor and almost non-existent thing—existent, perhaps, in some curious unexplainable craving of our nature—nothing more. But to those who have been in it and lived in it, it grows in certainty as its life grows, and it deepens and expands and rises, until it penetrates and comprehends the natural world on every side. Wherever the natural world touches it, it can form its judgment of its facts and of the meaning they will bear. If an attempt is made to persuade it that the soul is a mere expression, a kind of shifting focus from a play of light in a world of appearances, it can certainly judge. "I know that there is a spirit in man, not only from its first creation in its intelligent and moral structure, but from its new creation, from the assurance of its divine instincts and powers and aims. 'The inspiration of the Almighty has given me this understanding.'" If the natural world should grow in the hands of some men into materialism, and deny the existence of a personal God, the spiritual man can judge. He can say, 'I can not only feel Him in that sense of dependence, in that impression of responsibility with which He has created the soul, but I know Him as the Father of spirits, who has drawn me to Himself with an irresistible longing, whom I have learned in some measure to love, and in loving have learned to see.' If there be an attack made by secular history on the person of Christ, to reduce Him from the place He holds in the Gospel to some human level or shadowy fancy, the spiritual man can say with the woman of Samaria, "Come, see a man which told me all things that ever I did: is not this the Christ?" or, still more with the Samaritans, "Now we believe, not because of thy saying: for we have heard Him ourselves, and know that this is indeed the Christ, the Saviour of the world." 'We have learned through Him, not only to know ourselves, but to belong to ourselves, because we belong to Him; we have learned what sin is, but also what peace is; we have come to know not only the misery and loathsomeness of a corrupted nature, but also the joy and beauty of purity and love; and if we have yet taken in only a few of "the things that are freely offered us of God," they are so real and satisfying to our inmost nature that we are sure they must have a real source.' Or if there be an attempt made to interpose the laws of the natural world between the soul and God, so that the Holy Spirit cannot come down with heavenly blessings, or carry prayer up to the heart of God, the spiritual man can judge the case. He can say, 'But I know that prayer does reach God, as surely as I know when a plumb-line rests on the bottom. I have tried it again and again; it has done more than rest, it has become an anchor; it has held me in duty and temptation and storm and night, and brought into my heart confidence and hope and joy.

These things did not come from my own soul, it is too weak and empty; they did not come from this natural world which is interposing its cloud; they came from above, from the Father of lights.' It is in this way that the man who has entered the spiritual world can judge all things that touch it. But he can do more; he can judge all things in the natural world itself, not as to their details, but as to their spirit and tendency. The great and manifold facts and laws of nature may be, to a large extent, beyond his reach; but as far as he knows them he perceives the eternal power and godhead of their Maker. He can judge of the infinite whole. The learned treatment of the Bible may not be within his grasp, its canon, its history, its difficulties and solutions; but the broad highway of its truth, moving on from beginning to end, this he knows well, and he finds it conducting to the Lord Jesus Christ. While he holds this, his judgment of the Bible is sure. He may not be able to answer the objections to God's providence and to prayer, but when he has found a living God, and access to Him, a Father and a Friend to whom he can speak and listen, he can meanwhile pass by the objections, or through them, and reach the conviction of a world where the laws are not dead but living, and do not separate us from God but conduct us to Him. The judgment, then, which the spiritual man forms is founded on the new life which the Spirit of God creates in him, and which becomes to him as real as any other part of his being; which becomes indeed more and more true, for it supplies him with the only sufficient key to his own nature or to God's universe. The spiritual life in him becomes a test by which to try the truth of things, a compass by which to steer through them, a balance with which to weigh them. It is not infallible—far from it, but he knows that wherever he truly yields to it, it leads him in the true direction; it has its deficiencies, its chasms as it were, but he feels that whenever he is standing on even one part of it he is on sure ground; it has its intervals of weakness and strength, we might say of loss and recovery, but he is assured that if his heart follows it, it will reappear with a fuller conviction, like the star which was leading to Christ, and rested over Him; and when they saw it again, "they rejoiced with great joy."

II. We come now to consider the spiritual man's judgment in its *Independence*—"he himself is judged of no man," or "of no one." It is clear, again, that we are not to take these words without explaining them by the subject of which the apostle is speaking. It does not mean that the spiritual man is beyond the judgment of others when he has contravened human law. He puts himself before man's tribunal to answer to it, and, if condemned, submits to the penalty, within all the range of civil authority to which the law of man extends. Nor is he exempt from judgment in his spiritual life. He can never be freed from the judgment of God as expressed by his Word and by his Spirit, for this is at the very basis of his Christian life and of all that belongs to it. And he is not entirely free, in spiritual things, from the judgment of his fellow-Christians. They can never judge him in the sense of depriving him of his responsibility to God, and of forming his own faith and character in view of this. "Every one of us shall give account of himself to God." But his fellow-Christians may have it in their power to instruct and correct his judgment, as he on his part can do the like for them. They are in the same domain of life, and can be mutually helpful by counsel and friendly admonition. And we may say, moreover, that the apostle is not speaking of the judgment which men of the world may form of the outward character and deportment of Christians. Any man of the world can judge a Christian man's conduct, so far as it comes before the outward eye; he can approve it or he can condemn it, and he has a right to do so. The ordinary man of the world is a judge of the consistency of Christians, and we should be very glad oftentimes that we have this mirror in which to study ourselves. Not unfrequently it may distort Christian conduct, and discolour it, but at other times it may give very wholesome criticism which it would be foolish in Christians to disregard. We might be ready to fall into much one-sidedness and many extravagances if we had not some such judgments. We ought to have courage to act against all human criticism when conscience commands; but, on the other hand, we may be unwise if we do not take it into account for correction and instruction in our way of acting. We are to walk in wisdom toward them that are without: as far as we can, "not to let our good be evil spoken of." What, then, is the meaning of saying that "he is judged of no man"? The apostle, you will see, is speaking of an inward, spiritual region into which the Christian man has been introduced by God's Spirit, and of the judgments which natural men, that is, men who have had no experience of it, may form of it, and of him as he lives in it. A Christian man can say, 'My conduct before my fellow-men belongs to the world; my heart is for the Searcher of hearts; my inward, spiritual experiences are for fellow-Christians who have felt them; but this inner world is not open to the decisions of those who have never dwelt in it, or even visited it; they are not acquainted with its motives, its laws, its sorrows, its hopes, its joys; I cannot be judged by any one of them.'

Perhaps the best way of illustrating this is to take the

apostle Paul himself, and see how he had a whole world within him removed from the judgment of natural men around. Take, at the very first, the great truth of salvation by grace without the works of the law, which was the pivot of his preaching and of his life. It was looked on by many then and since as an immoral doctrine which, if followed out, would lead to all manner of sin. But they could not understand that in receiving this free grace there is a new nature received, the motions of which are always saying, "How shall we, that are dead to sin, live any longer therein?" Neither could he be judged as to the way his new life was supported. Men saw the persecutions to which he was exposed—wave upon wave of affliction, unappreciated labour, unreturned sacrifice, stripes, imprisonment—these were not so much; but calumny, disappointment, heart-sickness, and depression came over him, and he had to say of himself, "Without were fightings, within were fears." The world could not understand how the spirit in him was sustained, and rose up in fresh flames of consuming zeal. John Bunyan has given the explanation of it. In the Interpreter's house Christian was shown a fire burning against a wall, and one standing by it always casting much water upon it, to quench it; yet did the fire burn higher and hotter. And when he wondered, he was taken to the other side of the wall, "where there was a man with a vessel of oil in his hand, of which he continually cast, but secretly, into the fire. This was the oil of Christ's grace which maintains the work begun in the heart." Or, take the happiness of his life, and ask if the mere natural man could understand it. Let us only think of this chain which begins with hope and ends with it, like two golden nails fixed to the gate of heaven, while the links hang down into all the trials of life, which are touched and turned to gold by their divine fastenings. "We rejoice in hope of the glory of God. And not only so, but we glory in tribulations also: knowing that tribulation worketh patience; and patience, experience; and experience, hope; and hope maketh not ashamed; because the love of God is shed abroad in our hearts by the Holy Ghost which is given unto us." Could the world judge of the weight which his heart put into the scale, that weighed all else down—"What things were gain to me, those I counted loss for Christ;" or of the deep assurance of reality which enabled him to say clearly and calmly, "I am not mad, most noble Festus, but speak forth the words of truth and soberness"? Here was a man moving among men, but a mystery to them, knowing them well, for he had an intensely human heart and he had tried many of its ambitions and delights, but with a world within him which the world of natural men could not comprehend; and so he says, not in pride or bitterness, but in simple truthfulness and strong desire that they should share it with him, 'I know the world you live in, I have been in it, and am in it now; but you cannot know mine until you enter it; the spiritual man judgeth all things; he himself is judged of none.' Now, this was not peculiar to the apostle Paul. He had it from a greater, from Him who "was in the world, and the world was made by Him, and the world knew Him not"—who had a universe of spiritual possessions within Him, among which He lived, and for the bestowal of which on men He freely died; and then, to as many as received Him He gave power to become the sons of God. The humblest Christian, who can take this name, or who has entered in but a little way within the door, has begun this experience which is more to the understanding of the life of Christ and to the conviction of its truth, than all the commentaries and histories that have been written by the most learned men. These have their value, but what is the telescope without the eye? The experience of most Christian men will fall very far short of that of the apostle Paul, but it is the same in kind. It may be little more than the sense of comfort which arises from thinking of Christ as a Saviour, and the earnest endeavour to commit all to Him, the strength that comes in duty or temptation from the attempt to realise his presence as a helper, the gladness which springs up in the soul at the hope of his approval; but, though it be even less than this, and though hesitation and fear accompany it, there will be the deep sense of reality in the blessing desired, and the turning of the heart to this side as the one secure and satisfying thing—" One thing have I desired of the Lord; that will I seek after." If a man has got this length, it is a foothold in the land of promise, by which he can distinguish it from the shifting sand through which he has hitherto travelled; and by God's grace he can keep his own against hostile judgments, and entrench himself till he gains more. If he will only be true to the teaching of God's Holy Spirit, which has begun to enlighten him, he will have a growing experience of life within, which shall give him an answer to all objectors. He has a right to set this inner world, in which his spirit is living and moving, against all the arguments which the outer can advance. 'There is an outer circle which you know, and which I know also, but this inner realm is one you have no experience of. It has given me a new understanding and desire and aim, which enable me to judge the world as I could not do before. They are still very imperfect, but they are very real, and they give me the inborn hope of higher things. You cannot judge me till you know the world in which I have begun to live, and, when you do, I believe you will judge with me.' This is the basis on which any Christian man may be able to feel that he is secure in his faith—" it stands not in the wisdom of men, but in the power of God." The men who oppose it may be men of vast learning and high genius, but there is one little reason which replies to all, 'I was blind, now I see; my soul was dead, now it begins to live.' Let us join the Lord Jesus in thanking the Father for this foundation, safe against all adversaries, open to all friends. "What shall one then answer the messengers of the nation? That the Lord hath founded Zion, and the poor of his people shall trust in it."

III. It now remains for us to speak briefly of the *Guidance and Tests* of spiritual judgment. This part of the subject is not referred to directly in the text, but it is implied in all that precedes it, and, unless something were said regarding it, we might feel as if the judgment of a Christian man on spiritual things were in danger of personal caprice. It may be asked, 'Does not the apostle's view of the independence of Christian experience make it doubtful and unsafe? Is it not left with a rule without satisfactory tests, and cut off from contact with the world of common humanity, so as to deprive it of proper influence? Can anything be true and powerful which is thus isolated from all its environments?' Let us, then, without entering fully into the subject, indicate how the spiritual judgment of a Christian can both guard and guide itself by seeking contact with the things around it. First of all, it must never separate itself from its source. Its source is God's Spirit acting through God's Word. What is true of all Christians is true of it. Its origin is not natural but divine. It is born not of blood nor of the will of the flesh nor of the will of man, but of God—born of God by his incorruptible Word, "which liveth and abideth for ever." The spiritual judgment, if it is to be sound, can never be cut off from this fountain-head. Here it verifies and purifies and strengthens itself. The old song of praise on God's Word is always to be had in memory, viz., "The testimony of the Lord is sure, making wise the simple; the commandment of the Lord is pure, enlightening the eyes." But in order to this there are two things to be observed. We must not form our judgment on single texts, but on the breadth of Scripture—the letter may kill, the spirit gives life; and I know no better way of reaching the breadth of Scripture than by carrying it up in its final issue to the Lord Jesus Christ. All its parts, rightly understood, will agree with Him; but in Christ himself, in his person and character and work, the right of guidance for the judgment is more clear. Many things that are doubtful become simple when we ask, What would the example and spirit of Christ lead us in this case to say and do? The other thing to which we should attend, in bringing our judgment to the Word of God, is to ask reverently and lovingly the guidance of the Spirit which gave the Word, and which kindled any light in us that we may possess. To ask the Author of the book to explain it, not with a word or two in opening it, but with the heart in the upward and expectant look, is the true way of being guided aright (Ps. xxv. 6).

After this guidance from the Source, there is that which we may receive from the new nature formed within, and from the growth of it in obedience to God's will. It may be asked by some, 'But what if this new nature is, in my case, very doubtful and very fitful, if its experiences come and go till I can scarcely distinguish them from cloudland? Can I trust what is so variable?' The answer is, that if a man will think of his inner life he will find that there are some fixed things which remain amid the changing. When a sailor is coasting the shore, the headlands and clouds seem so mingled that he can scarcely tell what is fixed from what is fleeting. But he patiently watches till his eye descries what remains constant amid mist and shadow. Frequently it is some far peak inland which steadies his view, till the vision stretches down to the shore, and the dry land appears, hill and valley, field and river, and now he cannot doubt it. And if, besides, as in the first creation, the light should come out and strike the landscape here and there, and there should be finger-points of slanting sunbeams, he comes then to say, 'Here is something that can be relied on'—a house or church which visits him with thoughts of something he has known or should have known. He doubts no more. It is in some such way that our inner experience is to form itself into certainties—first to separate shifting fancies and feelings from principles, and with the confidence this brings, to let, it may be, some one principle stand out, some high hill of God far away,—the thought of God himself, of truth, of duty as supreme and sure; and then when light at some moment strikes these, light from a higher source, to ask ourselves, When is my mind clearest, when is my heart purest, and life most real? Is it not when light from above comes in to make things on earth sure that are of the best and most sacred? It seems then, not so much a learning of the new, as a re-learning of the old, a recovery of our true and proper self.

Yet some would say that, after all, this experience is single and personal, and may be the fancy of the individual; and the Christian himself feels the need of having it verified and corrected by something outside. He may be sure of God's Word, but is he always sure of his understanding and application of it? For this, there exists the guiding aid of those who have come under the teaching of the same Spirit. They cannot dictate, for the personal conscience, in the sight of God, is the last judge; but they can bear witness, and thus confirm. If any one charge the spiritual experience with being a fancy, we have to think of the great cloud of witnesses which compasses it about. As far as we can go back in time, we find like feelings and desires and aims, and as far as we go out in space, among different climes and colours and stages of civilisation, we shall find that God forms the hearts of Christians alike. No doubt there are differences about many things, and jealousies creep in because of them, but the love of God and the life of Christ, wherever they are received into the heart, bring forth essentially the same experiences and expressions. There is a Church of the living God going through the ages and through the lands, with which the spiritual man feels himself to be at one, and the more the inner spiritual realm is reached, the fuller is this unity felt to be. May we not with justice appeal to it as proving that the spiritual experience is not an individual fancy, but a testimony from man's nature to a wide and permanent power, the power of Him who has not only formed men's hearts alike in nature, but who by his Spirit in-forms their souls with new and higher life?

Still it may be said, Does this not cut off spiritual experience from the great mass of humanity, for take the Christian name as wide as you will, it is but a fraction of the family of man? And it is too true that the spiritual experience, in the form in which we have been speaking of it, has belonged to a minority in every age, and that it is only slowly extending. But we are not, therefore, to infer that this experience is an isolated thing, separated from man's nature by a hard, unsympathetic wall. It has its points of contact from which it draws evidence of its own reality, and through which it seeks to diffuse itself among those who are not sharers of it. The restlessness in the hearts of men, their sense of want of something more than they see and possess, their cry in sorrow for comfort which the world cannot give, and their shrinking from the blank future which a hopeless death presents, what are these but negative testimonies to the experience which the heart, taught by God's Holy Spirit, feels it has found? There are ruined chambers, there are strange indifferences, no doubt, deceitful opiates which the carnal nature takes to in its diseases and despairs, but in man, as man, there is the want which it is not in earth, in any of its forms, grosser or more glittering, to fill. Is it unreasonable to believe that He, with whom is the fountain of life, has opened a spring for these necessities? that as we see forms of existence each rising above the other till they end in man; and as in man himself we have experiences which widen until they beat at last against the barriers of the finite in moans and wails from great depths—is it unreasonable to believe that God has answered in some way so as to still and satisfy these cries? It is to bring men into a new and wonderful world, and can be done only by a wonder. It must be by some strange tokens that the heart of the Father of mercies breaks through to offer this, by a law, indeed, but by a law of love which bends the lower laws to its own will and way. And I know of no other way but that which has appeared in Jesus Christ, and in his opened heart, "Come unto Me." If there are those, then, who have this lower experience, the experience of want and heart-weariness, here is a way open to a higher. If you have felt that the heart knows its own bitterness, here there is a path to the joy with which no stranger can intermeddle. From the secret grief of the human experience you may reach the secret gladness of the divine, and for the sense of gnawing emptiness you may obtain the hidden manna. It is true that this can reach the soul only from God's own hand, and by his Spirit's power. Of this bread from heaven the Saviour says, "No man can come unto Me, except it were given unto him of my Father." And yet it is most certain that the refusal of it is the man's own act, and that the conviction of this pressed in on the conscience will be the sorest experience of all. A man has two ways before him, either to face this charge, Ye will not come to Me that ye might have life—or to come to this confession, Thou hast the words of eternal life; and we believe and are sure that Thou art that Christ, the Son of the living God.

If we have reached this experience in any degree, we should seek to strengthen and extend it by these means,— God's word brought home by his Spirit, our own spirit responding to it by growing love and obedience, fellowship with the like-minded, and communication of it to those who have it not. We shall thus grow in the knowledge of the divine life, and in the assurance of its reality. It will be increasingly our own by the surest of seals, the witness of the life itself; but it will be ours not to keep but to give away, and in giving it to possess it more fully. If Christians in this age of doubt and confusion are to have real power, they must go to men with this sure judgment of experience which has proved all things only to hold fast to the one good—That which we have seen and heard declare we unto you, that ye also may have fellowship with us: and truly our fellowship is with the Father, and with his Son Jesus Christ.

IX.

HADAD THE EDOMITE.

(LOVE OF COUNTRY.)

" Then Pharaoh said unto him, But what hast thou lacked with me, that, behold, thou seekest to go to thine own country? And he answered, Nothing: howbeit let me go in any wise."—1 KINGS XI. 14-22.

THIS narrative of Hadad comes in as a short episode in the later days of King Solomon, when he was being punished for his defection. The story has an interest of its own. Edom had been defeated many years before by David and Joab the captain of his host had returned to complete the conquest. With his unsparing severity he had slain every man capable of bearing arms, and crushed the reigning family. Hadad, who was very young, and of the seed-royal, was carried off by some faithful servants, and, after wandering from place to place, took refuge in Egypt, which was then and afterwards an asylum for fugitives. Here he was hospitably received, and rose high in favour. He had a fixed provision made for him, land given to him and his people, and in course of time he entered the royal family. The sister of Pharaoh's queen became his wife, his son was formally adopted into the household among Pharaoh's own children, and Hadad appeared bound to his new home by ties not to be broken. But news of important change reached him. David was dead, and, it is emphatically added, Joab the captain of the host—the terrible Joab—was dead, and the reins of Jewish rule were in weaker hands. The love of his old home awoke in Hadad's heart, and he came to Pharaoh with the request that he might be allowed to leave. It is evident that Hadad possessed a warmth of nature which attached men to him, for Pharaoh was unwilling to let him go. There is a simple beauty in the brief conversation, which makes one afraid to touch it by an attempt at expansion, " But what hast thou lacked with me, that, behold, thou seekest to go to thine own country? And he answered, Nothing: howbeit let me go in any wise." We have no intention to deal with the narrative and its bearings on Solomon, or Israel, or the future of Hadad. All this the narrative leaves in silence, and fixes our thoughts on this one feature in Hadad's nature, his love of country. We can scarcely doubt that it was the love of his country that was the ruling feeling in Hadad's wish to return to Edom. Had it been revenge or ambition, he could have named it to Pharaoh, and he would have been understood; but it is a feeling he cannot explain. It is an old Edomite anticipation of the saying of the Latin poet, " I know not what charm it is which leads us captive in the love of native land; it will not let us forget,"—a saying which one of our great philosophers could not help quoting when he left home to die in a foreign country. And it seems not less clear that the sacred historian wished to fix our eye on this feature. We are told of all that surrounded Hadad to keep him in Egypt—the royal favour, the good of the land, the ties of friendship and family—but Edom with its rocks and scanty pastures has a power that will not let him stay. He remembers it though he had been yet a little child, and the old memories come up afresh. He cannot put their power into words, but they draw him back to Edom—" Let me go in any wise."

We wish, then, to take this one feature—the love of country—and look at it as implanted in the human heart for a wise and divine purpose, passing beyond this simple instance, and drawing whatever light we can from God's providence and Word.

The first remark we make is, that it is *a feeling not only deep in our nature, as we do not need to show, but acknowledged and approved in the Bible.* This has been denied, and some have blamed, while others have praised, the Book on this account; but, whether it be to its blame or praise, the feeling is there. We cannot surely fail to perceive that the love of country was employed by God to build up the place He gave the Jewish people in preserving his truth in the long period of darkness, before the time came for the Gospel to go out into the world. Their love was drawn to it before they saw it as the land of Promise. Their lots were cast in it as if to give them so many separate roots in the soil. When they were banished from it, what a plaintive wail came from their harps in the most touching, if not the very first, of exile songs, " By the rivers of Babylon, there we sat down, yea, we wept, when we remembered Zion ;" and what a joyful counterpart we have in another song, " When the Lord turned again the captivity of Zion, we were like them that dream "! It is quite true they were sacred songs; the love of the temple was in the love of the land; but the natural beating of the human heart to the soil was also there, and God approved and used it. And, scattered through the Old Testament, we have passages ever and again which acknowledge this feeling—the case of Hadad here, the justice, if we may so say, done to the heart of an Edomite in this touch of nature, the patriotic pride of Naaman in the waters of Damascus, the admitted sacrifice made by Abraham when it was said to him, " Get thee out of thy country, and from thy kindred," and that dirge for the banished, old and deep, " Weep ye not for the dead, neither bemoan him : but weep sore for him that goeth away : for he shall return no more, nor see his native country." It is said we do not find this in the New Testament. But we are to remember that the New Testament accepts the Old, and it accepts whatever is true in man's nature. It comes to free from onesidedness, to enlarge and purify, but not destroy, whatever is human. I do not know that there is anywhere so intense a patriotic cry as that of the apostle Paul, "I could wish that myself were accursed from Christ, for my brethren, my kinsmen according to the flesh;" and may we not rightly think that it had its share in the heart of the Son of Man, when He looked out on all the world as He wept over lost Jerusalem, "How often would I have gathered thy children together, and ye would not!" It is, then, in accordance with God's Word, as well as with God's law in our nature, that our love should go out to native land.

But what purposes are served by this? There is one which may seem low enough to begin with, but which has its own importance. It is one of the ways by which God secures that the earth should be inhabited. There is a dispersive force in the world which began long ago, and which has been going on ever since, the spirit of adventure and energy which seeks action and change; so waste places are peopled and tilled. But there is needed not less an adhesive power to maintain what is gained. The world must have an anchor as well as a sail. Rocky Edom is dear as fertile Egypt, and bleak, storm-struck islands more than southern Edens. If it were not for this, wars for sunny spots would be more common than they are, and kindreds and peoples could not be gathered and held together to build up communities. But the building up of communities is a part of God's providential design. Each one in its own place brings out its own character, and, in the end, may be found to bring its own contribution to the interests of humanity. The wisdom of God's plan in scattering men abroad, and yet holding them together, and the part taken in it by this love of native land, may become more apparent as the world goes on—the love that tears men from it with pain, and draws them to return—" Let me go in any wise."

We may come to a higher view of this feeling when we think of its effect on the individual man. This love of the native soil has been one of the great springs of the poetry of the race; and, whatever we may think of poetry ourselves, we cannot fail to see its power. In the midst of the hard battle for material interests, and the hard laws of material things, men would be poorer and more pitiable without the fancy and imagination, which give them an escape from stern realities into the world of possible or probable or coming things, which may have more reality in them than what we see around us. God, who gives the bird wings for its safety and delight, has given man imagination It is certainly his gift, if men would only use it for Him. And it can be said with truth that, apart from the region of the spirit itself, it is never more pure and purifying than when it takes for its subject the things of native land and home. In all time, as far as we can trace it, and in all countries, this has found its way straight to the heart, and made men feel they had imagination who did not suspect it was within them. The kindling of this fire, the calling forth of tears when far away, helps men often to things more sacred. Many a youth has been led to think of a mother's love and a father's prayers and a neglected Bible, when his heart has been carried back over hills and seas to his native land. And so this feeling, as it affects the individual man, carries us to the thought of the home. The native land is dear, because the home has been there, where the soul found its way out first into the warmest affections which have been made ready for it by God as a welcome, and the thoughts first opened in their freshness to the wonderful things God has to show in the sights and sounds around. All the marvels of science afterwards through telescope and microscope are less than what meets the child's look on its first wanderings in its narrow round. The affections and the wonders of life grow out of this seed-plot. But to have a home, we need a native land, and to make it a true native land we must have a home. And here the practical may enter among things of imagination and heart. Next to religion, the great power for helping men to a better life is to improve the home; and it is certain that, without this, religion can never fully perform its work. If we are to do men lasting good, we must seek to keep them from constant drift, and have them grow up out of their place. It is in this way that they give mutual guarantees for worthy character, and that ties are formed which make men feel they belong to society, and are more than logs floating between sea and sand. And if we are to give men homes, we must give them houses. The man so far makes the house, but the house so far also makes the man. God, whose will it is that men should be men, has given us a house in the world He has made, which may well raise our nature above small and debasing things. When He bids us look to sun or stars or mountains or seas, He says, 'Think of this house, and be a tenant worthy of it.' We can do little more than help our fellow-men to look to Him and his world; but one of the helps is by making their house, as far as we can, capable of becoming a home. It is, indeed, a very difficult and complex matter, for there are different rights and interests to be considered, and while we seek justice in one direction we must not do injustice in another. But it is an aim to be kept in view steadily by Governments in giving equitable facilities, by philanthropists in their labours, and by Christians in their efforts to christianise the masses of the people. It is one of the good things of our time that more thought is bestowed on this than has ever been before. And until it is realised, the Church of Christ cannot be permanently healthy, nor our native land safe and strong. If in city and country the mass of the people could feel that they had homes in which they had some just cause for pride and pleasure, something which they could call their own, we should fear neither threats of invasion nor murmurs of revolt. True patriotism and true religion go hand in hand, for God has called Himself the God of families, and a happy native land is a land full of happy homes.

Another thought suggested by this feeling is that *it leads to acts of great self-sacrifice and endeavour.* Next to religion, there is probably nothing in human nature which has called out such a heroic spirit of martyrdom, or such long, persistent labour, as the love of native land. The grandest part of the history of nations has been the period when they have risen for independence and freedom, against the attempts to crush out their liberty or their separate life, and when they have left names of leaders which make hearts of men throb and thrill wherever they are heard. It is a poor Christianity, because it is not a true humanity, which affects to disregard this. There may be vanities and unreasonable jealousies, prolonged and hurtful irritations, which spring from these struggles, but in the struggle itself there is a true principle at work. Were the life of a nation destroyed, or hindered of its own proper development, every individual for long generations would suffer thereby. There is an heirloom of stimulus to a whole race in the heroic acts of those who have bequeathed them a name among the nations of the world.

It is one of the high motives, though not the highest, by which God's providence educates many men to rise above egotism, and take larger views of life than what they should eat and what they should drink and wherewithal they should be clothed. It serves some men, meanwhile, for a kind of religion, and keeps a people from being utterly materialised, till it comes in view of still loftier principles of life. Beacon-lights on land are valuable when the stars are hidden, and may have their use even when the stars are seen. But, besides such birth-throes of nations, there is their continuous existence, when long and persevering labour is needed to help them not only to live, but to live well. Philanthropy, the love of man as man, is great and generous; but we are not so rich in it that we can let patriotism go. There are men who can be reached by the love of fellow-countrymen, when they cannot be moved by the love of their fellow-men; and it is quite possible for a man to have both. The narrower is sometimes more intense and energetic than the wider. In the annals of the civil wars in England, an officer, who had fought in many battles abroad, tells that in his first fight on English ground he heard a cry of agony in his own tongue, and he looked behind him to see who of his men was killed. He discovered that the cry came from the opposing ranks, and then first he realised what a terrible thing it was to kill his own countrymen. There are many who feel it so in our quieter times, and who can be stirred more strongly to save from destitution and death those who speak their own language, and have a nearer blood beating in their heart. And though this in its turn may become selfish and exclusive, it has in it something that is natural and right. God's providence has connected us with a particular land and race, and nature prompts us to take a special interest in them. We should not hide our face from our own flesh. The Lord Jesus Christ has said, "Go into all the world, and preach the gospel to every creature;" and our hearts would be narrowed, and nearer interests themselves would suffer, if we ever forgot this universal commission; we need to keep it up for the assertion of our Monarch's claims, of the world's inheritance, and of our own full responsibility. But love of country has its rights in the very heart of Christianity. The apostle Paul was not wrong when, with all that he did as the apostle of the Gentiles, he said, "I have great heaviness and continual sorrow in my heart for my brethren, my kinsmen according to the flesh." When we become Christians we remain men. One of the songs of our native country which has come floating down through centuries, and which resembles some of the old historic psalms, but without the central Zion and divine breath, tells of a mother who found her two sons returned mysteriously for a single night to their home—" And she wrapped them in her warm mantle, because they were her own." We cannot escape from this strange tie of blood, and we should not seek to escape from it, but rather turn it to its proper use. It should lead us to care more tenderly for the sufferings of some, because they are our countrymen, and to work with more self-denial for the progress of our country in knowledge and righteousness and true religion, because it is ours. God did not form this strong tie without attaching a high duty to it.

Another thought suggested by this feeling is, that it should enable us to *understand the hearts, and work for the rights of all men.* There is a rule recommended by some religious communities, that their members should have no special friendships; that they should do nothing for each other as friends. And there are some philosophers who defend this. They say that "friendship is a barrier which hides from view the qualities of many who are more worthy of regard, that it is a kind of theft from the common good for the benefit of a few, and that, in a higher state of society, friendship will disappear;" which amounts very much to saying that if we put out our eyes, so as not to see things that are close to us, we shall be more likely to discover those that are far away. These are the theories of men who have either had no hearts to begin with, or have managed to cover them by cobwebs of speculation. God has not made his world on these principles, and no high society can ever be formed which does not take with it what is true in the lower. If we can discover a man who has no special love for what is near him, he is not likely to love what is a hundred or a thousand miles away, and still less to love some abstraction called humanity, in whatever fine terms it may be described. The heart is the inner eye, and it must be opened first to what comes close to it, if it is ever to see anything else in the world of man or God. Nor is it necessary that the nearest should be left behind to reach the furthest. Unless the nearest, if it be really worthy of affection, be taken up and on, the furthest will never be overtaken. Augustine has said that we may make a ladder of the dead things within us, to climb to the highest; but there is another ladder of living things by which we can rise as high, and by which our sympathies can be travelling to and fro like the angels in the dream of Bethel. The vision begins in the dreamer's own breast, and then it passes up into the skies. This is the very way in which God himself has dealt with us. He came from the limits of the universe into this world, and became our friend, that He might lead us step by step into the fulness of Him that filleth all in all.

Now, you will see that this is the course of Bible teaching in the growth of human duties—the family, the native land, the world; and if the Jew had been willing to carry his love of land into the world he would have kept his country yet. What we have to learn, then, from the New Testament is, not to love our native land less, but to use our love to it as a key of sympathy into the patriotism of others, with all their memories of what is noble in their past history, and what is praiseworthy in their aspirations and efforts to raise themselves in the scale of nations. The mere economy of things might teach us that, as the growing happiness of families in a nation is the good of every family, so the growing welfare of nations is the interest of every nation. But a Christian patriot has a more direct road to it. He will sympathise, from what he feels in himself, with the rights and just aims of other peoples, and will seek to help them to their due place. There is a golden rule which is intended to govern the duties of nations to each other as well as the duties of single men. If we are Christians, we shall feel that the one great means of gaining this for the world is the spread of the religion of Christ, the religion of freedom, of justice, of mercy, and of broad humanity. And even here, too, we might be helped to our end, if we studied with more sympathy the susceptibilities of different nations, and sought to present the Gospel in the way in which their history has prepared them for it. There is one Christianity, but there are different paths in which nations are conducted to it by the divine hand. The Jewish nation had the central place, "of whom as concerning the flesh Christ came," but the Greek in his love of wisdom, the Roman in his ardour for one empire, the Briton in his instinct for freedom, were led to find in it some lower good, purified and crowned by the highest blessing. There are nations still in this position, not far from the kingdom, if we were sympathisingly to study them, and help them to stretch out the hand to the hem of the healing garment. Even the weak oppressed races, among whom the consciousness of a nation has not begun to exist, have their claims on us. They seem placed like some of the maimed members of the human family about us, to excite a deeper pity, and to try our sense of equity in their feeble power of self-defence. There is nothing which shows a finer edge of patriotism, than the way in which a nation feels its honour engaged to deal tenderly with these races, as the prophet describes them, "scattered and peeled, meted out and trodden down;" and if God "deals a blow" at a haughty power it is most likely to be in behalf of some poor tribe that cannot strike for itself. If we love our own land, let us keep it free from this wrong and peril.

The last thought we suggest is, that this feeling may help *the conception of another and a higher country.* It is quite true that we find the spirit of patriotism filling the hearts of men with the highest enthusiasm, and spreading itself over masses of men and long periods, but bringing little spiritual desire. Yet it is one of the ways, as we have said, by which God keeps the heart above sensualism and utter selfishness—a kind of salt that saves nations from entire corruption. When his time comes for breathing in higher desires by his word and Spirit, He takes hold of this as of other natural human affections, to lift men to the "fatherland of souls," as one has named it. A Christian father has said, "The natural love (of man) builds the cities of men, and the divine love (of God) builds the city of God,"—they are the lower and higher planes of something in our nature. It is a token of our fallen state that, when they are so near, men so seldom pass from the one to the other. But we see in the Bible that the thoughts of native land and home are more than any others the figures which God has used to convey to us conceptions about the future. They are more than figures. They have been woven into his plan of education. He made the old patriarchs exiles, in order that he might create in them the longing which went further than any land, behind or before them, in this world. "And truly, if they had been mindful of that country from whence they came out, they might have had opportunity to have returned. But now they desire a better country, that is, an heavenly." He took their children into a land flowing with milk and honey, "the glory of all lands," as He called it, and they found disappointment and unrest in it, that they might look forward to "the rest which remaineth to the people of God." The last view given us of the heavenly world is that of a land and city which have over them a Father and an Elder Brother, and for friends the nations of the saved.

We sometimes ask ourselves, Can these distinctions which mark us out as kindreds and peoples, and bind us closely together in ties of affection and suffering and work, survive in another world? In their earthly form they must pass away, as flesh and blood cannot inherit God's kingdom, but there are differences of temperament and character, even in perfected beings, which may spring from the histories of this world, and contribute to the endless variety of another. The emblem which the apostle uses of the different kinds of grain, each receiving its own body in the resurrection, will apply not only to individuals, but to kindreds; for what are kindreds but individuals brought together according to their kind? If we can think of this, it will not take away from the perfectness of the affection of another world, but rather add to it. We are bound to one another by what we see of difference, as well as by what we feel of deep heart agreement. Meanwhile, let us make it sure that we come to the place where all these things and many more shall be made plain. "Let us fear lest, a promise being left us of entering into his rest, any of us should seem to come short of it." We should purify our affection for the lower, that it may lead us on and lift us up to the higher. The labour for the welfare of our dear native land should pass over into effort to make its people part of the kingdom that cannot be moved; the tender thoughts that make us long after it in absence, or when thinking of the great and good who have suffered and died for it, should transfer our hearts to the true native land, whence we have drawn our birth, if we are Christians, and where He is, who gathers round Him all whose eyes from many ages and countries have been turning toward his cross.

> "O sweet and blessed country,
> The home of God's elect,
> O sweet and blessed country,
> That eager hearts expect!"

There have been those who have had their affections so borne up by heavenly attraction that, though they had all the happiness of earth, they could not be satisfied with it, and would, if asked to remain, reply in the words, "And he said unto him, But what hast thou lacked with me, that, behold, thou seekest to go to thine own country? And he answered, Nothing; howbeit let me go in any wise."

X.

THE CHRISTIAN USES OF LEISURE.

"And He said unto them, Come ye yourselves apart into a desert place, and rest a while."—MARK VI. 31.

IF we look back a little way into the narrative, we shall understand better the occasion of this invitation. In the beginning of the chapter we are told that our Lord sent out his disciples to labour in the instruction of the people. They must commence under his own guidance the work they were to carry on after his death. They performed their mission with great ardour and success. A deep interest was created, and the crowds thronged around them till they had not time so much as to eat. When they returned, their Master saw their exhaustion, and made provision for it. They needed repose of mind as well as of body—the quiet that is required after excitement even more than after toil. There is a kindly considerateness in the words of Christ, a friendly sympathy with what may be called the lesser sufferings of our nature, which may give us confidence in still putting before Him the smallest wants and weaknesses. He had an end in view that took in the whole world, but He was not of those iron-hearted philanthropists who are cruel to men that they may work out their scheme for man, and who break their instruments in the passion for their theory. The zeal of God's house consumed Him; He had compassion on the multitudes, and spent Himself for them; but He devised hours of repose for his weary fellow-workers.

Another event recorded in this chapter had probably a share in this call to retirement. It seems to have been about the time of their return to Christ that the news came of the death of John the Baptist. It no doubt sent a strange shock to their heart. Some of them had been his followers, and knew him intimately; and all of them revered him as a divine messenger of extraordinary power and faithfulness. The details of banqueting and blood, the man of God meeting his executioners in the gloom of the dungeon, the glare of the lights above on the maiden and her frightful gift, strike us still with a shudder, and may help us to realise how those felt it who were in the presence of the event. It was not merely that they had lost a friend, but that God seemed indifferent to his own cause and its truest witnesses. Their faith must have been sorely tried, questionings must have been stirred within them to which they could find no answer, and it was to tranquillise their spirit, as well as refresh exhausted mind and body, that our Lord said to them, "Come ye yourselves apart into a desert place, and rest a while."

Before speaking of the uses which Christ intended this season of leisure to serve, we may make some remarks on the necessity for rest which God has imposed on our constitution. It is important to be convinced that there is a law requiring repose that we may avail ourselves of it without scruple, and give the advantage of it to others without grudging.

It is surely easy to see that God has signified it to us in his material creation. He has made the earth to revolve on her axis in a way that brings her at stated seasons under light and shade; and He has in a general but very marked way proportioned the physical strength of man to those seasons. The hands begin to slacken and the eyes to close when God draws the curtain. It is one of those adaptations which remind us that "the earth He hath given to the children of men." It is a general proportion, as we have said, not enforced nor rigid, but such as to show what his kindly purpose is. No man should transgress it in regard to himself or another. The thoughtless or covetous over-tension of our own powers, slavery, hard driving of those who may be under our control, the feeling that we can never get enough of work out of our fellow-creatures, the evil eye cast on their well-earned rest or harmless recreation, are all condemned by the laws laid down by God, and rebuked by this example of Christ. "The righteous man regardeth the life of his beast." He carries a shadow of mercy about him beneath which the meanest of God's creatures find their rights acknowledged —the night rest and the Sabbath rest, or their full equivalents. It is pleasant to think that Christ takes the bodily frame as well as the soul into his compassionate keeping, and that He looked as we do with a kindly eye on the signs which God has set in his creation that "man should go forth to his work and to his labour until the evening."

We may expect to find the same true of mental exertion. Even if the mind were not dependent in this world on the body, it would seem as if the continuous strain on any one object indisposed it for gaining its full end—the discovery of truth. It must learn at times to look away from things as well as at them, if it is to see clearly and soundly. It must close to thought with a kind of inaction, and must rest like the eye in darkness, if it is to preserve its health and have a true, undistorted view of God's world. There are some who reckon every pause in active thought so much of lost time; but when the mind is lying fallow it may be laying up capacity of stronger growth. There is an absorption of sunlight and air, an imbibing of common healthful influences, a comparative doing nothing which is as necessary to man's intellect as to his physical nature. When any one, who knows that it is not indolence in him, feels thought to be a heavy burden, and that objects of thought once interesting have lost all colour and freshness it is time to give the mind repose.

But the present subject leads us to speak more of the spiritual faculties. They are subject to the same law. There are cases in which there may be a constant strain of active religious work which at last deadens feeling and produces formality. It is true there are natures that have an inextinguishable fire of zeal and depth of emotion which enable them to go on unresting—burning more and more, as well as shining; but others, and these the greater number, feel the grandest objects become common, and the tenderest grow hard when they are incessantly handled. This is one of the dangers to be guarded against in seasons of strong religious excitement, in what are called revival movements; and we should either try to keep the movement healthful by dealing with the understanding and conscience as well as the emotions, or we should interpose a quiet, thoughtful interval. You cannot but observe how varied the Bible is as you read it; how, with the same truth all through, history succeeds poetry, and practical precepts follow up the most moving appeals; you cannot but see how Christ leads his disciples from the excitement of Jerusalem to the quiet of Bethany, takes them from the midst of the multitude to the fields and hillsides; and one purpose no doubt was that spiritual religion might not be lost through sensationalism. We have times of depression when we blame the temptations of Satan and the coldness of our own hearts, and no doubt we should jealously guard against the insidious chill that comes from these; but when we have earnestly struggled all in vain, it may be time to inquire whether we have not been losing our proper religious feeling through over-excitement, or the tension of too constant activity. This is the hazard that ministers, missionaries, and Christians devotedly given to sacred work have to avoid—not to go on in even the best of works till they become barren, external exercises, but to pause or turn to some other side of Christian occupation. This may be one of the ways of not becoming "weary in well doing."

Then, again, there may be those who, like the disciples, are not merely exhausted by labour, but perplexed by some painful subject of thought. The cruel death of John the Baptist was likely to make them feel that God had given up his government of the world, and that sin could go on without outward check or inward compunction. Difficulties of this kind are in some shape or other constantly turning up to perplex a certain class of thinkers. It is the besetting trial of their Christian life. They find it hard to realise a spiritual world existing beneath the face of the visible, to be thoroughly convinced of a great moral law working among and above all the ravages and temporary triumphs of sin, and to be sure that there is a God and a soul and an eternity. There are some natures which have such a passion for certainty that they can do nothing but dig down to the roots of these subjects to see that they are not mere artificial creations of man's device, but living realities fixed in, and growing up from, the soil of God's universe. The love of certainty can never be carried too far, but there may be a wrong way of satisfying it. Men may dig at the roots of things and lose sight of the evidence of life which humbler minds can gather quietly under the shadows of green branches, and from the nourishment of refreshing fruits. What some minds find it hard to gain by sore thought and toil, others can receive in unstruggling acquiescence. "A little child shall lead them." The passion to be perfectly certain about a thing in the way of questioning and argument makes one jealous at last about the most satisfactory reasons, and the proofs are pored over till the mind loses sight of their full bearing and power. There are times when, for the sake of full conviction, vexed minds should lay their difficulties aside, occupy themselves with quieter walks, and come back on their doubts as if for the first time. Now, for both these conditions of spirit—the dulness that might come from exhaustion and over-excitement, and the perplexed thought about spiritual difficulties—Christ proposes this remedy, "Come ye yourselves apart into a desert place, and rest a while."

Let us next proceed to consider what He offers in this leisure. It is not an indolent animal repose, but that rest of refreshment which befits those who have souls. We shall take the context for our illustration.

One element in it is *communion with outward nature.* Christ invites his disciples into a "desert place," not a waste sandy desert, as many figure to themselves, but a thinly peopled region away from towns and crowds. There can be no doubt that it was to the country east of the Sea of Galilee among rolling hills and grassy plains and quiet mountain flocks, with the blue sky overhead and distant glimpses of the deeper blue of the lake. One of the saddest things about our modern civilisation is that so many thousands of our fellow-creatures have so little opportunity for cultivating a pleasure in this side of God's world. Certainly He made the earth not only for the support of man's body, to yield him food and clothing, but for the nurture of his mind and spirit, to suit their moods and to supply them with thought and stimulus. Would a wise architect build his house only with an eye to stores and animal comforts, and with no regard to its being a home for a man, with windows opening on wide expanses of land and sea, or quiet nooks of homely beauty? This world has not been formed on the tame utilitarian principle of feeding so many million consumers, but with a regard to soul—to provide for the inner eye scenes of grandeur and sublimity—to train spirits to thoughts above dead matter by the spiritual forms with which matter is clothed; and hence the mountain wilds, the desolate moorlands, the terror of Alpine heights and boundless breadth of seas and desert sands. In these shapes of creative power, so far away from what we reckon the profitable employment of space, God is proving Himself not merely a former of men's bodies, but a Father to their spirits, lifting us up from the dull content of an animal existence to thoughts of illimitable freedom and range—and this not only when we look on such scenes, but when we hear or read or dream of them in fancy. Who does not see that the Word of God all through has interwrought these scenes of nature with a special fitness into its own revelations, as if it wished that man in his highest thoughts of his Maker should always feel himself in the face of his Maker's works? The awful rocks and oppressive solitudes of Horeb, splintered peaks and dumb wastes, were an appropriate birthplace for the stern majesty of law,—the hill of the Beatitudes, with fresh flowers and singing birds, a throne for the Teacher of mercy,—and the island of Patmos, looking away between sea and sky to the boundless regions of the west, a watch-tower for the inspired seer who beheld the triumphs of the kingdom of God filling the earth, and rising to heaven. We should endeavour to make the inner world of our thoughts about God and spiritual things not a separate life from the outer world of creation, but with a union like that between body and soul. If we could learn to do this rightly, it would strengthen us in good thoughts, and relieve doubts and calm anxieties. Many a fevered brow and cumbered spirit might feel a soothing hand laid upon them, pointing them, as it did Abraham long ago to the broad heaven (Gen. xv. 5), or Christ's disciples to the grass of the field, that they may learn tranquillity. Nature can do very little for us if we have no perception of a divine spirit breathing through it, but very much if the great Interpreter is with us. There are many, indeed, who have little opportunity for any lengthened access to her fair, wide pages, but few are altogether shut out if they will keep an open eye and heart. The grandest things in all the world are at the door of those who will admit them. If we can steal glimpses for a few hours of green fields and clear waters, they can be our own for ever in memory, and, blessed be God! give us glorious hopes of brighter scenes. We are never excluded from his wide sky, from sunsets that stream momentary glory over our dusky cities, and calm moons that look so compassionately through the clouds upon our vain turmoil; and if a man be so inclined, he can be more quieted and comforted by the sight of a little flower in his window or a star shining down through piled-up roofs, than another may be who has the leisure of all his days, and the breadth of continents to spend them in. The world of nature is like its God, entire wherever we see a touch of its finger. And if we surrender ourselves to this Teacher, He can show us wide views through narrow windows, and speak lessons of deep calm in short moments.

Another element of rest to be cultivated in leisure is *intercourse with fellow-Christians.* The wish to cultivate a life of repose separated from the active world has shown itself in almost every religion. There is a yearning for it in certain natures; and if the state of society be very corrupt and the mind quiet and self-inspective, it becomes very strong. We know how early and how often it has shown itself in Christianity. It is many centuries since the monks of Egypt hid themselves among the dreary sands of the Thebaid; and the most lonely islands of the Hebrides have the cells still standing in which solitary recluses, who found Iona too social, sought to perfect their spiritual life. Perhaps most of us have felt times of weariness of the toil and temptation and strife, when we have thought that if we might reach some isolation of this kind we could become wiser and better. And yet few things have been more repeatedly proved by experience than that tranquillity of spirit is not to be attained in this way. The very austerities and penances that these men practised is one of the surest tokens that they had not gained quiet. They had to do battle with their own hearts, and the conflict was all the fiercer that it was a single combat. And nothing is clearer from Scripture than that this seclusion is opposed both to its spirit and its example. It is against the stern witness-bearing of the Old Testament and the human tenderness of the New. Elijah, who may be thought to have approached nearest to it, and who has been taken as the model of anchorites, was a man of the world and of courts, and retired to Carmel and Horeb only to come back again stronger for the duties of public life. There are times when complete retirement for prayer and heart communion is good for every one. He can never stand firmly among others who has not learned to be alone; but the retirement should never shut out thoughts of his fellow-men, and should prepare for renewed intercourse with them. When Christ invited his disciples to come apart into a desert place, it was that they might be more in each other's company. He wished to give them an opportunity for the quiet interchange of experience, which they could not enjoy in their work among the multitude. They had much to say about what they had learned of the power of their Master's words over their fellow-men and over themselves. Many dark forebodings would flee away when they felt that their thoughts and fears and hopes were part of a new world that was common to them all, and that God had formed their hearts alike, not only by nature, but by his grace. What a refreshment a man finds it to be when he comes from the outside world, with its chill and its frequent selfishness, back to the warmth of his hearth and to hearts he can entirely trust! How he thanks God who has given his spirit the rest of a home! Let us ask ourselves, Do we use our leisure for cultivating a feeling like this in our intercourse with those who hold the same grand Christian faith, or are we eager when released for a short time from the world's work to run into the worse disquiet of the world's frivolous pleasures? What society and converse do we seek when we are left at liberty to choose them? Do we ask ourselves, 'How am I to gain most readily refreshment and strength, that I may be able when I go into the active work of life again to do my part manfully and Christianly?' To hold conference with the best of men in books is a great thing, and to converse with God in his Book, and in our hearts, still greater; but there will always be a want in a man's Christian nature, if he has not come into contact with hearts around him that are beating with a divine life to the pulse of the present time. Every age, every circle has its lessons from God, and no one can learn them all alone. We are all of us to blame in not being more frank and confidential in these matters of our mutual faith and hope. Let us, above all things, be natural, and say no more than we feel, nor affect a formal and conventional talk, but let us not unnaturally close up our feeling and be as much hermits in our spiritual life as if we had vowed ourselves to a cell or a wilderness. If we use our leisure to make our Christian intercourse what it should be, we shall find it a rest to our spirits whether they are exhausted with labour or perplexed with doubtful thoughts. It is not merely the refreshment of hearing what may quicken and comfort us, but the relief of unburdening our own mind. Many a trouble which seems to have an unfathomed depth, when we let it stagnate in our breasts, clears itself when we give it vent in a stream of Christian fellowship. Let it be remembered, too, that such an interchange of feeling has one of the last blessings promised in the Old Testament and one of the first bestowed in the New. When "they that feared the Lord spake often one to another, the Lord hearkened and heard it" (Mal. iii. 16); and when the two disciples journeying to Emmaus spoke together of Christ, He listened and joined Himself to their company, till their "hearts burned within them," and their sorrows and doubts were all consumed in the flame (Luke xxiv. 32).

This brings us to the third element of rest to which the leisure of the disciples gave them access, *a closer converse with Christ himself.* He offers to accompany them, and withdraws them from the crowd that He and they may be more entirely together. There are some professing Christians who speak of leaving their religion aside for a little when they go on recreation or into certain kinds of society. They seem to think it belongs to particular places or seasons, and can be laid by when they cross the sea, like a fashion or a dress. It is very evident that they do not know what religion means. If it is to be with us at any time, it must be with us at all times. We should be able to part with it no more than with the heart that beats, the soul that thinks within us. We should never go where we would blush to see the eye of Christ upon us, and we should try to make our intercourse with nature and with friends deeper and dearer from a sense of his presence hovering always round us.

And yet, as there are times when we are more alone with our own souls, so there are times when we can be more alone with the thoughts of Christ. When we are doing our appointed work in God's world, or labouring actively for the good of others, our minds are dispersed among outward employments; we may be serving our Master very truly all the time, but we are careful about many things, and have not leisure to sit at his feet and speak to Him about our own individual wants. Now, this last is most necessary in its place. The flame will not burn very long or very bright, unless you have oil in your vessels with your lamps. You will find it an arid and formal service, a distasteful work that cannot well be permanent, if you do not seek seasons when you can go apart with the Saviour of souls and confer with Him on things that concern not other men and the Church, but yourselves and your own soul's position towards Him. Let us remember the zealous watchfulness of the great apostle, who was careful "lest that, by any means, when he had preached to others, he himself should be a castaway." It is very unwise to take the matter so easily for granted when we have the example of one who had the care of all the churches, and had done so much for Christ, and who yet found time, and felt it to be needful, to inquire about his own spiritual wants. We do not pretend to give any rules for conducting this exercise of the heart, and have very little faith in them when they are imposed by one man upon another. They will be best found out by a man's consideration of his own circumstances and necessities, and the spirit of them all is to be found in this, that he should go to Christ's Word, and to Christ in it, not thinking about what he is to say to others, or how he is to shape its truths into logical and persuasive forms, but about what it says to the profound wants of his own nature, and how he himself has found it to be bread and water of life. A Christian man who has been handling truth throughout the week, like a sword and shield, battling with the anxieties and temptations of business, or who has been urging it in formal shapes upon the attention of other men, will find it like a rest in green pastures and beside still waters, when the Commander of the Lord's host becomes the Shepherd of his people, and invites them to speak with Him as a man talketh with his friend.

And from that other cause of exhaustion, the perplexity of difficult questions in God's Word or God's providence, this use of our leisure will also give relief. There are things which startle and stagger you, mysteries of evil and misery through which you cannot find your way with all your thinking. It may be well not to surrender thought, but to rest a while; and there is no better rest than that of quiet fellowship with Christ himself. There are questions which are solved, not by hard thinking, but by practical experience. If we have made trial of Him for our own sin and sorrow, our own emptiness and unappeasable yearnings, and if we have found that He can touch our souls, and strengthen and comfort them, as no other in the world can, then the hard sayings which offend the multitude will not separate us from Him. When He puts the question, as He did shortly afterwards, "Will ye also go away?" we shall reply, like those disciples who had rested with Him in personal fellowship, "Lord, to whom shall we go? Thou hast the words of eternal life; and we believe, and are sure, that Thou art that Christ, the Son of the living God."

There are these three elements of rest, then, provided for those who are able to gain leisure—communion with outward nature, true human fellowship, and closer and simpler access to Christ himself. It will be understood that, though we have said nothing of the claims of the body and the mind, of their need of repose and recreation, or of change and stimulus, we are very far from wishing to exclude them. God knows our frame, and Christ never deals with men in the one-sided, ascetic way which a false spiritualism affects—an extreme which in all ages has produced a corresponding recoil. But we have sought here to deal with the use to which leisure should be put in regard to our spirit, because, if this is attended to, all other occupation in leisure will be healthful and capable of happy reflection. The great thing for us is to have a guiding principle directing our lives; or, better still, an atmosphere pervading it, that shall take in all natural human things, and extract the evil and leave only the good. When we retire for a time from the turmoil and perplexity of life, we might learn to employ our leisure in a way that would make us not less fit, but more, for the great work to which God calls us. This is the only rest worthy of men and Christians; for true repose is to be gained, not by dissipating thought and degrading feeling, but by giving them true salutary employment—not by sinking, but ascending. The higher atmosphere is calmer as well as purer; and if we used our leisure rightly we might go down again into the hard duties of life like strong men reinforced for battle.

Such seasons of leisure, let it be observed, are not the object of life. They are given to those who have been working, and given to them that they may work again. "Come ye apart into a desert place, and rest *a while.*" The thronging importunity of the multitude soon broke in upon their quiet, and called them to fresh exertions. And though we had no command from Christ, "Son, go work to-day in my vineyard," and no such words as " Pray ye therefore the Lord of the harvest that He would thrust forth labourers into his harvest," yet the sight of the waiting fields all around might well break our repose. When we see sin and misery and sorrow, should we sit still—we who believe we have the healing word? Be sure that those only have a right to a season of rest, and those only truly enjoy it, who have done real work, and who mean to go to work again. This world is not for enjoyment, not even for self-culture in the highest things, but for taking our part in it as God's fellow-workers, and as the followers of his Son who went about doing good.

I know that there are some to whom very few, if any, such seasons of outward repose are granted—sons and daughters of toil, who welcome the evening as " a servant earnestly desireth the shadow"—who say, not of the Sabbath, but of the week, " When shall it be gone?" that they may give out of their one day's rest much work for God and for their fellow-men. They have quietly toiled on, I know, year after year, bending to the six days' burden, and having but the one on which they can look up more calmly heavenward, and look abroad and do their deeds of mercy. They have little experience of what the Christian poet means—

> "The calm retreat, the silent shade,
> With prayer and praise agree;
> And seem by thy sweet bounty made
> For those who follow Thee."

Yet God can make the light of that one sun to them as the light of seven; and if there be a peculiar heaven of enjoyment to those who have filled up Christ's sufferings, there will be one of special rest to those who have followed Him in his patient labours of love.

Finally, let us all seek to feel that we can have true tranquillity of spirit, whether in work or retirement, only through a heart that looks trustfully to God as a reconciled friend. That perfect peace goes everywhere with the man whose heart is stayed on God. The quiet scenes of nature have a song of constant joy in them (Ps. lxv. 13), and the wildest tempests a voice passing through them—" Peace, be still." The friendships formed within such a circle have a depth which gives the pledge of their perpetuity, and they begin in the retired spots and little companies of earth to be perfected in the gathering together of all things to Christ. The heaviest yoke of labour will be lightened, and the solitary place be made glad, when He shares them with us who can give even now to the most weary and heavy-laden a foretaste of the very rest of God.

XI.

THE ARK TAKEN AND RETAKEN.

LESSONS FROM AN OLD DEFEAT AND VICTORY.

> *"And the Philistines fought, and Israel was smitten, and they fled every man into his tent; and there was a very great slaughter; for there fell of Israel thirty thousand footmen. And the ark of God was taken; and the two sons of Eli, Hophni and Phinehas, were slain."*—1 SAM. IV. 10, 11.
>
> *"And when the men of Ashdod saw that it was so, they said, The ark of the God of Israel shall not abide with us: for his hand is sore upon us, and upon Dagon our God."* —1 SAM. V. 7.
>
> *"So David and all the house of Israel brought up the ark of the LORD with shouting, and with the sound of the trumpet."*—2 SAM. VI. 15.

THE whole of this history which gathers round the capture of the ark, and its return to the land of Israel till it found a home in Jerusalem, is of very great interest. We shall not try to give even a summary of it, but shall ask that the full account may be read in the books of First and Second Samuel. It was evidently a history which made a deep impression on the minds of the Israelites. It found its way into their worship in the 78th Psalm, which is an inspired comment on it, a kind of divine illumination traced around the narrative in a series of pictures which bring into connection with it the great events of the past life of the nation. All the previous defections and disasters are called up and explained, and then the transference of the ark from Shiloh to Mount

Zion is presented as the beginning of a new and brighter period in the nation's future. Our purpose is to use this part of the sacred history for a lesson to ourselves, and we shall do so under two points of view,—man's declension leading to defeat, and God's victory calling us to higher duty.

I. Let us first, then, look at the connection between declension and defeat. At the root of the calamity which befell the nation and the dishonour to the cause of God, there was a deep moral apostasy. The spiritual condition of the people had never sunk lower, from their abasement in Egypt to their captivity in Babylon, than at this time. The character of the priesthood had become thoroughly corrupt, and this is one of the most ominous signs that can appear in any society. They turned God's ark into an instrument of selfish speculation, and made their office a means of gratifying their covetous and sensual appetites. The brief description given of them is very powerful: "The sons of Eli were sons of Belial; their sin was very great before the Lord; for men abhorred the offering of the Lord." And yet the abhorrence of the worshippers seems to have proceeded as much from dislike of the rapacity of the priests as from the recoil of conscience from their inconsistency. The priests have the heaviest responsibility, no doubt, but sins of priest and people generally go hand in hand. They act and react on each other, and stage by stage a state is reached where conscience becomes blind, and shame is cast aside. Then, if there is to be recovery at all, convulsion is not far away. There is not perhaps any country with the name of Christian where such a condition of things could now be long borne. A growing light has so penetrated the darkest places that any nominal ministers of Christ would shrink from gross and open immorality, and the feeling of men would rise in revolt. So much we have gained since Christianity entered the world. But we have to remember that with the higher light we have higher responsibility. Churches and ministers with a very decent exterior may be standing in the same relative position as the people and priesthood in this olden time. We may be as far beneath the Sermon on the Mount as they were beneath the commandments of Sinai. If ministers put the service of the church above their own spiritual character, if they look upon their office merely as a means to their own profit and comfort, they are acting in the spirit of the sons of Eli. If the people indulge them in this, and willingly accept indulgence in return, then the whole tone of the Church of Christ is lowered to self-seeking, and under the respectable exterior there may be a hardness and selfishness which break out from time to time into overt acts, to startle us and give us warning. We must never forget that the great test of all religion is its moral results. Is it making men lead higher, purer, more self-denying lives? Is our Christianity presenting itself in the spirit of Christ? Are ministers following the example of the apostle who could truly say, "I seek not yours, but you," and keeping before them his great Master who forgot Himself in the thought of God and for the good of man? "For even Christ pleased not Himself; but, as it is written, The reproaches of them that reproached Thee fell on Me." To have Church and land safe, it is not enough to be free from the profanations which led to the capture of the ark; we must be in some conformity with the Christian standard.

There was another feature of the declension of the people of Israel connected with this. They had changed their religion into a formal superstition. After their first defeat by the Philistines they began to think of higher help. But it was not of God they thought, the living God, but only of his ark. "Let us fetch the ark of the covenant, that it may save us out of the hand of our enemies." And like all men when reality begins to fail, they are great in lofty phrases—"The ark of the covenant of the Lord of hosts which dwelleth between the cherubim." How far they are away from those who saw "the goings of their God and king in his sanctuary, and his glorious marching through the wilderness"! It is evident that the ark has been changed into a fetish; the name of it is to be their deliverer; and He who passed in cloud and fire through the sea, who "rideth upon the heavens of heavens of old," is to be shut up in that chest to be carried hither and thither in the hands of priests, foul with avarice and pollution. When religion comes to this it sinks into a hideous idol, and the petrified shell must be broken in pieces if the spirit is to be saved. It is the natural result of the corruption of the word of life. Whenever religion loses its hold of the conscience and the character, it loses all real meaning. It leaves the heart and becomes a thing of the hands, while the soul of it dies.

So it was with the Pharisees in the time of our Lord. They made broad phylacteries with texts on them, and washed cups and plates, and made much of tithing little things, and then religion ascended a cross and hid itself in a grave. And then came the time in the Christian Church when a small piece of the wood of that cross was put for Him who suffered on it, and a fragment of his dress coveted more than his spirit, and his gospel covered with embroideries and ribbons till its meaning was hidden under its many-coloured vestments. How deep it is in human nature to put the letter for the life! And when we take the Bible into our hand and call ourselves evangelical Christians we are not safe from this same danger. It is quite possible to possess an orthodox creed and put it in place of a true, unselfish life, to hold fast by our Bibles, and make the having them and reading them a charm, as truly as did the Israelites with the ark of Shiloh. There comes perhaps a great quickening of religious life to the Church of Christ, an evangelical revival. The gospel is preached with earnestness and fervour by lips touched with a live coal from God's altar, and men listen to it as if the angels were singing for the first time in human hearing, "Behold, we bring you good tidings of great joy which shall be to all people." It is a message of love and power, and those who can remember such a season look back on it as a "visit of the dayspring from on high, through the tender mercy of God." But in time it loses its efficacy. The same truth is preached, the very same words are used, but they have passed into a formula which glides over the tongue of the speaker, and falls on the ears of the hearers without any movement of the heart, or perhaps any distinct significance to the mind. The freshness and fervour, the solemn awe which stirred and bent to submission the souls of thousands, have gone, and bequeathed only phrases of doctrine which have ceased to work any deliverance. When such times of depression come to the Church of Christ, it will generally be found that the truth of God has been held in unrighteousness. The revival of Christian doctrine will ere long lose its power, unless it lead to a corresponding revival of Christian life. The gospel of the grace of God may not be turned to lasciviousness, but it may be suffered to sink into self-indulgence, into a mere desire to escape from fear here and suffering hereafter. The Gospel gives this, but if we are to retain it in its power we must receive from it far more. It must make us willing to court suffering, to meet self-denial for noble ends, and to forget self for the cause of God, and for the good of man. This was the Christianity of Christ, and this must be ours if it is to continue with us. But when men wish to have a gospel which stops short of the cross, or which makes Christ bear it that they may have nothing but comfort; when they look on God's mercy as, in its beginning and end, only a passport to heaven, they have turned the glory of God's sanctuary into the wood of the ark, and are near delivering it into the hands of the enemy.

Now, there is a further stage in the ark's history before it reaches its lowest fall. It has been dissociated from the living God, and has become not merely a common but a desecrated thing. To redeem the Israelites from their error, they must learn that the ark is powerless if God forsakes them, and that the symbol cannot save without the living presence. In this stern lesson God uses their enemies as teachers. We cannot help admiring the patriotic spirit of the Philistines, their manly courage, and love of freedom. The Bible is a broad book, and just to what may be called natural human virtues. At first, when they heard the shout that welcomed the ark to the Israelite camp, they were struck with fear. They remembered the history they had heard of its God, and said, "God is come into the camp." But Jehovah was to them only one out of many deities of the nations; the conduct of his worshippers had not filled them with high regard, and the blood of patriots and freemen is in their words: "Be strong, and quit yourselves like men, O ye Philistines, that ye be not servants unto the Hebrews, as they have been to you; quit yourselves like men, and fight." This has the ring of an old battle-song, and it may have been such, one of the utterances of fire which have made hearts swell and swords flash in many lands over the world, and not least in our own. "Ah, freedom is a noble thing," begins the story of the patriot king of our country by a poet centuries ago, and we must be permitted to sympathise with men who were ready to face the Hebrews and their gods, as they reckoned them, that they might be free. In this case the Philistines were on the better side. It was not man against God, but man against falsehood under his name; and the battle ended as one might anticipate. "The Philistines fought, and Israel was smitten, and the ark of God was taken." Natural human courage proved itself stronger than corrupted religion, and hypocrisy was broken and scattered. No doubt the Philistines imagined they had vanquished Israel's God, and some of his sincere but short-sighted friends thought the cause of religion lost, but the victory was for God and truth.

The history of this battle has been often repeated. It was another form of it when the King of Babylon carried away the sacred vessels of the temple to have them made drinking-cups at his boastful feasts; when the temple itself was laid in ruins, and the prophet bewailed the holy and beautiful house which was burnt up with fire; Titus was repeating it when he destroyed the Jewish State, and carried the seven-branched candlestick in triumph to the Capitol; Mohammed, when the decayed churches of the East were trampled down beneath the feet of his fierce horsemen; and the French Revolution, when its cry for human liberty shook and is shaking the despotism of the church of Rome. "The corruption of the best thing becomes the worst," and life, in some lower form, rises and overthrows what has lost its spirit, though it may still bear a higher name. We may think that catastrophes like these are very far from our own country, and from the churches of God among us, but there may be a slow decay which brings about the same end. Unless we can raise our

Christian life in some measure up to our profession, and make it higher than the natural virtues which are found outside the Church, we shall suffer defeat in point after point, which shall bring on us serious detriment. If, for example, dishonesty and faithlessness to engagements be permitted among us, which would not be suffered in the common walks of life, we cannot maintain our place as the guardians of righteousness. If we are surpassed by men who have no regard for Jesus Christ in patient, self-denying work for the redress of wrong and the relief of suffering, we cannot claim to lead the way as friends of humanity. If men of science show an unwearied love in the study of nature, an enthusiasm in gathering stores of knowledge from earth and sea and sky, and a skilfulness in applying them to practical use, while we are indifferent and inert in the pursuit of spiritual truths, careless about the hidden treasures of wisdom which cast light on the ways of God and meet the wants of souls, we shall not inspire confidence in our sincerity, or give men much interest in the contents of God's Word and the work of Christ's Church. The question which will condemn us may be, What do ye more than others? or even, What do ye equal to others? The world is ready to judge a cause by the spirit it creates and the fruit it produces, and if we do not surround the ark of God with all the things that have virtue and praise of which the apostle speaks, if we do not let the hidden light which is in it shine out through our character and work, men will not believe in us, and may come to treat it with contempt. There may be no sudden disaster, but it may be passed by for more palpable and active interests, the name Ichabod may be written on it slowly, letter by letter, and it may fall into a neglect as saddening as would be its captivity in the hand of an enemy. There are lands where this has happened, and should it ever befall us it may take long to repair the loss.

II. We come to the other side of the subject, God's victory. The Philistines carry the captive ark in triumph to Ashdod, their capital, and set it up as a trophy in the house of Dagon their god. But the ark, which could not be defended by great armies, and round which thirty thousand men fell in vain, showed the power of the God of Israel when it was alone and in exile. Dagon fell prostrate before it, and when the priests set up their idol again it brought on it a heavier ruin. Disease spread through their coasts, and they began to feel that they were in conflict with a mysterious power, though they were slow to admit their weakness. They carry the ark from place to place, with the idea that change of circumstances will bring the balance once more to their side. For Ashdod they try Gath, and for Gath, Ekron, but with the same result, till priests and diviners, though they do not acknowledge Jehovah's supremacy, own their perplexity and defeat; and the ark, so late their trophy, is sent back with propitiatory gifts to the land of Israel. This is a lesson which the world needs to learn, and which God wrought out in his own way long ago, and has recorded that men may read and ponder it. It is that when they think they have gained a victory over God they are on the edge of a sore disaster. What to do with God is the world's great trial, as what to do with Jesus was the difficulty of Pilate, "What shall I do then with Jesus which is called Christ?" For the world cannot make God to its mind, and in the end the world cannot do without Him. It carries his ark hither and thither, seeks to bring Him to the level of its own conceptions, to subject Him to its own idols, but finds in all its efforts no true rest till it suffers Him to take his own way to his throne, from which in his own time He shall make good his word by still higher victories—"Over Philistia will I triumph." We are still in the midst of this history, but we have reached a wider phase of it. We see it now more frequently, not in the attempt to put Dagon above the God of heaven, but to put man above Him. Man—his own divinity, with neither ark nor altar, God nor immortality, is the last form in which the trial of strength is being carried on. There can be no other beyond it. But the result in Ashdod shall work itself out once more, although the process may be longer. Man cannot stand without God any more than against Him; time after time this self-worship will be defeated, and sifting trials and pains will overtake those who follow it. As there can be no true religion without morality, so there can be no permanent morality without religion, and without morality no possible society among men. All civilisations have fallen to pieces as they lost their faith in the Highest, even though that faith had much alloy. The world cannot revolve unless it is held by something outside itself. This has been verified again and again in what we call Christian lands. When the supreme Judge has been driven from his place in the soul, conscience reels to and fro and is at its wit's end. Men theorise it into a thing of natural growth which some will call a flower, and some a weed. And then come the rivalries and rancours, the sensualities and hates which are unappeasable, because the time is short, and there is nothing more. Ah! but we shall educate men to sweet reason, and train them up in morality, and teach them to moderate their passions, and the planet will all the while be rolling round into new regions of light! Fools and blind! You will educate human reason by denying the reason that is supreme; you will train in morals while you cut the roots of conscience and plant its empty stalk in sand; you will moderate passion by giving it the present and earthly for its portion, and you will have the world roll into light when you have quenched its sun! Men must come at last to perceive this, if not by the sunlight of God's goodness yet by the fire of his judgments, for He retains his hold of the world though the world may lose its hold of Him. And there are tokens that such seasons are coming. When atheism opens the gulf of anarchy, and the foundations of the earth are out of course, men begin to recoil, and look to religion as a safeguard. After the first French Revolution this reaction set in, and we see signs of it again in our day. We may be glad of it as a confession and a preparation; but true homage to God cannot come from this motive. The diviners may make their new cart for the ark, and put their jewels of gold in a coffer by its side, but after all they send the ark away; and if we take to honouring God, only from motives of policy, and in order to escape some threatened evils, it is the same as rejecting Him. In whatever way God may overrule the times "when men's hearts are failing them for fear, looking for those things which are coming on the earth," the only obedience which He accepts is that which is given Him out of love, and for his own sake.

This brings us to the last remark, that if the ark of God is to find its true place it must be committed to the hands of men who love it. Men who have no real faith in it may be made instruments in God's providence of showing its powers, even by their extorted acknowledgments; but if it is to reach its throne it must be set within the border of its own land, and be borne from house to house and village to village till it gains Jerusalem. Even the God of the ark will not carry it to its end without human agency. He vindicates his honour when it is all alone, redeems it from the enemy, transfers it to its own domain, and commits it to the care of its friends. We may call all this a type if we will, and so it is, if by a type be meant an illustration of the way in which God is accustomed to have his work done. There are some things which men cannot do for themselves, and God performs them; but there are others where they can work for Him, He all the while working in them, and in these it is their privilege and their profit to be God's fellow-workers. He takes them to the brink of the Red Sea, bids them stand still, opens its waters, and then afterwards the march through the wilderness is their share. He prepares the cross of Christ, rescues it from the weakness and shame which men ascribed to it, fills it with divine power and love, and then puts it into the hands of its friends that it may move on its way to its final conquest. That cross is our ark of the covenant, and in the joy that welcomed it to Jerusalem, when "David and all the house of Israel brought up the ark of the Lord with shouting and with the sound of the trumpet," we seem to catch far off the anticipation of that time when "the temple of God shall be opened in heaven, and there is seen in it the ark of his testament: and there were great voices in heaven, saying, The kingdoms of this world are become the kingdoms of our Lord, and of his Christ; and He shall reign for ever and ever" (Rev. xi.).

And so let us, in closing, gather up the spirit of the history as it applies to ourselves. We need never despair of the cause of God; it has had its defeats where all seemed lost, but every defeat has been the herald of a new victory and of a higher rise. From Shiloh to the house of Dagon; but thence to Jerusalem to put on more spiritual beauty, and to be surrounded with those songs which go deep into Christian hearts. Let us not faint at its many vicissitudes. The history of the Church of Christ has been the history of the ark, lost in many a battle, covered with many a cloud, spitefully entreated by many an enemy, forgotten often in its own land when it has been expelled by the stranger, but having the record of one of its heroes for its own watchword, "persecuted but not forsaken; cast down but not destroyed; as chastened and not killed,"—going on all the while from strength to strength, if we read its record not by man's days but by God's years. The days sometimes indicate decline and defeat, the years tell of widening circles and growing power. On which of the slopes are we at present placed? Are we going down, it may be, to some reverse, or upward to a higher position? Is the ark meanwhile on its way to temporary capture, or has a new movement begun toward a lasting home? It would take a long survey to speak of this, and there would be among Christian men conflicting judgments, but our duty in either case is clear and urgent. It is to surround it with high lives and sincere hearts when it goes out to its battle with the world, "by pureness, by knowledge, by longsuffering, by kindness, by the Holy Ghost, by love unfeigned, by the word of truth, by the armour of righteousness on the right hand and on the left;" in these we shall ward off every danger. And if we are still under the impulse of one of God's past victories, if God has turned our captivity, we should lament for it when it seems to be abiding long in one place, we should give it room in our houses, that we may be blessed like Obed-edom because of it, seek it out from obscurities like the "fields of the wood," bring it into the open highways of life, give no sleep to our eyes, no slumber to our eyelids, till we find habitations for it, where it may rule and bless men with a wider empire and greater gladness. God has given us a view of its past and its future beyond all measure clearer and larger than could be possessed by the men of this ancient period of its history. We may still have surgings to and fro, decline and rise, defeat and victory, but each time to something better, and the last time to a final and central home, and a universal kingdom. With loftier purpose, then, should we survey the future, with deeper personal interest should we claim a share in it! "Arise, O Lord, into thy rest; Thou, and the ark of thy strength!" "I will make mention of Rahab and Babylon to them that know me: behold Philistia, and Tyre, with Ethiopia; this man was born there. And of Zion it shall be said, This and that man was born in her: and the Highest himself shall establish her,—all my springs are in Thee."

XII.

THE CRY OF THE ORPHANED HEART.

(FOR A COMMUNION.)

"*Doubtless Thou art our Father.*"—Isaiah LXIII. 16.

If this chapter is read, it will be seen that these words came from the heart of the Jewish people when they felt themselves "aliens from the commonwealth of Israel, and strangers to the covenants of promise." They had wandered from the God of their fathers, and they feel as if their fathers had cast them off. If Abraham were to appear on earth, he would not know them; if Jacob were to return, he would not acknowledge them; and what then can they do? They cannot endure life, cannot bear the burden of its sorrows and struggles without a father and a friend. What can they do but pass up beyond men, and seek a father in God? Their heart is an orphan everywhere else, and is forced to this door of refuge—"Doubtless Thou—Thou art our Father." It is thousands of years since this cry was uttered, but it has never died out, and it is present still in many a spirit. Let us listen to it, and think of some of the things which it suggests.

1. The words express *a deep longing of the human heart.* With all its folly and frivolity and sin, the heart of man has been made to feel after these words: "Our Father—our Father which art in heaven." The lower creatures

have not this cry, because they have not our wants, our aspirations, or the possibility of our hopes. God opens his hand, and casts down their food, and they look down for it; but there is something within man's heart which bids him look up and see God's hand, and seek from it something higher. "Your heavenly Father feedeth them;" their Provider is your Father. There are wonderful instincts among them—most wonderful often in the most minute. The bees and ants have their policy, their regulated industry, we might almost say their civilisation. But what curious microscope ever discovered among them a spire pointing heavenward, or tokens of prayer and praise? The magnet which is passed over the earth to draw things upward finds nothing in this world which trembles and turns to it save the human heart. It is very true that many hearts make little visible response, and seem to bear the want of a heavenly Father very lightly. But even in them there may be discerned the heart-hunger that shows itself in unnatural cravings which the lower creatures do not feel. The void may be discovered in the restless attempts men make to fill it. It is true also that there are times when the evil fumes of material sin deaden the hearts of men of whom we could wish better things. But, when we look at the length and breadth of man's history, it tells us that this cry constantly returns, sometimes exceedingly great and bitter, sometimes sinking to a low moan or a suppressed whisper, "O that I knew where I might find Him!" There have been men in all ages to whom the answer of this cry has been the one necessity of life, and if you could convince them that it is impossible to find a heavenly Father they would smile no more. Good were it for us, good for all of us, that we had never been born. Better never enter the world, than find it a world without God and without hope.

2. And yet it is often *difficult to speak these words with full assurance.* The struggle to reach them is evident in the men who use them here, and is felt in the very word "doubtless," with which they begin their claim. When a man says, 'Surely, surely, it must be so,' he shows how hard it has been for him to make the truth his own. We may appeal to many still if it is not so. You will say, 'I long for it, I will not give up the hope of reaching it—no, not for all the world. I think I can sometimes look up and truly say it; but to have it as a clear and constant possession of the soul, this is very difficult. Would that I had always a cloudless spiritual sky above me when I look to God! Doubtless Thou art our Father.' It would take long to number up all the difficulties, but we shall mention some. There is one, which belongs specially to our time, in the *mind* of man as it deals with the universe and its laws. There is a form of science which says, 'I have ranged the world, and there is nothing in it but material law, iron links riveted, each to each, so fast that prayer can never pass up through them, or the hand of a heavenly Helper come down. I sound the depths, I scale the heights, and there is no door or window, not a chink or eyelet-opening through which a Father can be seen. There may be a heart in man, but there is no heart beyond to answer it; or, if there be, the heart of man can never reach it.' Let us thank God that it is not all science, nor the clearest-eyed, that speaks thus; but the voice is loud enough to fill some with fear. And, besides the mind, the *heart* finds difficulties in itself. There are so many things in life which make it hard to believe in the love of God. There are the losses and crosses, sore bereavements, terrible agonies of doubt and spiritual darkness, from which God could surely keep us free. We say with the man in the gospels, "Lord, if Thou wilt, Thou canst." It is not want

of power; is it then want of will? Can it be true that "like as a father pitieth his children, so the Lord pitieth them that fear Him"? It is easy, very easy, when the sea is smooth, and the ship in full sail, to talk in a general way of the Fatherhood of God; but when gulfs are yawning, and cries of drowning men are around, and deep answers to deep in our own soul, then to say, "Thou art our Father," does not come so readily to the lip. And still beyond the mind and heart there is the *conscience*. When we think of a Father in heaven, we must think of a righteous Father, of one "who is of purer eyes than to behold iniquity." The weak, indulgent fatherhood, which is passed so lightly from hand to hand, will not fit into the parts of the world's history which show the terrible penalties of sin; it will not satisfy the soul when it is brought face to face with the majesty of God's law and the holiness of his character. When I look within, I may please myself in comparisons with others, or in little complacencies of my own temperament; but should the Spirit of God lead me into his presence, can I help feeling how I have defaced his image, and given over to the vainest and basest things the love which belonged to Him alone,—how I have dethroned Him from his place, and put up too often the most unworthy idols in his room? It would be very ill for us if we could take all this with a light heart, and imagine that if we frame our mouth to the word "Father," it will cover all. The conscience, when stirred, forces a man to a harder struggle.

3. But, with all these difficulties, it is *a feeling which can be and has been reached.* Yes, it can be reached. We could never believe that such a deep longing had been implanted in man, to be for ever unanswered—a cry pressed from his heart to be mocked with endless disappointment. If a man cannot trust in a God for this, he

might in some ways find hope in the structure of the universe, and infer that the most profound cry of the heart shall have something to meet it. And it has been reached. In view of all the difficulties of mind and heart and conscience, there have been men who could look up and say, "Doubtless Thou art our Father." They have said it not only in sunshine but in storm and in the shadow of death; have given up their lives, that they might testify to it clearly and fearlessly; and have shut the door, and said it to their Father who seeth in secret, that they might not seek the praise of men. Those who have been able to say it in times past have been more than the stars of the sky for multitude; and let us bless God they are round us yet, in duty and trial, in the world's work, and on solitary sick-beds, doing their Father's will, and bearing it.

But we are here to think of One, the greatest of all. Even those who take the lowest view of Jesus Christ will admit that He, beyond all others, taught men to think of God as a Father, and gave the example of it in his own life and death. How strong it made Him, and how patient, how active in doing good, how comforted in solitude, that his Father had sent Him, and was present with Him, putting the cup of suffering into his hand, and ready to receive Him when He said, "Father, into thy hands I commend my spirit!" But his example, his influence, wonderful as they are, would not enable us to follow Him to God as a Father, unless there was something in his death which laid hold of us with stronger power. It behoved Him to be made like unto his brethren, to make reconciliation for the sins of the people. He drank the cup we deserved to drink, that He might put into our hand a cup of blessing. "This cup is the new covenant in my blood, shed for many for the remission of sins." It is this which enables us to go to God the Judge of all with confidence, because we go through the blood of sprinkling. In the storm of soul which an awakened conscience rouses, this is the anchor which holds—not my character or repentance or the new life formed in me by Christ, for these still remain imperfect ; I need a perfect righteousness to meet a perfect law, and I can find it only when I am found in Him. Here the conscience may have rest for all the guilty past, that it may begin its new service of love to the God and Father of our Lord and Saviour Jesus Christ. And when the conscience can say, My Father! the heart begins to say it also. "He that spared not his own Son, but delivered Him up for us all, how shall He not with Him also freely give us all things?" New comforts and hopes come down into the soul, like the angel that came into the agony of the garden to strengthen Christ himself—nay, Christ himself returns, as He said, "I will not leave you orphans : I will come to you." And then, when the heart finds a Father in God, the difficulties of the mind about the laws of nature disappear. These laws are but the expression of his will always and everywhere. Every blossom, ay, and every blight, every sunbeam and every cloud, are in his hand for good to me if I love Him. It needs no door or window, no chink or eyelet-opening through which we may communicate, for all the earth and sky are transparent, and material laws are no impenetrable armour laid on nature, but are "touched and turned to finest air." When the heart has found a Father in God, all the world's laws cannot lay hands on it to imprison it; it moves "through the midst of them, and so passes by."

4. But this full sense of God's Fatherhood is *not generally gained at once*. We do not say that the position is not gained at once. As soon as any one comes to God through

Christ, he is no more a stranger and an enemy but a child, and all the dealings of God with him are paternal dealings. But he may fail to recognise a Father's voice and hand. When his conscience comes under the shadow of guilt, he says, 'I am no more worthy to be called thy son, make me as one of thy hired servants; I would be in the house, but I cannot be in the family.' Or, when his heart is sick and sore with loss and pain, he says, "Surely against me is He turned; He turneth his hand against me all the day." Or God seems so far away, shut out by heavens of iron, that he cannot reach Him. "Also when I cry and shout, He shutteth out my prayer." All this has been felt, and is felt now, most of all by those who desire to have God not as a name, but as a living God and Father. Is it so, then, that you feel yourself in this state, and that you wish to rise from it to a more clear and assured use of the words, "Doubtless Thou art our Father"? Then think of these ways by which it may be gained. Come, first of all, by a more simple and loving faith to the death of Christ in the fulness of its meaning Bring all sin and shortcoming, and acquaint yourself with God through Him, and be at peace. He will take you by the hand, and lead you to Him who is reconciling sinners to Himself, "not imputing unto them their trespasses." And then, if you would retain it, seek more fully to give Christ entrance into your heart and life. He himself has said, "If a man love Me, he will keep my words: and my Father will love him, and we will come unto him, and make our abode with him." Whether He comes with a word of active duty or a word of patient suffering, let us take it and put it into our heart, and we shall find ere long God's fatherly kindness in it. As the heart is purified, we see God. And that we may have power for this, we must realise more constantly the presence of Christ's Holy Spirit. It is He who leads us to be Christ's guests in his house, and brings Christ to be a guest in ours, and conveys to the soul at last the full sense of sonship. To have God for our Father is not merely to be forgiven, it is not even to be sanctified; it is to be one with Him in thought and feeling, to listen to Him and speak with Him, as one speaks with a friend. It is peculiarly the work of the Holy Spirit to lead us into this inmost sanctuary of sonship. "As many as are led by the Spirit of God, they are the sons of God." But to be led by Him, we must not grieve Him by sin or neglect, but welcome his whispered admonitions; and then, as we listen and obey, we shall reach the innermost room where "the Spirit beareth witness with our spirit, that we are the children of God." There are three chambers, then, by which we advance to the assurance of Fatherhood in God. The first is the upper chamber of Jerusalem, which comes to us ever and again in the Lord's table, with its offer of pardon and peace. The second is the chamber of the heart, to which we give Him admission in love and obedience. And the third is the home, where the Holy Spirit teaches us to cry, "Abba, Father." Every Christian should know something of all of them at first; some reach an intimate knowledge of them very soon; but in general the progress is gradual, from the peace of forgiveness to the house where we can say, "Doubtless Thou art our Father," with an entire conviction which fills the heart and the life.

5. We say, last, that to use these words truly is *a matter of infinite moment to us all.* Here is a friend we need in every stage of life, and in every event of it. It comes with its invitation to the young: "Wilt thou not from this time cry unto Me, My Father, Thou art the guide of my youth?" In years long ago, when the world

was in its spring-time, the voice of the Lord God was heard in the garden, and it is so still. The world is not safe or truly happy without his guidance.

> "Now seek Him : in his favour life is found,
> All bliss beside a shadow or a sound."

And when the world seems growing old to us, and the autumn leaves are falling, and the woods are bare, and we look up straight into the sky, it is cheerless if the face of a Father does not meet us there, who knoweth our frame and remembereth that we are dust. And if there be some young man who has wandered far from his true home, it will never be well with him till he comes to himself and says, "I will arise and go to my Father!" Or if there be some who in the world's work have despised the better portion, it is time to come with the prayer, "Bless me, even me also, O my Father!"—while they can recover the birthright, and the full inheritance of the elder-born. Whatever our estate in life may be, it will find what it needs in this name, if we can truly use it. The cup of happiness will be sweeter when a Father's hand provides it, our sorrows soothed when He pours in comfort, our burdens lighter when He sustains declining years, not lonely when God says to old age, "I am He;" and death will not be dark, with the promise, "If children, then heirs; heirs of God, and joint-heirs with Christ."

It is in Jesus Christ that all the promises of God are "Yea and Amen;" and in the memorials of his death and sacrifice He is willing to certify and seal them to us, if we draw near in faith. Let us listen, as He speaks of a Father's love of heart: "Therefore doth my Father love Me, because I lay down my life." "As the Father hath loved Me, so have I loved you: continue ye in my love." And then, as He leaves, He points to heaven and says, "I ascend unto my Father, and your Father: and to my God, and your God." Coming down to our level that He may attract us, He thus raises us to his, that we may look away to the infinite and endless hope, "Father, I will that they also, whom Thou hast given Me, be with Me where I am, that they may behold my glory: for Thou lovedst Me before the foundation of the world." If we could only take one of these words, we who were far off might come nigh, and claim God by the name which will make life happy, death hopeful, and eternity safe—" Doubtless Thou art our Father, though Abraham be ignorant of us, and Israel acknowledge us not: Thou, O Lord, art our Father, our Redeemer: thy name is from everlasting."

XIII.

THE STRUCTURE OF THE BIBLE.

" Thy word is true from the beginning.—PSALM CXIX. 160.

THE object of Christian faith may be compared to a jewel enclosed in a casket. The jewel is the Lord Jesus Christ; the casket is the Bible. Now, we believe that a man may possess the jewel who has never seen the casket, or who has got it in his hands in an imperfect and broken form. There is such an efficacy in the Lord Jesus Christ, such a fitness in Him for the sins and sorrows and wants of poor fallen humanity, that the Holy Spirit of God can bring Him home to the soul with saving power by a small portion of knowledge. A single Gospel, a single Epistle, a psalm such as the twenty-third, or a verse such as " God so loved the world that He gave his only-begotten Son, that whosoever believeth in Him should not perish, but have everlasting life," if explained simply and brought home by God's Spirit, may become Gód's power to salvation. The Bible came to men in fragments, piece after piece, through many generations, and a fragment of it can still do its proper work. It has a principle of life that is complete in its separate parts, and you may see all its truth in one text, as you can see all the sun's image in one drop of dew in a flower. This is a wise, divine arrangement, which may reassure some who fear they are losing Christ, when the question is about the meaning of some parts of the Bible. If a man were so driven about on seas of difficulty, that he could only have a board or broken piece of the ship, it would "bring him safe to land." Nevertheless, the care and completeness of the casket are of very great moment. Our salvation may be gained by one word about Christ, but our edification, our Christian comfort and well-being, depend on the full word of Christ. Wherever He is set forth, however dimly, there is something for us to learn, something needful to make us thoroughly furnished unto every good work. Here the Bible may be compared, not to a casket enclosing a jewel, but to a piece of tapestry on which a figure is inwoven. If it be mutilated, or the golden threads that meet and intermingle be torn and tarnished, we lose, so far, the complete image of truth that is the inheritance of the Church of Christ—the inheritance which the apostle thus describes: "Whatsoever things were written aforetime were written for our learning, that we through patience and comfort of the Scriptures might have hope."

We purpose, then, turning attention to the structure of the Bible as a whole, and we shall try to show that it bears evident marks of being a complete book. It is not a number of stones accidentally thrown together; it is a building that has grown up, with all its variety, into a symmetrical shape. In trying to do this, we shall not enter into any questions of criticism, higher or lower, and we shall take no part in controversies that are at present proceeding. Our desire is to avoid details, and to deal with the Bible in its great, broad features, but in such a way that any intelligent Christian, who knows nothing of Hebrew or Greek or the rules of criticism, may feel, with God's help, that he has the Bible in a self-attesting, consistent form. As a man may have such a hold of Christ that, with his life dwelling in the soul, he can stand fast against all scepticism, so an earnest Christian, who studies his Bible and compares part with part, may be able to say, This book is attested by its structure as one unbroken work : "Thy word is true from the beginning."

The Bible, as one sees at first sight, consists of two great divisions, the Old Testament and the New. These are very unlike each other in many ways. There were several centuries between the end of the one and the beginning of the other. You turn the leaf from Malachi to Matthew, and you forget that there is a wide sea of time rolling between them. They are like an old world and a new. They speak two different languages. The one is Hebrew, with all the ways and thoughts of the Jewish people gathering round Jerusalem. The other is Greek, beginning at Jerusalem, but going out to visit Ephesus and Athens and Corinth and Rome and the great civilisations of the world.

And yet these two halves of the Bible are necessary to supplement each other. Although the Old Testament has the knowledge of the one only living and true God, it could never by itself have brought the world to worship Him. It might have a proselyte here and there, but it could never gather all nations to the temple at Jerusalem once a year, nor lead them to adopt all its rites and ceremonies, which were a heavy burden to the Jews themselves. It was impossible that their ceremonial law could ever become a universal law, for one of its purposes was to be like a close wall round the truth of God in a cold, dark time, and to keep the Jews a separate people from all the nations of the earth. And so we find that the Jews who have held by the Old Testament alone have never been able to spread their religion. They have indeed no desire to do so, and they remain alone and unmixed. If we had only the Old Testament, we should have an incomplete and broken monument of the past, with hieroglyphics and pictures on it to which there was no key.

On the other hand, if you were to take the New Testament alone, you could not clearly understand it. Many of its truths about God and Christ and the eternal world are clothed in language and figures drawn from the Old Testament. Christ is a priest, He offers sacrifice, He makes atonement, He enters in within the veil, there to appear in the presence of God. When the apostle tells us what we reach in the New Testament, he says, " Ye are come unto Mount Sion, and unto the city of the living God, the heavenly Jerusalem;" and after leading us through one shining circle after another he says, "And to Jesus, the mediator of the new covenant, and to the blood of sprinkling, that speaketh better things than that of Abel." Before God sent his Son into the world, He had to create words and figures and moulds of thought, into which to pour the truth, else we had not been able to think or speak rightly about Christ and what He is to us; and that is one reason for saying that Christ "came in the fulness of time." Philosophers tell us that, without the outer world of nature to draw a language from, we could not have expressed a single thought. Every word we use is some figure drawn from the outside world; so much so that Locke said, "There is nothing in our intelligence that was not before in our senses;" to which Leibnitz replied, "Nothing, except our intelligence." The senses would be blind and dead without the intelligence; but the intelligence would be dumb without the sense and the world of sense. And so what the world of nature is to the soul of man the Old Testament is to the New. God first made his creation, and then He made a living soul to use it and interpret it; He first made the old world of type and symbol and history, and then He sent his Son to fill it with spiritual truth, and use it for a language to tell us about divine and eternal things.

And yet we should not have given a true view of the connection between the Old Testament and the New, if we made the one merely language, and the other thought. For the Old Testament has also thought. There are thoughts breathed in, as we believe, by the Spirit of Christ before He came, thoughts somewhat like those that He breathed into the souls of the two going to Emmaus, when they did not know Him, yet said, "Did not our heart burn within us, while He talked with us by the way?" These were frequently not shaped into distinct expression, not articulate, and clearly they were cries of longing, of want that went forward to a great Object out of sight, but their very hopes tell us something of his nature. The trees of the field rejoiced before the Lord when He was coming, for his Spirit's breath was already in the leaves. When you sit in the house at night, and hear the wind blowing as it listeth, you cannot tell whence it cometh or whither it goeth; but when you see it bending the trees, you know how it is setting; and the whole bent of the Old Testament is from the soul in breathings and desires that go forward to the Lord Jesus Christ.

The study of the Old Testament and the New in some systematic way is one of the most instructive and reassuring ways of reading the Bible. The Epistle to the Hebrews was written for the guidance of such study, and our Lord has urged us to it: "Search the Scriptures; they are they which testify of Me." No other religion has a book that resembles this in structure, or that at all approaches it—two independent halves that were formed separately, and that fit into each other like a lock and a key, the one needful to complete the other, and yet framed at a distance of centuries.

But we may advance now to look at the separate structure of the two parts.

1. We cannot read the Old Testament without seeing that the whole of it rests on the basis of a history—the history contained in what we call the books of Moses. The life of the Jewish nation is continually turning back to the covenant made with Abraham and Isaac and Jacob; and, above all, to the great deliverance from Egypt by the hand of Moses. It is impossible to understand the subsequent history without this. What was it that inspired all the battles against foreign enemies and internal revolts and corruptions, but this memory? Men like Joshua and Samuel are fired by it, and, if there be any truth at all in what we are told about them, it is impossible to account for it without the history of Moses having gone before, for they are constantly speaking of it, and inspiring the people with its recollections. Or take the great historical psalms, or the psalms generally, and the prophets; you find their appeals always made to it. "The waters saw Thee, O God, the waters saw Thee; they were afraid: the depths also were troubled" (Ps. lxxvii. 16). "Then He remembered the days of old, Moses, and his people, saying, Where is He that brought them up out of the sea with the shepherd of his flock? Where is He that put his holy Spirit within him? that led them by the right hand of Moses with his glorious arm, dividing the water before them, to make Himself an everlasting name?" (Isa. lxiii. 11, 12.) You might as well describe a tree without a root, as explain the great body of the Old Testament without the knowledge of the history contained in the five books of Moses, both by the men who spoke and the people who listened to them; for you will observe that they speak to the people as acquainted with the events. How they gained that acquaintance we do not here inquire, but that they had it very fully and circumstantially most reasonable men will admit.

Now, if you turn to the New Testament, you will find

that it begins, in like manner, with a history—the history of the four Gospels; and what the Pentateuch is to the Old Testament, the Gospels are to the New. You cannot understand, you cannot account for, the rest of the New Testament, the labours and sufferings of the apostles and the letters they wrote, without admitting that the writers and those to whom they wrote were acquainted familiarly with the life and death and resurrection of Christ, as these are related in the Gospels. Indeed, we could reconstruct the chief events in the life of Christ from the first four epistles of Paul, which the most daring criticism admits to be genuine.

Here then is a symmetry in the two parts of the Bible. Each begins with a history which pervades and inspires all that follows. Only, the two histories are different, while they are connected. The one is that of a divinely chosen people selected for a special purpose. The other is that of a Divine Person, and a person is superior to a people merely as a people, as a corporate body; for a person has an immortality, a nation has not, and a person can be charged with far higher lessons than a nation. The two histories are on two planes, a lower and a higher; the lower is imperfect without the higher, and the higher assumes and completes the lower.

2. If you look to the Old Testament, you find that there is a second stage, after the Pentateuch. It is a struggle to obtain a place where the original history may find a firm footing, and may unfold itself for the good of the world, though as yet those who act in it do not understand its full bearing. This is the history of Joshua, and Judges, and Samuel, and those that follow after. There were great truths about the unity and character of God committed to this nation, that they might preserve them in the midst of the darkness and chill which then prevailed; and they

must have a land to themselves where their law is to wall them in from the world around. The struggle of the nation is to secure this separate place, and the struggle of those who lead them is to secure the permanence of the law which God had given them. We cannot read these books without seeing that there was this twofold struggle, first the land and then the law. They are to be a people who dwell alone, and who are not reckoned among the nations.

In the New Testament there is a similar period, contained chiefly in the Acts of the Apostles, but it penetrates also the Epistles. The apostles and disciples are struggling to find a lodgment for the history of the great Person with whom they have come in contact. Only, the place is no more one country, but the whole earth. They have heard the word, "The field is the world." "Go into all the world, and preach the gospel to every creature." And the weapons are not now "carnal but spiritual, yet mighty through God to the pulling down of strong holds." They have to lodge these truths in the hearts and souls of men by argument and suasion. The one period draws its force from Sinai—"The soul that sinneth, it shall die;" the other from Calvary—"I, if I be lifted up, will draw all men unto Me." But they are connected as battles for truth and grace, and the two leading men in them, Joshua and Paul, have similar features of courage and zeal and fidelity to death—the one dying with the words, "As for me and my house, we will serve the Lord;" the other, "I have fought a good fight, I have finished my course, I have kept the faith."

3. If you turn again to the Old Testament, you will find a third stage. It is the period of reflection. After the battle for the land has been fought, and the land itself to some extent secured, the question rises, What have we gained in

our conflict, and what is the meaning of the history through which our nation has passed? Leisure has been given for this question, and it is in the course of things that the eye turns from the outside world to the inner. Thought is folded over on the past in meditation. This brings us into the centre of the Old Testament—to the books of Psalms and many of the Prophets. It is a meditation in which they are guided by God's Spirit. They are ready to acknowledge this, and it is seen in the character of the teaching, but at the same time it is carried on by the musings and reasonings of the spirit of man. This is what makes it so human, so natural, so attractive to us. They pore over the old book of the law, and see wondrous things in it about God and his government and works and ways, about themselves and God's will to be fulfilled in them. That history, which in the Pentateuch is in a great measure general, something done for the nation, becomes individual, as a promise of what God will do for every soul that trusts Him. The very law which seems an outward and ceremonial thing, at best a map of moral duties, becomes deep and searching and spiritual. Compare, for example, the psalms of David and Asaph and many parts of the prophets, with the song of Moses and Miriam or the death-song of Moses or the song of Deborah and Barak, and you see what an advance there has been in the depth of the spiritual life. The eye of the earlier believers is turned outward to the grandeur of God's deliverances, the eye of the later is turned inward to the needs of the soul—"My soul thirsteth for God." "Create in me a clean heart, O God, and renew a right spirit within me." "The sacrifices of God are a broken heart." You can see that these men live after the days of ceremonial law, long after it, and that they have learned to see beyond it and through it, to another cleansing in which their hearts rejoice. It is as impossible to take the ceremonial law, and put it after these words, according to any rule of progress, as it would be to take a tree, and put its roots in the air and its branches and blossoms in the earth. In all real development, insight into the spiritual follows the outward events.

Now, in the New Testament there is a corresponding period showing the same marks. It is in the Epistles of Paul and of his fellow-disciples. The Gospels give us great events, but the conclusions are not fully drawn, and Christ promises the Spirit of Truth to guide, to show the way into all truth. What the Psalms and Prophets are to the early history of the Old Testament, the Epistles are to the Gospels; and the Epistles are above the Psalms and Prophets, as the Gospels are above the books of Moses. The view they give of God is more clearly " God in Christ." The grand attributes of power and justice are still there, but mercy, condescension, tenderness, have come into full view, and gather round Him who is Son of God and Son of Man. The questions of the soul as to how righteousness, acceptance with God, and likeness to Him may be gained are answered in Jesus Christ. Compare the 51st psalm, which is one of the highest reaches of spiritual life in the Old Testament, with the 8th chapter of the Romans, and you will see how like David's use of the law is to the apostle's use of the knowledge of Christ, and yet how much clearer and fuller is the New Testament form.

4. We shall now ask you to look at one closing period in this comparison. We may call it *the sense of incompleteness*. This is the period of prophecy proper—of many of the psalms, of Isaiah and the later prophets. They expect a king who is to be greater than David, a prophet who is to speak truth without a veil, a priest who is to present a perfect offering and be king as well as priest. All through we find sparks of such an expectation breaking forth, but,

as the ages roll on, they gather into a deep, burning desire. The look that turned in memory to the deliverance from Egypt is turned in hope to One who is to give liberty to the captives, the opening of the prison to them that are bound, and to preach the acceptable year of the Lord—the desire of all nations, the Messenger of the Covenant, who is to come and fill the rising temple with his glory. As the sun of the past is setting, another sun rises, the Sun of Righteousness, with healing in his wings, and that Sun shall no more go down. The Old Testament closes with this intent, bending gaze on the future, and closes, not having received the promise, but being persuaded of it and embracing it.

And the New Testament has this period also. It is true it does not occupy so large a place, for the New Testament is the revelation of fulfilment and possession. But even its possession is imperfect. Christ, when He left, pointed forward, and spoke of his return; and the Book of Revelation is full of it, and cannot end until it shows us, in the grand sweep of the Word of God, the second paradise resting above the first, and surpassing it at every point. For though the Gospel of Christ has in it that which gives present peace and power, it has such promises on its lips, such presentiments in its heart, such infinite desires infused into its life, that we feel these mortal eyes can never measure it, nor this finite world hold it. And so, as the Old Testament ends by looking for his first coming, the New finishes with a cry for his second. Its last word breathes out a response to his promise, "Behold, I come quickly." "Amen. Even so, come, Lord Jesus."

The view we have given of the structure of the Bible shows us two great divisions of independent formation, and yet connected, the Old Testament and the New answering to each other as childhood to manhood, or as the younger plants in a nursery-garden to the trees. When you look into the two parts, you find these stages —a history at the base of each, the Pentateuch and Gospels, in the one that of a selected nation, in the other of a Divine Person—then a struggle to find a place in the world—then reflection on what has been gained, bringing out the lessons—then the sense of incompleteness awaiting something fuller. I think an unprejudiced mind will acknowledge that there is a plan here. We hold it to be a divine plan, and that there is no other possible way of accounting for it. If a man will not admit this, he may say that all these remarkable agreements have been the work of *chance*. But a reasonable man will see that they are so many and striking, they will so grow upon him as he studies, that he will reject such an explanation. He will come to the conclusion, as some one has said, " I had rather believe in the miracles of God than the miracles of chance." Or a man might say that this agreement is the work of *concert*. But when you look at the length of time over which the formation has extended, at the independent way in which its different parts have sprung up, you will see that this is impossible, even if the writers had been dishonest enough to try it. It would be impossible to make up the New Testament by concert, much more the Old Testament and the New. Neither of these two ways of accounting for the Bible will stand serious consideration, and I do not know of any one who would now urge them.

But there is still another way a man might take. He might say the Bible is a thing of *natural growth*. It has gone on through mind propelling mind, each carrying on the growing torch of light, first in the Old Testament and then in the New, till it has become what we see. It is a formation, wonderful, beautiful, but still it is only a human formation. Now, let us frankly admit that more can be said for this explanation than for the other two. As we have tried to show, the Bible *is* a growth, a growth up through the minds and hearts and lives of men. On one side it is a growth in humanity. But we have this to say: You have not only to account for a growth in the mind of man, you have to account for facts and events well attested, which meet and supplement one another, and some of which are proceeding in our own day, carrying out words written down long ago in the Bible,—for example, the condition of the Jewish people, and the spread of the Gospel of Christ. You have to account for this, that there is no other natural development like it, none even of a secular kind, none certainly of a religious kind. No religion has a book which in its formation can compare with the Bible, still less in its character and contents, in its power to elevate, to transform, to regenerate human nature. And you have this to account for, how the Bible has had to force its way against ordinary human nature. Do we not feel it in our own experience? It has had to fight for its position, foot by foot, in the world and in men's hearts; cast down, crushed out of existence like its great Subject, and then rising by a miracle from the grave. It is a development *in* man's nature, but not *from* it; it comes from a power that causes it to rise up through the surface strata like a great mountain peak with its forests and fields and streams, till it forms a new and higher law for itself, a supernatural that becomes divinely natural, and that proves it to be from Him in whose hand are the "deep places of the earth and the strength of the hills." We are very hopeful that, if a man will so study the Bible, he will come to the conclusion that it is a plant of " our heavenly Father's planting, that cannot be rooted up."

There are three things for which we should thank God. —First, that He has given his revelation in the form of a history. Science has her sphere in nature, philosophy in thought, religion in a divine history. This gives it a variety, an interest, a life, which it could not otherwise have possessed, and allows of its being put in a book which every man can read for himself, so simple, yet so profound. Secondly, that He has given his revelation in such a form that it bears the marks of its epochs on it, and shows us an advancing education of the human family from the natural to the ever more spiritual, from the outward lessons of symbol to the inward lessons of life; so that every intelligent Christian can judge of the current of revelation as a whole, and say, 'This way it flows, not so.' Criticism has its place and rights, but it cannot touch the strong current. It can study the bank eddies here and there, but it can never affect the place of broad rivers and streams. There, our common Christianity can judge of the course of the river. And, lastly, that He has so connected Christ with the Bible that, by carrying the thought of Him through it, we may bind it into one unbroken Word. From first to last it is the revelation of Jesus Christ. All through He is in it, from the first promise to the last. If we fear about the Bible, let us follow Him through it, and the Word of God will not be broken. He passes through it, reads its writings, opens its seals, and is worthy to do it all, because He was slain and has redeemed us to God by his blood. And that He may so open the Bible to us, let us open to Him our hearts, and all shall be sure about the Bible and its truth from beginning to end. Amen and Amen.

XIV.

THE WOMAN OF CANAAN.

"Then Jesus answered and said unto her, O woman, great is thy faith: be it unto thee even as thou wilt."—MATT. XV. 28.

WHEN our Lord Jesus Christ lived on earth, He did not carry his mission beyond the land of promise. He has given the reason of this: "I, if I be lifted up from the earth, will draw all men unto Me." He must first ascend his cross, and then ascend his throne, that divine love and power, his gospel and his spirit, might be ready to move forth with the command that "repentance and remission of sins should be preached among all nations, beginning at Jerusalem." But in his journeyings He came, ever and again, into gracious contact with mankind-sinners from beyond the Jewish pale, that He might show Gentile and Samaritan what was in his heart. He travelled close on the border line of heathendom, that the light of his presence might shine across on some of the longing souls that were in darkness and the shadow of death. In one of these walks of compassion He came near the coasts of Tyre and Sidon, where the remnants of those nations dwelt which had been driven from their land for their sins. One of this race, a woman of Canaan, was suffering from a sore affliction in her family, and she sought Him out and followed Him with an urgent prayer for help. At first He turned a deaf ear to her and repelled her petition with a coldness which rises into what seems harshness. But He knew the strength of faith which was in her heart, and He wished to bring it out for the perfecting of her own spiritual nature, and for an example to us. When at last her faith appeared in its marvellous strength and beauty, He looked on it with wonder. It is said of the first creation, " God saw it, and behold, it was very good ; " and of the second, " The Lord Jehovah shall be satisfied in his works." And so, when a part of this new creation appears in a human heart, Christ sees of the travail of his soul and is satisfied. It is an earnest of the joy set before Him, for which He endured the cross and despised the shame. We shall make the faith of this woman the subject of thought by trying to answer two questions : (1.) What made her faith so remarkable ? (2.) What enabled her to hold on and at last to triumph ? We shall thus have a view of it first on its outward, and then on its inward side.

I. WHAT, THEN, MADE THE FAITH OF THIS WOMAN SO REMARKABLE ? The first thing which strikes us is that she had much against her in *her original circumstances*. She was, as you see, a woman of Canaan. She was not of the Jewish race, nor even, as it would seem, a proselyte; but an " alien from the commonwealth of Israel and a stranger to the covenants of promise." She was not only a Gentile, but of that family of Gentiles which must have had most dislike to the Jews. Her forefathers had suffered from their hostility, and she no doubt had felt their haughty bigotry and exclusiveness. There was a frontier line of dislike to cross, far wider than any distance between Tyre and Palestine. But it did not keep her from finding her way to the great Teacher of the Jewish nation. Then, think of how her circumstances must have affected her knowledge. She addresses Christ as Lord, with reverence and trust, and speaks of Him as the Son of David. But how dim was her light, compared with that of those who had heard the Scriptures read in their synagogues, who had joined in the services and sacrifices of the temple, and had been prepared for the coming of Christ as a Saviour from sin and sorrow! How little did she know compared with Anna the prophetess who departed not from the temple night and day, with Martha and Mary who heard his words in their own home, or even with that woman in the city who was a sinner, who had listened to Him without, and was then drawn into Simon's house to weep till her heart was like to break! All these had remarkable faith, but we do not know of any who had so little knowledge on which to base it, and so little room to take home the promise to their own case. It is an instance of faith like a grain of mustard seed which can remove mountains, or wing its way over them.

God has bestowed on man two great powers, reason and faith. They are not opposed to each other, though they are sometimes spoken of as if they were. But they are very different. The field of reason is the things which are seen and temporal; the field of faith, the things which are unseen and eternal. Where reason can go no farther, faith passes forward on stronger than angels' wings, grasping the hand of God; where reason is blind, faith has eyes for a world in which it dwells, like those men of old who lived "as seeing Him who is invisible." Let us thank God for reason, but let us thank Him above all for faith, for the power by which the soul can find a way through all the thick folds of matter straight to the living God, and, through small privileges and what to us seems hard treatment, can find out Christ and fall at his feet with the burden of its need. It is often impossible for us to ascertain the laws by which faith operates, and the ground on which, in individual cases, its strength rests. Its object is unseen, and so also is its work in the soul; but its effects are very sure and palpable. "The wind bloweth where it listeth, and we hear the sound thereof, but cannot tell whence it cometh, and whither it goeth;" but we can judge of its power in the barriers it breaks down, and of its sweetness when it comes to wake up flowers and blossoms. Some of us may have seen it in poor, lone, agonised sufferers who held fast to their hope in God and repelled every doubt, and we wondered how their faith had learned to begin and maintain its hold. It was the "good pleasure of his goodness, and the work of faith with power." The case of this woman is one of these. What are many of our arguments but doubts answering doubts, the taking and retaking of outposts, when she and others like her pass right into the citadel through all obstacles and enemies, and claim for themselves Him who alone can help a stricken spirit! "They shall come from the east, and from the west, and from the north, and from the south, and shall sit down in the kingdom of God." "And, behold, there are last which shall be first, and there are first which shall be last."

Another thing which made the faith of this woman remarkable was that *she had little countenance from Christ's disciples.* It is very strange to see the burning love of the disciples to the souls of men after the ascension of Christ compared with their coldness while He himself was with them. Think of how they pleaded with men to come to Him as a Prince and a Saviour, while in his lifetime they often surrounded Him like an icy wall! It becomes clear to those who consider it that something very decisive had happened in the interval to change their views of Christ's relation to men. Nothing less than his death and resurrection and the disclosure of his purposes of mercy can account for this. Observe them here:—they do not, indeed, rebuke the woman as they rebuked the parents who brought their children to Christ; they only ask Him to send her away. In all charity let us hope that they wished her request to be granted; but the reason they give takes the heart out of their petition—" for she crieth after us." It appears to be not so much sympathy with her sorrow as annoyance at her importunity, and a desire to be freed from the trouble of her presence. No doubt she felt it, felt that they looked on her as an annoyance and a shame to them, and that they would gladly be quit of her, in the way some cast an alms to a persistent beggar. Weaker faith would have felt the chill which surrounded Him, and would have retired. But it is not from them that she expects an answer. She will take it from none but Christ himself, and she presses past the disciples into his presence—" Lord, to whom but to Thee?"

And is there not a lesson here for us Christians as to the spirit in which we should deal with those who are, as it is called, outside? Are we approaching them in the spirit of the disciples before the day of Pentecost, or after it; with the heart of those to whom the cross of Christ had as yet no meaning, or of those to whom it opened the infinite sympathy and long-suffering of God? If we carry the Gospel to men with no pity in our own souls for their misery, but merely to quiet the disturbance of their cries, to preserve social order, and save ourselves and society from danger, we cannot expect great progress in our works. Men know very well when a gift comes from a loving heart, and when it is thrown to them to get ease for ourselves. God did not cast down his benefits from the door of heaven; He came down to earth with his heart in them, and this makes the difference between a benefit and a blessing. If we are to win men we must go to them in Christ's spirit and, as it were, in his person. " As though God did beseech you by us; we pray you in

Christ's stead, be ye reconciled to God." And yet if there are any who keep back from Christ, because, as they say, Christians are so cold and inconsistent, let them know from the example of this woman that they are not thereby excused. Christ invites them to come to Himself, to judge of Him not by what his disciples do, but by what He himself has said and done. "Look unto Me"—" Come unto Me, weary, heavy laden "—" Him that cometh to Me I will in no wise cast out." It is to Him at last we have to give in our account, and we cannot be justified in our rejection of Him, until we have taken our decisive answer from no lips but his own.

And yet here the woman's faith reaches its greatest trial, in *the conduct of Christ*. The disciples, cold as they are, seem merciful compared with their Master. She breaks through outward difficulties to find an iron wall about his heart. The story is so told that we can see it in each appeal, and each repulse. As she cries, and pours her heart into her prayer, He is moving away from her with silent neglect. "He answered her not a word," as if she were not only beneath help but beneath being soothed or spoken to. Have we not sometimes felt this ourselves, when we have prayed to God in our trouble ? He not only withheld the deliverance we asked, but left us all alone with our bitter, helpless cries. That dreadful silence of God ! it is harder to many a poor heart than the sorest word which can be spoken : " O Lord my rock, be not silent to me; lest, if Thou be silent to me, I become like them that go down into the pit." If He would only speak, though it were to reprove me, I could bear it. " Show me wherefore Thou contendest with me." Anything but this stony silence, this desolate forsakenness which gathers round me, and makes me ask if there be a God who cares for me at all. This woman must have felt it when He answered her not a word. Still she cried after Him, and at last He spoke. But his words, were they not harder than his silence? For He did not speak to her, but only of her, and what He said appears to quench all hope. "He answered and said, I am not sent but unto the lost sheep of the house of Israel." The Son of Man is come to seek and to save the lost, but there is a chosen flock, beyond which He cannot meanwhile go. "Then came she and worshipped Him, saying, Lord, help me." She bent before Him, cast herself on the ground to bar his way, and so she waits an answer. Does she drop the title "Son of David," as if it told against one who belonged to the Gentile race; or is it the emotion of her heart which makes her words pass into broken sobs, "*Lord*, help me"? At length she draws an answer from Him to herself: "It is not meet to take the children's bread, and to cast it to dogs." Are these the words of Jesus Christ? They startle us who know the close of the contest between Him and this suppliant creature; and how must they have been listened to by those who did not know the end—with wonder by the disciples, with sinking of heart by the woman? What can she do, but rise and leave in anguish, if not in anger? 'I have prayed in vain; thy gifts be to Thyself; this boasted deliverer is as hard as He is helpless.' So it would have been with ordinary human nature, so it might have been with many a one of us. But Christ knew what was in her soul, and his own hand was upholding her against his words. "Though Abraham was ignorant of her, though Israel acknowledged her not," the faith of Abraham was in her heart, and she had the spirit of that night-wrestler who contended with the Angel of the covenant and prevailed: "I will not let Thee go until Thou bless me." And she said, "Truth, Lord: yet the dogs eat of the crumbs which fall from their masters' table." It is marvellous. There is a faith, a humility, a sacred ingenuity in her reply which has no higher example in the Word of God. A dog, yet the dog has a place in the house, and has its claim on the master's care. She yields all, and in the same moment gains all. It was for this victory Christ was waiting, and He welcomed it and gave her her heart's desire: "O woman, great is thy faith: be it unto thee even as thou wilt." And when He grants it, He raises her from the ground and seats her at the table and gives her the children's bread. And now, as of another woman, it may be said, " Wheresoever this gospel shall be preached throughout the whole world, this also that she hath done shall be spoken of for a memorial of her." Nor is it written for her sake alone; but for us also it is written, "The humble shall see this and be glad; and your heart shall live that seek God."

II. We shall now, as it were, turn a page and look at the inner side, if we may discover *what helped her faith to hold on and triumph*. We do not speak of the first cause of all, which was Christ's eye watching her steps, and his hand bearing her up. It is impossible to exclude the divine nature of Christ in considering the way in which He deals with souls. It is this which saves his conduct from the charge of hardness, and of unnecessary exposure of them to fatal peril. He knew what was in them by his own grace, and He knew that it could be maintained. What the psalmist felt was, no doubt, true of her: " My soul followeth hard after Thee; thy right hand upholdeth me." We do greatly err if we think that, when we seek God, we are self-sustained. It is He who holds us up and guides us to find Himself. It is not, however, of this first cause we speak, but of the mediate causes by which this woman's faith was upheld.

One of the first was that *she had a deep home and heart sorrow.* Her daughter lay at home grievously vexed with a devil. A malignant disease with torturing pangs had seized her child, pointing directly to the power of the wicked one, who was permitted to make his hand more open in the face of Him who came to challenge his power. Even yet there are calamities which speak more distinctly than others of the disorder sin has brought into our world. We sometimes see suffering so deep, so long, so apparently meaningless, that we cannot connect it with any natural order of things, or with a moral government in a sinless state. We must say, "An enemy hath done this; this is the hour and the power of darkness." There is, indeed, no ground for connecting special suffering with special sin; we have been warned against this; but we may very well believe that sin is sometimes permitted to show its effects in terrible shapes, that we may be driven by the sight to the only refuge. It was so with this woman. She had in her home and heart a terrible and constant affliction. She had tried man's skill, and it had failed. She had called on her country's gods, on Baal and Ashtaroth, but they were as deaf as in the days of old Elijah. If she had known of Epicurus with his divinities above the clouds who do not trouble themselves with human sorrow, or of the pitiless Fate of the Stoics who bid us submit to the inevitable, would it have quieted her heart when it was agonised by her daughter's moans? But a new name was now heard in the world, a wonderful soul of compassion seemed to be moving among human diseases and sorrows, and word of it had crossed the heathen border and reached her ears. Something told her that, if what she had heard were true, there was hope here, after despair—a plank of deliverance after utter shipwreck,

It was this which nerved her hand to cling. Can she go back to her dreary home and look on her daughter's convulsions and listen, helpless, to her cries? The torture of her child is in her heart, pleads through her, and presses her petition till it is granted. And when she gains it she secures a blessing for herself. For saving faith begins oftentimes in some crisis of the life in which the soul casts itself on Christ as far as He is known, and then it learns to trust Him with all. The door of hope in the valley of Achor becomes an entrance to Him who says, " I am the door : by Me if any man enter in, he shall be saved ;" and so this woman returned to a changed home with a changed heart.

Now, if there be any with trouble in the soul for which they have found as yet no cure, is it not for this it has been sent? It may be some shadow of fear or grief thrown in from without ; it may be some deep wound of the conscience when sin is realised in its guilt, some fainting of the spirit before the yawning hollow of a world in which there is no divine Friend ; whatever it be, do not let it quit its hold of you, until you have laid hold of the great Helper. Beware of forgetting it, of having it drowned in the world's noise, or discouraged by seeming delays. If you have some grief where all other help has failed, turn your ear inward till the sense of it urges the appeal, Lord, help me! The greater the feeling of the trouble, the more surely will it carry you into the presence of the only Saviour. There are easy paths in life when men feel as if they could do without a God, and there are smooth speeches of the conscience when they persuade themselves they do not need the ransom of a Redeemer; but when the heart is convulsed with grief, when the conscience is stirred into storm, the deep currents of the soul will bear men, if they will yield to them, on to Jesus Christ, and to none but Him.

Next, this woman's faith was strong because she *had learned to take a very humble view of herself.* She has no plea but, Have mercy on me! no appeal but to her misery, with that upcast look to Christ's face, Lord help me! And when He seems to spurn her and take up the language of the common Jew, who spoke of the Gentile as a dog, she accepts the name, and founds an argument upon it. The reproachful word has nothing in it which she had not felt in her own heart. How she got her spirit of humility it is impossible to say. God's Spirit must have been her teacher, and his first lesson is to convince of sin. There are times when a soul enlightened by God feels that nothing can be said of it which it is not ready to say of itself. We have made such a miserable return to God; we have so defaced and defiled the nature He gave us; such mean and selfish and unholy thoughts have festered and swarmed within us, that the words of the Psalmist rise to our lips, '" So foolish was I and ignorant; I was as a beast before Thee." These poor dumb creatures do their part in the world better than I. I am higher, and so I have made myself lower. If I could only yield to God the unquestioning obedience, the affectionate trustfulness which a dog yields to its master, how much worthier a place I should fill in the world than now I do!' Some of us may have felt this; which of us should not feel it? but who could bear to be told it, and to answer, Truth, Lord?

But, then, there is the dignity of human nature! Does not the Bible say, Remember this, and show yourselves men? And it is true; but to show ourselves men in God's sight is to humble ourselves. An old writer has said, "There are times when we must be a man, and no worm, but there are times when we must be a worm, and no man." To come into the view of that infinite purity and be abased, is the only way to rise to it. We are on the path to the dignity of human nature, when we see the indignity we have done to God and to ourselves. It is not till the prodigal sees his sin and shame among the husks and swine that he comes to himself—to his true and proper self—remembers his sonship, and says, "I will arise and go to my father." As humility goes deep down, faith rises up high and strong, for humility furnishes the roots by which faith holds on. If you would come to Christ, you must let humility take faith by the hand and lead it to Him, and then He will lead faith to God, and open to it all the treasure-house of grace: "For thus saith the high and lofty One that inhabiteth eternity, whose name is Holy: I dwell in the high and holy place, with him also that is of a contrite and humble spirit." It is by this wonderful *also*—with him *also*—that faith passes from defeat, and even from despair, to victory. If we could but use the word "yet" as she uses it, we should, like her, gain all when we surrender all. "Truth, Lord; yet!" "I am poor and needy, yet the Lord thinketh upon me." "I said, I am cast out of thy sight; yet I will look again toward thy holy temple."

Lastly, her faith was so strong because it *had hold of another Christ, greater and more merciful than her eyes saw.* But for this, she could never have persevered,—unless her soul, by some secret reasoning or divinely-given instinct, had found out a heart of sympathy beneath the looks and words which covered it. We cannot help poring over the narrative, and wondering if there was any ray of hope allowed to escape through the thick folds of indifference in which He had wrapped Himself—any board or broken piece of the ship to cling to in her death-struggle. Was it possible to draw comfort from the way in which He speaks of the Jews? With all their gainsaying and rebellion, they are still "the children." Or is it possible that there was something in the word *dogs* being a diminutive, and having a touch of pity in it? It is the "little dogs," which belong to the house, and are therefore the objects of kindly care. Certain it is that her woman's heart seized this point, and that through the chink her faith glided into his heart's citadel, and gained the day. She could not have found it had He not left it open. Or were there not suppressed undertones of pity which her heart, rather than her ear, caught trembling in his voice—relenting looks of sympathy which her soul, more than her eye, saw in his face, breaking beforehand like sunbeams through a cloud they are about to scatter? In any case we know that she had already learned some things about Christ which her faith could use as a support under her repulse. She had heard of his works and how He had helped others. She knew something of his errand as the Son of David. There was a reasoning of the heart which told her that a mercy like his could not be limited to place or nation, and so she set her trust in his nature above the coldness of his demeanour, and cast herself at his feet in the spirit of the ancient sufferer, "Though He slay me, yet will I trust in Him."

In what way soever she had learned it, her faith went beyond appearances, and fixed on something in Christ which her soul told her must be true and real; in some such way as the needle will turn to the pole, though testing fingers may turn it aside, and winds blow and thwart it in its struggle. If you ask, as Nicodemus did, How can these things be? we can only answer, God has so made the soul of man. There is a world of atoms and forces with their gravitating law; but there is a world also of souls which has its attracting power, and which will lead those who yield to it on to the Father of spirits, whose heart is felt in Jesus Christ. It leads by a way which the lion's whelps, if we may use the figure—the strong assurances of the senses—have not trodden, which the "eagle's eye"—the keen vision of science—has not seen ; "God understandeth the way thereof, and He knoweth the place thereof;" and He can touch human souls and make them sure of the road and the end. It is by reason of this divine gift, even in its lower form, that wherever we find men they are capable of going beyond things seen and temporal, to things unseen and eternal. Those who deny these things prove, in their denial, the power to think of them. And, if we would but think deeply and tenderly, our thoughts would lead us on. In spite of all the pressure of material laws, often so cold and crushing, there is in man what the poet calls "the heat of inward evidence, by which he doubts against the sense." The persuasion grows that there is more in the universe than he sees, and that what he does not see is better and higher, and more akin to him, than all that meets his eye. It is this which prevents men from believing, in their deepest moments, that the evil comes from God—which enables them to cling, in their sorest trials, to the faith that "Behind a frowning providence He hides a smiling face," and that, though "He chastens them sore, He will not give them over unto death." Thick thunder-clouds of Atheism and Pessimism sometimes hang lowering over the earth, and threaten to quench all the higher hope ; but God has given to the spirit a power by which it can pass up through them and sing like the lark in the sunshine and the blue sky. It is the work of the Lord Jesus Christ to educate and strengthen it by drawing it, often through much tribulation, to Himself. This history has been given to us as a glass wherein we may see the way in which He deals with many souls still, that we may not think some strange thing has happened to us in the trial of our faith, and that we may hope to the end for the grace He will bring. He gives faith ground for trusting Him, tries it whether it will trust Him with all, hides Himself that it may find Him, puts difficulties in its way that it may break through them, makes Himself stern that it may wrestle with Him, and then, when He yields, faith is stronger, and a grander Christ is revealed than the eye had seen. His aim is to bring faith to the resolve of another daughter of the Gentiles long before: "Entreat me not to leave thee, or to return from following after thee: for whither thou goest, I will go; and where thou lodgest, I will lodge: where thou diest, will I die, and there will I be buried: the Lord do so to me, and more also, if aught but death part thee and me;" or to the clearer resolve of the apostle, who saw through death to life: "Whether I live, I live unto the Lord: or whether I die, I die unto the Lord; living or dying, I am the Lord's."

And now that we have looked at the hindrances and helps to the faith of this woman, let us put her example to its use. First, let us give our soul into the hand of Christ, as we have been taught clearly how to do, knowing Him whom we trust, and being persuaded that "He is able to keep that which we commit unto Him;" and then let us confide to Him every care and trial, whether they touch our outward or our inward life. Let us go with humble thoughts of self, and high thoughts of Him; and let us hold on in trust amidst delays and seeming repulses. He conceals his purpose for a while, to surprise us with more than we could ask or think. We read of Joseph that before he made himself known unto his brethren, "he made himself strange, and spoke roughly unto them, and turned himself about from them and wept, and returned to them again and communed with them."

When we call up the scene we sometimes wonder if their hearts did not yearn to his, though it was hidden under that Egyptian mantle; and although the tears were dried on his face, and his voice made cold again, did they not whisper to themselves, 'May not this be Joseph, our long-lost brother?' Nature has wonderful instincts, but grace is still more marvellous and sure. If we have learned to know the Divine Friend even in a dim and feeble way, it will help us to wait for Him when He is under the veil of strange and stern events, until his voice is recognised from out the cloud: "It is I, be not afraid." And then we shall receive Him gladly, and be immediately at the land where faith passes into blessed vision: " Ye now have sorrow; but I will see you again, and your heart shall rejoice, and your joy no man taketh from you." Wherefore, " Wait on the Lord; be of good courage, and He shall strengthen thine heart: wait, I say, on the Lord"

XV.

THE LORD'S QUESTION TO MARY.[1]

"Jesus saith unto her, Woman, why weepest thou? whom seekest thou?"—JOHN xx. 15.

THROUGH all the first Sabbath after the crucifixion of our Lord, we have no trace of his disciples. A terrible cloud had fallen on their hopes, and they were brooding over their past in darkness and silence. At the end of the Sabbath, when it began to dawn toward the first day of the week, some of them went to visit the sepulchre. Those of us who for the first time have traversed the road which leads to the new and strange home where our dead lie, can understand their feeling; when the heart tries to pierce the grave and see the face which in so short a time has been put so far away, and when the thought of what is lost and lying below the ground hides what is before and above. They came and looked, and perplexity was added to their grief; for the sepulchre was empty, and the body of their Lord and Master was gone no one could tell them whither. They lingered for a while and left, all save one. Love may be equal in sincerity, but it may differ in intensity; and the deepest love has the reward of the first and farthest vision. Mary Magdalene remained, and stood without the sepulchre weeping. It was true of her, as of another woman, that she had been forgiven much, and she loved much. She stooped and looked again, with the wish to see the place, if she might not see Him; or with a hope which reason told her all

[1] Preached in Eyre Place Church, Edinburgh, on the occasion of the death of John Brown, M.D., May 21, 1882.

the while was hopeless. The place was still empty, but at the head and foot, like God's heavenly guards, when the keepers had fled, were two angels in white. They put the question to her, "Woman, why weepest thou?" a question of pity such as angels may feel at the sight of human sorrow, but with no authority to add the question of hope which must come from the Saviour himself. Mary answered naturally, as if to a human questioner, "They have taken away my Lord, and I know not where they have laid Him." If she felt surprise or fear, it is not recorded. Either she did not recognise them, at first, for what they were, or the convulsion of feeling in her soul made her think nothing strange. There are moments of agony which bring a paralysis of calm, and neither wonder nor terror would be felt if the unseen were to open. She turned again from the grave, and Jesus himself stood beside her; but she knew not that it was Jesus. The mists of morning still lingering, the change in his face and form as He hovered between two worlds, passing from his cross to his throne,—and, with these, the absorption of her heart, which still sought its lost among the dead, prevented her from recognising Him. It was in this moment of doubt and bewilderment that He put the question which we shall here consider—a question not only of pity, like that of the angels, Why weepest thou? but a question of hope and guidance, Whom seekest thou? We shall try to lift it out of the circumstances of the narrative, while we preserve its spirit; and we shall look at some of those to whom it may be still addressed, at the answer which is implied in its form, and at some things worthy of notice in the recognition which followed.

FIRST. *Let us look at some of those to whom this question may be still addressed.* There is a sense in which it may be put to all men in as far as they have not yet found rest for their souls in God. Man's heart lost the true centre of life and peace when it abandoned Him, and to this at last it comes—a sepulchre where its dead desire has been buried, and it looks in and finds it empty and bare, without the Saviour's memory and the angels' presence. If God be in the heart, there are many ways in which a man may enjoy and serve Him; and, if God be absent, there are as many by which he may seek to fill up the vacant place. Power, fame, worldly pleasure, knowledge and affection limited to the human sphere, are some of the things which men cast into the felt void in hope to fill it. For a while they are deceived by the ardour of pursuit, or the first glow of possession; they benumb the pain and forget the loss. But God, in these things too, does not leave Himself without a witness. There comes the frequent disappointment, "the check, the change, the fall," the death of their hope, their grief before its grave. The object they coveted is taken away, or, if it remains, the joy of its promise is felt to be false and empty. And so, if their nature be of the common superficial kind, they begin the chase after new shadows, and fulfil the old picture of the languid worldling who will not learn: "Thou art wearied in the greatness of thy way, yet saidst thou not, There is no hope." Or, if the nature be deeper, they turn in upon themselves to lament the vanity of human endeavour and the misery of the soul, with its infinite desires hemmed in and mocked by the finite and perishing —fatal shipwrecks of cherished hopes in mid-sea, or landings on dreary desert shores, where life has lost its highest interest and meaning. Is not this the case of many if they would but speak aloud, or confess it to themselves—Mary before the sepulchre, without the consciousness of her loss, or the search for her Lord? And yet the Christ is there, near the place where they are groping among the ashes of buried hopes. He is seeking them, though they see Him not; and these deaths of desire come to them to make them feel after and find Him. "Why weepest thou? whom seekest thou?"

There is, however, another class to whom the question may be put more directly, as being more nearly in the case of Mary at the grave of Christ. Some, like her, have had a deep sense of the soul's exceeding value, and of Christ as a friend who could meet its need. But they seem to have lost Him. The Christian life has its changes. Those who speak of it as an unclouded walk, an unbroken assurance, offend against the generation of God's children. What makes the book of Psalms a Christian book for all time, but that its cries out of the depth still find an echo in the souls of many who seek after God? What makes the Gospel record a mirror of the spiritual life of the universal church, but that we can recognise ourselves in the disciples of Christ, left alone by Him in the storm, crying out for fear of Him when we mistake his face, chiding his absence when our friends are dying, and despairing of his cause when He bears once more his cross and his shame? May we not appeal to your own experience, and ask if you have not felt it so? You have had your hours of darkness as well as of light, seasons when the candle of the Lord was shining on your head and your path was clear; but seasons, also, when you had to grope out your road with both your hands, and pray, "Lighten mine eyes, O Lord, lest I sleep the sleep of death." May we not remind you of the experience of Christ himself, who had to pass through a night where He saw neither moon nor stars, and cried, "My God, my God! why hast thou forsaken me?" He had something to bear for us which we cannot share, but something, also, in which we may touch the edge of his terrible eclipse. It is very hard and bitter; to have seen the most blessed of all sights, a Father in heaven, and opening behind his face an eternal home, and then to feel, or to fear, that we have lost them. It may come in different ways; it may be through a shaking of our faith in the divine and eternal as real, or it may be through a loss of our own personal hold of them, or, as often happens, through an intermingling of both. But, however it comes, whether as it seems from heaven above or earth beneath, it is a horror of great darkness, and those who feel it are of all men most miserable. Now, in these days of rebuke and blasphemy, when the great stone is once more rolled to the grave of Christ, and men put their seal on it, when there are anxious hearts to which his memory is dearer than all the world's hopes, here is a question which was put by Himself in a cloudy and dark day to a downcast, desponding spirit. The cause of the Gospel was never so despaired of as in the hour of its birth, and the question which was then put by its Lord may be repeated for the encouragement of those who are seeking Him whom they seem to have lost: "Why weepest thou? whom seekest thou?"

But there is still another class to whom the question may be put, and we mention them that we may not exclude any. There may be Christians who are beyond Mary's position, who have the comfort of knowing that they have not only a dead but a risen Lord, who can pierce with the eye of faith the cloud which closed the door of heaven upon Him, and who can see Him preparing to reopen it and come to make all things new. Yet even they are not beyond this question. Have they realised Him in their own life, in the power of his resurrection, and looked so steadfastly on the face of the ascended Christ that their face shines with his likeness, and that the spirit of glory and of God is resting on them? We may have seen Him in his risen majesty, but, for ourselves, we are still on this side death, tainted with earth and sin. A little view of his greatness made one of his disciples say, "Depart from me; for I am a sinful man, O Lord;" and the sight of it, with the spiritual eye, filled the apostle with an eager longing, "If by any means I might attain unto the resurrection of the dead." There are times when evil around and evil within make Christian men feel this so strongly that it rises to a pain, and is heard in a cry, "O wretched man that I am! who shall deliver me from the body of this death?"—looking for the blessed hope and glorious appearing which shall bring in this great and joyful change. We have too little of this sacred sorrow and high desire, but, if there are those who feel it, the question comes to them with a promise in it, "Ye now therefore have sorrow; but I will see you again, and your heart shall rejoice, and your joy no man taketh from you." Why weepest thou? whom seekest thou?

SECOND, *we come to the answer, which is contained in the form of the question.* When we look at it, we see that the question is composed of two parts, and that the one is connected with the other. The first part directs us inward to our own heart, with its want and sorrow, the other, outward to what is to meet and relieve it. It was not without a purpose that the Lord put it in this form to Mary. He surely meant that the multitude of her thoughts within her should be drawn out and fixed on the thought of Himself, and that doubt might feel its way to faith before faith ended in sight. And still there are these two witnesses, the soul's cry within, Christ's voice without, and their testimony agrees. Let us look at them.

It may be that it is speculative unbelief which is

troubling your soul, the fear that the resurrection and the life which you had hoped for in Christ have no reality, that there may be no voice of God in this world, or no God to speak. Observe, then, how in all the works of creation around us, and in the nature of man, there is an agreement between the inner need and cry, and the outer provision. There is everywhere in life an effort at advance, and a preparation to welcome and answer it. The seed hidden beneath the clod has its brooding secret which cries for help to disclose itself, and to reach the perfection of its nature; and the voices of spring are soliciting it above, the showers, the soft breezes, the gentle influences of the sky. Everywhere there is seed and climate, and every climate matures its own seed. Or observe the eye, with its delicate and complicated organism, and the light of day so sweet, so pleasant, like some angelic minister leading it out through all the fields of earth and heaven. There are, in our daily life, hunger and bread, thirst and water, the breathing frame and the vital air, and the manifold necessities and supplies which are like prayers and answers in every place and through all time. And, beneath us, there are the innumerable instincts of the smallest creatures, so strange oftentimes, so mysterious, yet not one of them made to be disappointed, as if their necessities were a look and cry to an unfailing hand, "These wait all on Thee."

If a man will say there is no thought or plan in this, then there is no more any room for argument; it must be decided ultimately by each man's spiritual vision; but let it be understood that it is a question on which the humblest mind can form its own independent judgment, and form it quite as surely when it is unblinded by the microscopic dust of details. Or, if a man will say that all this has arranged itself by some cunning mechanism of

Nature's laws through which instinct and object act and react until they create their mutual adaptation, and harmoniously fit into each other;—yet still the great fact remains, that so it is; every want has its provision, every instinct points to an object and end out of, and beyond, itself. And let us ask ourselves, if it be so in the lower wants, shall it fail to approve itself in the higher? Shall a wise and provident nature, to call it by no better name, show itself perfect in every step of its meaner mechanism, and then call out the deepest desires and loftiest aspirations only to visit them with disappointment and defeat? Or, may we not pass to more fitting language? Shall God have regard to the animal necessities and turn a deaf ear to the cries of the soul, to those longings so unutterably profound, which, in our calmest and most impartial communings with our spirits, we feel to be so true and real? A universe so carefully constructed, or developed if you will, in all its other parts, cannot at last fail in its topmost blossom and crown. The ear which hears the young raven's cry cannot be deaf to the sobs and prayers of human hearts. And let it be considered that these prayers in their best moments are not for a mere immortal existence, a life of self, but for a life in God, which, from its very nature, must be an eternal life. When Mary sought his grave, it was not for herself, but for Him—to see Him living, if it might be, and to forget all else as she cast herself at his feet; if this might not be, life had for her no more aim. And let us thank God that He has made the soul so that when it is truly wakened by Himself, none but Himself can satisfy its need. It must press through his works, through his laws, to the living God, without whom the universe would be a vast sepulchre, and immortality a perpetual weeping before it. If there are such breathings of desire in human spirits, and nothing can be surer than that they have been and are, there must be an object and end for them. If we have felt them in any way, as our souls open inward, we shall find a reality in Him who can interpret, and meet them as no other can. The word is nigh thee, even in thy heart, and then the living Word himself is near who answers it: "Why weepest thou? whom seekest thou?"

But it may be that the trouble of your heart is not so much that you doubt the reality of Christ, as that you feel unable to lay hold of Him. Then the question still comes with its own answer. Ask yourself of your pain, and see if there be not in Him the remedy you seek. Is it that you are oppressed with the burden of guilt unforgiven, rising like a thick cloud between you and God, and hindering your free, child-like approach to Him? Here is forgiveness from his hand in a way which should meet your heart's desire. It is free, it is full, and it is immediate; offered to you not as the end and prize of a life of service, but as the beginning and strength of it; and offered by Him who has the right to bestow it, for He bought it dear that He might give it free. "Who is he that condemneth? It is Christ that died." Is it that life is a battle to you, with daily cares and anxieties, troubles and temptations, others leaning on you, and you without strength for yourself, ready to fall like a weary soldier out of the ranks and die by the wayside, while the strong pass on unheeding? There was One who was weary and heavy-laden with the burden of others, and who sank at last beneath his cross; but He drank of the brook by the way and lifted up the head, and He comes back to help the fallen that they who wait upon Him may renew their strength. Is it that you feel the loneliness of life when lover and friend have been put far from you, when "the coal which was left is quenched," and the world outside is bleak and bare? There are not only promises for you, there is the Promiser himself: "Behold, I stand at the door and knock: if any man open, I will come in." What whisperings of cheer He has, even now, for lonely hearts, and what words of hope when He shall come in another way to open sealed sepulchres, and lift up his feet to the long desolations, to give beauty for ashes and the oil of joy for mourning!

It is by putting such questions as these that we learn the fitness of God's answer to our heart's cry, and find it all in Jesus Christ. It is the way God himself has taken in the Bible; for what is the Old Testament, with its utterances of want and longing desire, but a pressing of the question, Why weepest thou? and what is the New Testament but the unveiling of Him who answers the question, Whom seekest thou? And when He comes in person what is his earthly life but a touching of the deep chords of man's nature, that He may awaken him to a consciousness of his misery and sin, and that then, from beyond his grave, He may assure him of his power to save and satisfy? And what is this life to many of us, when we come to understand its meaning, but a questioning us of our heart-sores and losses, with strength and comfort interspersed like pledges which make us say, Lord, to whom but to Thee? in order that He may prepare us for the answer which shall be given when the weeping of the night gives place to the joy of the morning? "I will come and take you to Myself." "Amen. Even so, come, Lord Jesus."

THIRD, *we shall advert to some things worthy of notice in the recognition which followed.* One of them is that Christ reveals Himself to the heart before He discloses Himself to the eye. He stood at first beside Mary as a stranger, led her to review her past, and seek and find Him in her sorrow; and then He removed the cloud which had come between, and appeared as the risen Saviour. You will recollect the history of the Emmaus journey, which has been given us that we may understand his way, as it were, step by step. He joined the two disciples as a wayfaring man, unknown at first, and put his question, "What manner of communications are these that ye have one to another, as ye walk, and are sad?" He brought them to tell their story of disappointed hopes, to revolve and unfold their grief; He presented Himself to their inner eye, taught them to seek for Him amid their troubled thoughts, constrained them to constrain Him, and then revealed Himself as the Lord they sought. It is this method which explains to us the gloomy hours and long questionings of some whose hearts are seeking Him with a despondency which touches despair: "O that I knew where I might find Him! O Lord, my rock: be not silent to me: lest, if Thou be silent to me, I become like them that go down into the pit." We wonder that God does not show Himself, and speak out. But He means to deepen the sense of need, to render the choice more free and decisive when it is determined by the inner bent and struggle of the soul, and to make the revelation of Himself more blessed when the hands clasp on Him after long doubt, "My Lord and my God!—whom having not seen we love." It is a sore trial to be beside such sufferers and feel ourselves unable to give relief; and yet we have this comfort that, as Pascal says, "Those are blessed who seek, for they have already found; they need only to know it." If our eyes were opened we might perceive Christ himself standing beside them, ready, here or hereafter, to step out of the cloud, and let the eye see what the heart was seeking—see it better than it sought for it, the Man of Sorrows rising up into the Lord of Life.

For ourselves we have to learn here that Christ makes Himself known when we seek Him in the way of duty. Some make comfort the guide of their spiritual life, and, unless they possess it, they neglect every Christian service. But this recognition of Christ came to one who had no sense of comfort, and who could scarcely be said to be seeking it. She came to Christ's grave because she could not stay away. Grief, loyalty, love drew her there, and she had her reward. She came comfortless, and she left with the joy of the resurrection in her soul. And still, however desirable Christian comfort of spirit may be, it is not the only, it is not the chief, thing. Our part is to go in the way of duty where God bids us, to do what He tells us, to wait where He appoints us, and in time, in his own time, He will turn the shadow of death into the morning, and change Him for whom the heart weeps into Him whom it seeks and finds.

There are some things, further, in the recognition which may be noted, because they give us doors of hope, or at least some light through chinks in the door, as to Christ's way of revealing Himself in this world, and, it may be, in the world to come.

"Jesus saith unto her, Mary. She turned herself, and saith unto him, Rabboni; which is to say, Master."

A human historian would have constructed a long speech, but Christ used a single word—so simple, so natural. It is like that God who sets his power in the heights of the firmament and the breadth of seas, but shuts up his tenderness in drops of dew, and spring flower-cups; or like Him who has distilled his mercy into short Bible words: Immanuel, Jesus, Saviour, God is Love,—making it small that it may enter feeble hearts, as He makes the drops of water small to visit the blades of grass.— The single word was a name. It spoke of personal knowledge and interest, singling out the heart He addressed, and coming close to it in friendship. We read of it as great in God that "He counts the stars and calls them by their names;" but it is something greater in Him that He calls by name the children of men: "Jacob whom I have chosen; the seed of Abraham my friend." He is a personal God entering into personal fellowship with his creatures, and this makes Him grander than his almighty power. It is in Jesus Christ that this personal approach is nearest; and therefore the Great Shepherd of the sheep, when God brought Him from the dead, begins to call them by their name: "To Him the porter openeth; and the sheep hear his voice: and He calleth his own sheep by name, and leadeth them out."—It was at the name that she turned and knew Him. What He put into it of tone and thrill, what He breathed through it by his Spirit, as the Risen One, we cannot tell; but it said, Thou mayest mistake Me, and fail to recognise Me, but I am still the same! "And she saith unto Him, Rabboni; which is to say, Master!" No more, for her heart was full, and no more was needed; her soul was poured out in her with that word. And may we not say that it was more grateful to his heart than her own name could be to hers? In that hour Jesus rejoiced in spirit; it was the first welcome to Him from the grave, given in the name of a countless multitude who shall yet confess Him Master and Lord, and who shall form "the joy set before Him, for which He endured the cross and despised the shame."

And may we not, perhaps, in this way of recognition, have a hint of how Christian fellowship shall be restored, as restored it shall be, in the world beyond death? It seems so strange to us, and so far away. Our friends, do they think of us? When we follow them, by God's grace, shall they know us, and meet us with a welcome? What joy would that be! A father, a mother, a wife, a husband, a sister, a brother, to step forward as the cloud breaks, and call us by the old familiar name, with all our human memories clinging to it, and heaven's new tones of pity, wondering pity, at our fears and faithlessness! Can this ever be, we sometimes say, O Saviour, Lord, can this ever be? And this great Friend, who carries all other true friendships in his heart, named Mary from beyond his grave, to bid us hope and trust that He will meet and name his friends on the heavenly threshold. Christ surely first, as well befits Him, but afterward they that are Christ's, and ours. For, if He names us, they too shall know us, and in his light we shall see light. "I know my sheep," He says, "and am known of mine;" and then, "we shall know even as also we are known."

While we have been speaking of the Lord's question to Mary, and what it suggests, I feel sure your thoughts have been accompanying mine to the friend for whose loss we are this day sorrowing. The history of this first visit to the grave of Christ, the grief for the loss, the cloud between, the heart which holds what it cannot yet see, and doubts its hold of what is deepest in its nature, have been repeated ever since in some of the most earnest spirits. The pain of the struggle is keenest where the faith in the eternal truth and the depreciation of self meet together in unusual strength. But the history is also a prediction of the way in which such search must end; and we need carry the application in this respect no farther. Nor is this the place to speak at length of the writings by which he was so well known. We may be permitted only to say this much, that while there was not a line in them which his friends could wish to blot out, there was a fragrance all his own which has wafted them across broad seas, and which will carry them down to men not yet born, as things of beauty and joy. There is a tender, tremulous humanness in them which is close under the shadow of the Divine. Sunshine and tears sparkle through each other—the purest, kindliest humour, and, rippling up from beneath, a deep well of pathos. His human nature flows out through God's world of nature, which was to him a garden, and takes delight in all the things and creatures in it. And yet we cannot help feeling that in the garden there is a sepulchre, and that his thought is often drawn to it. As he looks in, he sees the angels clothed in white, and hears their question, and, between them, there is the empty place of Him whose absence makes the soul sad. But, as he communes with the gardener, we have the assurance that the great Presence is hidden behind, and that, by and by, the cloud will lift and reveal the living Lord. And so it was.

His personality, beyond that of most men, was in his writings, and yet, like all true men, he had something more. He had a singular power of winning affection, and carried, wherever he went, the box of ointment which fills the house with its odour. His friends feel what a rare nature has been taken from them; how this city will be long darker that we miss his well-known face, and its fellowship poorer that we can no more converse with his mind and heart. He was one of those beloved physicians who can help the spirit as well as the body, and help it in the steps of the Great Physician, by taking, in sympathy, "their infirmities, and bearing their sicknesses." He suffered much because he gave so much of himself away. In this he had no little share of the spirit of Christ. When broken in heart, he lightened and comforted others, and the thought that they are not to see his face again makes many hearts sore this day.

Every true man has his own peculiar perfume of soul.

When he goes, he leaves no other like him. When flowers die, we know we shall have them back again, and feel no difference. Next spring and summer will renew the violets and roses with the same old fragrance. But it is not so with the perfume which belongs to a true human soul. Each one is a species, a genus in itself, a kind which is extinct to us when death takes it, and which the whole world, in all its seasons, never gives back again. Our hearts tell us there are losses which are irreparable. And yet is there not in this a hint and token of a life beyond? What cannot be replaced here must exist there, and have a world to itself in which it shall grow on. His was one of those rich, rare natures which make us feel this. His looks, his words, his glances of thought and eye belonged to himself. He saw things, and said them, as other men do not; and yet all was simple and natural and true. Is there not in the recollection of him, in his life and look, such a forewarning?

> "Gone before
> To that unknown and silent shore;
> Shall we not meet as heretofore
> Some summer morning?"

But we have a word more sure from that great Lord who has said, "I am the Resurrection and the Life." He sought Him long and bending low, looking into his own heart, it may be, too much and too narrowly, but looking also into the sepulchre where the Lord lay. Such search can never fail. The simple word of trust before he left, the quiet spirit, told that in the eventide there was light, and that the parting of the cloud was revealing Him who sometimes hides Himself long, that we may find Him more gladly at last. Doubtless He was there to lay his right hand upon him when he fell at his feet as dead, and to say, "Fear not; I am the first and the last: I am He that liveth, and was dead; and, behold, I am alive for evermore, Amen; and have the keys of the unseen and of death." Wherefore let us comfort one another with these words; and let us thank Him who has the key of the eternal world, who openeth and no man shutteth, that He used it so wisely and tenderly in the death of our beloved friend.

XVI.

THE BEST GIFTS TO BE COVETED.

"*But covet earnestly the best gifts.*"—1 COR. XII. 31.

WHEN we read the close of the second chapter of the Acts of the Apostles we seem to be in a different Christian atmosphere from any the world has since known. The footsteps of Christ are so fresh, and the fragrance of his presence so felt, that the disciples are borne up on eagles' wings to follow Him. "All that believed were together, and had all things common; and they, continuing daily in the temple, and breaking bread from house to house, did eat their meat with gladness and singleness of heart, praising God and having favour with all the people."

It is the kind of feeling which sometimes falls on a household after the death of a beloved member, who has gone so visibly into a better world that the gate of heaven seems thrown open, and those who remain think that all the rest of their life they can walk straight on in that blessed and holy light. But soon there come the chill and damp of the outer world with its work and temptations, amid which it is so hard to preserve the higher spirit.

We have many of us experienced this, and lamented the decline. It was the experience of the primitive church, and this epistle to the Corinthians shows how soon and painfully it began. The gifts bestowed in that remarkable time, by which the descent of a new life into the world was signalised—powers of knowledge and speech, of healing and administration—became the occasions of jealousy and division. The questions of the understanding and practical life, which are all right in their own way, came to disturb the heart and spirit. The apostle Paul shows the means of cure. It is not by casting aside the questions and occupations that concern divine truth and church administration, not by treating them as insignificant or spreading over them a haze of indifference, but by choosing and aiming at the best. By the best I have no doubt he meant those gifts which tend most to Christian edification, which tell most directly on the conscience and spiritual life. And then he passes on to the best of all—to what we may call better than the best: "Covet earnestly the best gifts; and yet" (besides this) "show I unto you a more excellent way." Like a true poet, as he was, he takes his harp in his hand, and in the thirteenth chapter he sings that noble hymn in praise of charity, of which the world had never heard the like till Christ entered it, and which is still so far above the reach of the Church in the full height of its tone and in the compass of its harmony.

We shall take these words and try to show what some of the best gifts are, and what frame we are to cherish towards them, and, in doing so, we shall take the guidance which the apostle himself gives us—the touchstone of charity. He means us to prefer those which group themselves most readily round this great centre.

I. First, then, let us consider WHAT SOME OF THE BEST GIFTS ARE.

It is very evident that they are not those which are external to the soul's nature, such as money or power or reputation. These are certainly gifts, and a Christian man is not forbidden to seek them in the right way and measure, and when gained they may be employed for high ends. Yet a heathen has said of such things, "Scarce do I call them our own;" and we need not say that neither the apostle Paul nor his Master would number them among the best gifts.

Neither does he speak of all the gifts that touch our inward nature. Intellectual ability, and taste, and culture— the qualities of mind and imagination which lift man above sense, and give him a life that takes in the compass of the world of humanity—these are very precious, and no enlightened Christian man will underrate them. We wish that Christian men would seek them more, as they well may do with the words in their hearts, "These are parts of thy ways." The apostle Paul was far from despising these gifts, and yet we feel that he would be as far from describing them as " the best."

Evidently he meant to point us to those gifts with which the spirit of charity, as he has described it, is connected— the love of God, as it is presented in Jesus Christ, flowing out into the love of man, or shall we not say into the love of all that God has made, desiring and labouring that it may be freed from the evil, which is not of his making? Even faith and hope, which we may reckon among the best gifts, have their value in this, that they lead on to something better than themselves; and in coveting the best we are not to rest in them, but to press on to that of which God has made them the heralds and ministers. The apostle Paul agrees entirely with John as to the nature of true religion—a heart that has been reconciled to God, and that strives to carry its feeling of reconcilement down into all God's ways, and out among all God's creatures. If you wish to know what it is by its fruits, let us mention some of them. In regard to God himself, there will be a spirit of reverence and humility, an earnest wish to know his ways, and a willingness to pause when they transcend us, with the conviction that we have only to wait to find out the grandeur and goodness of what we cannot meanwhile understand. True love to God will carry with it this reverential trust. As regards our fellow-men, there will be a spirit of candid and generous judgment, a freedom from jealousy, a readiness to forbear and forgive, a desire to sympathise with the sorrows and rejoice in the happiness of others; for we have the highest authority for saying, "that he who loves God will love his brother also." As regards ourselves, the best gifts are patience and cheerful contentment, courage to march in the path of duty when it leads to the deadliest breach, and calm fortitude to endure hardship when God appoints us to watch. That these are not inconsistent with the spirit of love, the long roll of Christian heroes and martyrs proves; and it could easily be shown that out of the sweetness of a heart at one with God there comes the highest strength. As to things around, there will be the temperance of chastened desire, not grasping at the immoderate, nor pining for the unattainable, not unduly depressed by any outward loss, nor elated by gain; for when the heart is kept by the peace of God it may be harassed, but cannot be conquered, by such assaults. The general mark of them all is that we are not trying to make everything and every person pay tribute to self, but that we are learning the lesson of self-control, still better of self-sacrifice, and all this from the love of God shed abroad in the heart. These, I believe, are some of the gifts which the apostle meant to pronounce the best; not gifts of the hand, nor gifts of the mind, but gifts of the heart and spirit; and that we may be convinced of their superiority, let us see how they differ from others.

These gifts *enter deepest into our nature.* The outer things of the world, its wealth and power and sensuous pleasure, can scarcely be said to enter into our nature at all, except when their abuse corrupts it. They lie on the face of it, oftentimes, like a fire on ice burning the surface while the deep is freezing. A man's soul can be utterly cold and miserable in the midst of all that to an onlooker is fitted to give warmth and comfort.

As to intellect and culture and the prize of reputation, they may go deeper, but can they reach the centre? If the heart and spiritual nature are left uncared for, the mind, even if illuminated by the light of genius, is a very cheerless home for happiness. The coveted laurels are sprinkled over with the corroding acids of envy and jealousy; or vanity and pride gnaw at the root like the worm in the ancient gourd; and the prophet or poet sinks into a peevish cynic, and quarrels with God's sunshine. It is only when a man has better gifts than intellect that he can escape such heart-burnings.

The value of the gifts of love in the soul is that they go deeper than all these, and reach the centre where happiness lies. Even if they abide alone, they are sufficient; and, if other gifts are there, they touch them and turn them into gold. As they go deepest, they become the ruling power, and make all else that a man possesses a blessing to himself and others; and so the apostle (Col. iii. 15) says, "Above all these things" (that is, over them all, like a girdle compacting the garments) "put on charity, which is the perfect bond." That which is deepest in our nature becomes most comprehensive and all-controlling.

These gifts *are the most lasting*. We know how very quickly outward possessions may take their leave. They have wings like birds. Every day shows it in an age like ours, and a city like this, where the first chapter of Job is repeated according to our time, and storms at sea and fires and false securities and swindlers as remorseless as the Chaldean plunderers attack a man's property, till he is brought down from wealth to sit among cold ashes.

And intellectual gains are not over secure. The stores of knowledge are in the keeping of a treacherous memory. Age comes to steal a man's mental treasures, dim his imagination, and pluck the wings of his fancy, till he creeps beneath the summits where he soared. More melancholy than the loss of empire is the saying of poor Swift, when reading one of his own works, "What a glorious mind I had when I wrote that!"

But let a man have the gifts of a loving, patient, self-renouncing heart, and the rule is that they grow richer and mellower as life advances. I do not say that the surface of them may not sometimes be ruffled. There come sore shocks of the physical and nervous system, which seem to afflict the most loving natures with impatience and despondency. But these are exceptions; and, when they do happen, we feel that they are temporary jarrings which do not belong to the real self. Such cries of the physical frame are mercifully passed over by God, and they will be more than compensated in a coming time with the garments of praise for the spirit of heaviness.

There are gifts of God without repentance, and the surest among them are those that have charity in their heart. The fashions of the world of culture and knowledge make some forms of it out-dated; and we can conceive a time when all the experimental wisdom of this life will be inapplicable, like hills and headlands on the shore which are no landmarks in the mid-ocean. But if the lessons have gone into the soul, and made it a sharer in divine possessions, they are the same through all time and space, for they make a man partaker of God's nature. These gifts are not the laws of his hand; they are the pulsations of his heart.

And therefore such gifts are best, because they *are most God-like*. It is in a small degree that we can share God's wisdom; in a still smaller degree his power. These attributes of his nature must always be over and around us rather than within us. But of his love it is said, "God is love, and he that dwelleth in love dwelleth in God, and God in him!" It is as much ours as our home—nay, as much ours as our heart. And therefore, when Christ tells us how we are to be like God perfectly, He says, "Be ye perfect as your Father in heaven is perfect," and interprets it in another place, "Be ye merciful as your Father in heaven is merciful." When God had displayed his power and wisdom in creation, when He had shown the majesty of justice in the vindication of moral law, He came at last into the world in Christ to exhibit sympathy and self-renunciation—the lowest step, the highest manifestation—the hiding of his power, the unveiling of his grace. For when the Son of God visited men, He left outward wealth and power behind, that He might show that the highest ends of life can be gained without them, and He did not choose the arts and arguments of the schools, but He went about doing good, He surrendered all that the world holds dear for those who gave Him only ingratitude and reproach, and was nailed of free consent to a cross that He might bequeath a legacy of pardon and eternal life. It was the opening of the heart of God, and, when we look into it, we find a stronger power than all human law, and a deeper wisdom than all man's philosophy; and those who realise most of it in their nature, and breathe its spirit to their fellow-men, are partakers beyond all others of the life of God.

A man of a doubtful mind,[1] who has found, we trust, in a better world the certainty he painfully groped for in

---

[1] A. H. Clough.

this, has left this record of his melancholy perplexity—"My own personal experience is most limited, perhaps even most delusive. What have I seen, what do I know? Nor is my personal judgment a thing which I feel any great satisfaction in trusting. My reasoning powers are weak; my memory doubtful and confused; my conscience, it may be, callous or vitiated." And then in another place, ignorant of what he should desire, he says:—

> "Would I could wish my wishes all to rest,
> And know to wish the wish that were the best."

Even if this description of the feebleness and untrustworthiness of the human mind were true, there is a way by which we may make our escape to certainty. Can any one doubt that love is better than envy, self-sacrifice more noble and divine than selfishness? In wishing for patience, sympathy, and mercy, we feel and know that we wish for the best things in all the world; and inasmuch as these things are the centre and soul of the gospel, we have a token that the gospel is of God. Whatever sad misrepresentations of it we may have in some of its adherents, when its great Author and Lord comes into view the heavenly dove is hovering over Him with the testimony, "This is my beloved Son, in whom I am well pleased."

II. Let us now look at THE FRAME OF MIND WE ARE TO CHERISH TOWARDS THESE GIFTS.

We are to covet them earnestly. It seems strange that the apostle should have chosen a word that is stamped with disapproval in the commandments of God, "Thou shalt not covet," a commandment from which he himself has told us he was first brought to see how deep sin was lodged in his nature—not in his actions only, but in his heart. It is probable that he uses it with a reference to the conduct of the men he was addressing. They were coveting each other's place and honour and talent, engaged in a struggle to depreciate and supplant one another. 'If,' he says, 'you would only set your hearts on the right things, you may desire what belongs to your neighbour, and you may strive to appropriate it to yourselves. Covet if you will, but let it be the gifts of charity and self-denial.' Here, you will observe, the word "covet" ceases to have any sin in it. This is the only case in which it can be used with constant and perfect safety. In every other thing we may sin against and wrong our neighbour, but here never. If we covet his material possessions, we shall desire to dispossess him, or give him less than their value. If we covet his intellectual gifts, there will be jealousy and envy in the very look of admiration we cast on them. But if we covet his loving spirit, his forbearance and kindliness and self-abnegation, we are yielding to him our deepest affection and reverence. We are not so much taking from as rendering to him, lighting our taper at his fire, and adding it to the flame. In the fullest sense we are allowed to envy our neighbour's loving spirit, for in that envy our own love is given to him. The word of prohibition in the law thus becomes a word of command in the gospel. We may covet if we set our heart upon the best gifts, for we are restoring that which we took not away.

We are to covet these gifts earnestly, making growth in them a constant and supreme desire. We are to pursue them as an avaricious man pursues wealth, or an ambitious man power. Observe how they think and toil, watch opportunities, treasure up the smallest gains; and do you go and imitate them. Instead of entering into detailed rules, I shall give two general counsels for your intercourse with others, so that the spirit of this admonition may be carried out.

Try to discover what is best in those around you and to rejoice in it. This is one way of making what is good in them your own without taking anything from them—a just and Christian coveting. I do not mean that you are to surrender your powers of discrimination, and to fall into the easy and stupid indifference that makes no distinction between right and wrong, good and evil. But I mean that you are not to attribute evil to men till you have sufficient reasons for it, and that you are to judge even wrong appearances in a large and generous way. You are to remember how many things look so evil in the rehearsing, that could be explained, or might turn to good, if we had all the setting and circumstances; and how a tone or a look in the saying or doing of a thing would alter all its complexion. It is a blessed work to go through the world trying to put men and things in the best light that is consistent with truth, removing misconstructions, casting a shield over those who cannot answer for themselves, and striving to bring into prominence excellence that is overlooked. The pity is that sharp criticism should have the credit of strong-mindedness, when its chief ability often lies in want of capacity to see what is good, and want of feeling to refrain from saying what is disagreeable. When we do discover good in any man where it was hidden, we have a right to rejoice in it as a covetous man would rejoice in some unlooked-for profit. It is so much gain to the cause of our poor human nature. Every noble and beautiful action performed by a man belongs to us as men, and when it comes gleaming out of some dark spot, some poor, abject life, it is token that the world, outcast as it is, is not utterly cast away.

And if this is our duty as men, surely not less as

Christians. When any one stumbles or falls who bears the Christian name, instead of pride or self-congratulation, we ought to feel it to be a family dishonour; and, when any disinterested or heroic deed is done by a Christian man, a glow of gratitude to God should warm our heart. How rich we should be if every gift and grace which we saw thus became our own—for his the possession is whose soul is rejoiced by it! And we must also cast our eye over and outside sectional walls, and take pleasure in the advance of spiritual life everywhere. Whatever is going towards God is ours, if we are striving to be on God's side. What was true of the possessions of the primitive Christians should always be true of Christian gifts. "They that believed were together, and had all things common." In this sense also "all are yours; for ye are Christ's, and Christ is God's."

The next counsel is that, while you look out for what is best in each character, *you should mingle much with those who have it in large degree.* It is very difficult to live long among selfish people without becoming like them. It is not merely that their example, their maxims, the atmosphere they breathe, are infectious, but that they drive us to their own temper in a kind of self-defence. When they draw unscrupulously to their own side, we can scarcely help trying to redress the balance by drawing to ours; and so men who are much in this element come at last to believe only in the law of self-seeking. But there is an unselfish world—what Prévost-Paradol has called "the great nation of generous spirits." Try to find it out around you, live in it in your free hours of intercourse, and when it opens its heart you cannot, if you have any heart within you, fail to respond. However restricted you may be in your living friendships, you have your choice of books. Take not to the hard and cynical, but to the generous and broadly human. Above all, you have your Bible. What a noble breadth and generosity there is in it! How it teaches us to compassionate human nature without contemning it—the very opposite of the current literature of our time! Seek out its noble characters, make them your friends, and grow with their growing life. Follow, for example, Jacob's earlier and meaner self into his later and higher, when the lurking folds of selfishness were taken out of his nature, and, as in old men the face of some ancestor is said to reappear, the grand features of his progenitor Abraham rise up anew. Come much into the company of the man who spoke the words of our text, the apostle Paul—so ardent for truth, yet so large, so candid, so forbearing. One cannot admire such gifts without coveting them, nor covet them earnestly without gaining them. Above all, be much in the company of Paul's Master. We shall learn breadth and nobleness where he learned it, in the life of Christ, in his death, in the view which his life and death give us of God himself—so long-suffering and forgiving, so ready to accept our poor mites of service, and to remove our burdens of sin. "Ye are taught of God to love one another."

We shall conclude with two thoughts which may serve as encouragements to seek these gifts.

In coveting them as earnestly as we may, we can never harm any one, either ourselves or others. Is there aught else of which this can be said? Many other things on which we set our hearts may, through our abuse of them, become a stumbling-block and tend to ruin. These make whatever we gain wholesome and safe. We may hurt our fellow-creatures by our very desires. Our struggle for wealth may impoverish them; our efforts to rise may cast them down; our contest for reputation may throw them into the shade. But when we are coveting these gifts we are bestowing unmingled blessing on others, setting all they do in a kindlier light, and giving pledge that whatever we acquire shall be used for universal good.

In coveting these gifts earnestly, we are sure to gain them. To desire them with all the heart is to have them. Of what else can this be affirmed? We may covet wealth and power, but how few succeed of those who seek! What pining eyes look up, what panting hearts break on the craggy steep, where a few ascend! Or we may covet pre-eminence in talent, while an iron barrier seems drawn about our brain. This is one of the most painful things to witness—a man with admiration for genius, with the passionate desire to possess it, and the road to it inexorably closed. He sees it leap from the thought of others, but no spark will come from his own, pray and labour as he may. The consciousness of an inferior intellect, and the impossibility of ever escaping from it, is one of the sorest things a man can bear, who has made intellect his god. But here is something best of all, which is open to all—the spirit of love and self-sacrifice. Each one of us has a way to what is above the glittering of gold or the fire of genius. The weakest intellect can touch and take possession of what is most divine, of the most glorious attribute of the God of heaven. And this may be a token to us of a gracious order in the universe, of a principle of righteousness that will redress all the inequality and wrong—a beam of light amid the dark. The Highest stooped to be the servant of all, that He might beautify the meek with salvation, and say of those who learn of Him, "Where I am, there shall also my servant be." "He giveth grace to the humble," and He who gives grace will also give glory; which, if we understand it rightly, means—"He addeth more grace." Wealth shall be very little when we tread upon it in the golden streets, and genius not so predominant when in God's light we shall see light. But better than its gold and much fine gold, and sweeter than all the honey of its knowledge, shall be the love of the heart that looks upon and is made like unto the Son of God. Such a heart now enables a man to draw happiness from every other man's good, and it is heaven's seal in his soul that he is the heir of all things. "The humble shall see this and be glad; and your hearts shall rejoice that seek God."

XVII.

THE HEAVENLY HOME.

"In my Father's house are many mansions."—JOHN XIV. 2.

WE cannot read the life of our Lord Jesus Christ in the Gospels, without observing how it gathers and grows in intensity as it nears its end, that last great act of self-devotion when He is lifted up to draw all men unto Him. And there is a like progress in his words and manner of speech. Compare, for example, the Sermon on the Mount, its guidance for the practical Christian life, and its lessons from nature for confidence in God, with this discourse in the upper chamber at Jerusalem, and you feel the change. It is like that between the fresh meeting in the morning sunlight, with the day spread out before them, and the parting under the solemn shadows of the nightfall. We feel as if the voice must have sunk at times to whispers, but it has a depth and earnestness which it could never express before, because it had never found the season and the listeners. His soul is about to be poured out in death; his disciples have a dim feeling that such an end is at hand; and his heart is now opened in most tender pity to them for all they have to suffer when He shall be no longer in the midst of them. Such is the undertone which pervades the whole discourse. But while the earthly sun is sinking the stars are coming out in the sky, to tell of a grander universe, and of purposes beyond the narrow homes under whose roofs we now meet and part. Nowhere in any part of his teaching does our Lord point to these so distinctly, for as stars shine in the dark his hopes brighten amid life's shadows. There is not anywhere in all the Bible a view of the heavenly world so clear and full, and yet so brief and simple, as is contained in his opening words. It is like the firmament itself, "inlaid with patines of bright gold." We have, first, his description of heaven, "In my Father's house are many mansions;" next, the assurance of it, "if it were not so, I would have told you;" then, the fitting up and furnishing of it, "I go to prepare a place for you;" still further, the safe conduct to it, "If I go and prepare a place for you, I will come again and receive you unto Myself;" and, last of all, the essence of it, "that where I am, there ye may be also."

We shall turn attention now to the first of these, that, if we are under the shadow of partings, as indeed we always are, we may, with the help of Christ's Spirit, share in the comforts He offers.

The first remark we make is that our Lord teaches us to connect with heaven the thought of *permanence*. It is a place of "mansions." Both the English word and the Greek intimate this — a place where the dwellers shall abide, like a city to wanderers in the wilderness. 'You have known Me,' He says to his disciples, 'for a few years, moving to and fro, but I leave you for the city of God, where you also shall enter in, to go out no more at all.' The promise answers a very deep desire of the human heart. "All things change," the old heathen poet says, "and we with them." But the change in things around us is like fixity to the change that is in ourselves. It may be that the earth and sun and stars and all material things are slowly moving from their old forms into new, their light paling, their vitality decaying, to be renewed we know not how; but their slow, stern cycles seem to us changeless when we think of ourselves. Let any one who has advanced but a short way in life look round. Old times are away, old interests, old aims: the haunts, the friends, the faces of our youth, where are they? Gone, or so changed that we dare not think to recal them. Or, if we try, we cannot; they are so different, so far away, such a mist has come up from the stream of time, that they are shadows dim and broken like things in a dream. And we are changing within. If we could keep up the life and freshness there, it would be less sad. But there are few who can say the spring-leaves are as green, the flowers as sweet, the summer days as long and sunny, the heart as open and free from distrust, as when life was young. There is indeed compensation for this, if we will seek it. If we have a home in God through Christ, it brings in something better than youthful brightness, even a peace which flows like a river, a joy and gladness at times, the taste of which is like the wine of Christ's higher feast, that makes the guests say, " The new is better." But here, too, there is frequently change. The anchor of our hope seems to lose its hold, our sense of pardon and peace may be broken, and the face of God, if seen at all, may look dim and distant. The disciples who were in possession of this fellowship with Christ at the close of the week were, before another, scattered from around his cross, or hopelessly seeking Him in his grave.

It is from such changes that the promise of Christ carries us to a fixed place of abode. The permanence of the dwelling shall ensure permanence in all that belongs to the dwellers in it; otherwise the home and the inhabitants would be out of harmony. There must be, indeed, the change of progress; it is the permanence not of death but of life; and so the changes of decay, of loss, of bereavement, of the unreturning past, these are gone with the last great change, which ends the perishing and opens the eternal. There shall be no wavering of faith, no waning of hope, no chill of love. Faith shall see, and yet go on into the unseen; hope shall enjoy, and yet look forward; love shall be perfect, and yet have increase. Here, change at every step leaves some lost good behind it; there, change shall take all its good things forward into fuller possession, and thus become a growing permanence. Many a heart has said with David, "O that I had wings like a dove! for then would I fly away and be at rest;" and has found it no more in the solitude than in the city; but the hand that is put out at the window of this ark of refuge will ensure to it peace always, by all means. "There remaineth a rest to the people of God." We can rely on nothing else but his promise for the fulfilment of it. Sometimes it looks so strange, so unearthly, so utterly away from all the laws of nature and life as we see them here, that it seems incredible. We stand before him like Nicodemus—"How can these things be?" In what part of this changing universe, by what reconstruction of this unstable soul? He has the same reply: "No man hath ascended up to heaven, but He that came down from heaven, even the Son of man, which is in heaven." It admits of none other; it is for faith, not for sight; for the trust of the heart, not for the telescope of science. If God has given us spirits that cry out for such a home, and if Christ has given us one fixed point in God's love, we can commit all the rest to Him. He who can create a spark of love in a human heart, which all the floods of change cannot quench, can raise it to a sun that shall no more go down. Heaven is a state before it is a place. It is being in God, then with God. The locality will flow from the heart. The way to be sure of a permanent home is to keep fast hold of Him who is the same yesterday, to-day, and for ever.

Our Lord teaches us to connect with heaven the thought of *extent and variety.* It has "many" mansions. This saying gains wonderful grandeur when we think of where it was spoken. The humble chamber where He and his friends are met is to be exchanged for a palace where there shall be room for them and all who shall believe on Him through their word—for the children of God scattered abroad from the beginning to the end of time. We narrow the walls of these final abodes in our imagination as well as our heart, but both Scripture and reason give us conceptions of their vastness that widen to the infinite. Our present life is related to it as that of childhood to manhood. Let us think of the dwelling of the child, where it looks from its little window on the few houses or fields which make up its world, and then let us compare it with what the man knows of his present world-residence, when he has surveyed with his eye or his mind the breadth of the earth with its oceans and lands that stretch over continents by Alps and Andes. The difference, we may well believe, is not so great as that between childhood here and manhood there. Let us think, moreover, of the way in which the Bible speaks of the inhabitants; for we can judge of a city as we look on the roads and multitudes that make it their centre. There is indeed but one gate: "No man cometh unto the Father but by Me." Yet by it there passes in "a multitude which no man can number, out of every kindred and tongue and people and nation." It is a heart-reviving thing when we can feel sure that numbers without number have entered consciously by that wide door, reading over it his own handwriting, "Him that cometh unto Me, I will in no wise cast out;" and joyfully singing, as they pass through, "This is the gate of God."

But there enter at the wicket-gate Christiana and also the children, many Ready-to-halts and Feeble-minds, and far-off pilgrims for whom we can find no names, but who are written in the Lamb's Book of Life. Infants are carried through the door sleeping, who wake up in the heavenly city to read their deliverance first in the face of their Deliverer; and it is not for us to say by what far-off rays in dark nights, by what doubtful paths amid many imperfections, hearts have been yearning to this home. There have been Simeons and Annas outside the temple waiting for the consolation; and to desire and wait is, with Christ, to reach the door. The notices of Rahab and Ruth, of Ittai and Naaman, of the wise men of the East, and the Greeks who came up to the Passover, of the Ethiopian eunuch and the devout Cornelius, are hints for the enlargement of our hopes about many who had the same yearning in their hearts, though they did not see the walls of any earthly Jerusalem. And, if we believe the Bible, there are long eras to run, when the flow shall be toward God more than it ever has been away from Him. Though it seems at times, when great material conquests are gained, as if the soul were depressed and almost crushed out under its own discoveries, it must awake to its true birthright in the spiritual and divine. The ages of faith are not behind us, they are before; for we can never be persuaded that the world's advance is to the gulf of despair. From many sides and in different ways, from regions of the shadow of death and from realms of light, Christ will gather inhabitants to the final dwelling-place, and make good the assurance that He shall see of the travail of his soul, that He shall bring many sons unto glory, and be so satisfied in his works that He shall call on his universe to join in the satisfaction,—"Be ye glad and rejoice for ever in that which I create: for, behold, I create Jerusalem a rejoicing, and her people a joy." And then we have to think, with all this, that there are to be other inhabitants. From the beginning of Scripture to the end, we have glimpses of spiritual beings, other than men, who serve God in carrying out his purposes in this world, and who are to be joined with men at last in work and fellowship. There is to be a gathering together of all things in Christ, and the holy angels have relations to Him which will give them their share in his home. When we think of this, how the extent of the heavenly world grows!—mansions which shall contain the innumerable company of angels and the myriads of saved men, where they shall have room to expatiate and be at large! It is not well for us to attempt a premature union between the discoveries of material science and the revelations of God's word,—or to say that in some particular sphere of the firmament, near or far, the mansions may be forming; yet the discoveries of science may help us to extend our hopes. When the astronomer's glass shows us worlds on worlds, suns of systems and systems of suns spread through the sky, under whose magnitude and distances imagination faints, we may feel it not presumptuous to expect that He who has done so much for the temporary lodgment, so to speak, of his intelligent creatures will have at least something corresponding for their final residence. And if in the history of this world, from the rude inorganic mass up to present forms of life and thought, we can see every epoch bringing forth something more allied to spirit, may we not trust that this world does not show us the close, but that other forms higher and more akin to spirit will be found extending beyond these, or growing up through their ruins? In some way, we may be sure, there will be abodes for the inhabitants, suited to their number and character and wants.

But this promise of many mansions holds out the prospect of *variety* as well as extent. In all God's works the many means the manifold. When we visit new lands we expect new forms of life. There is no tame monotony anywhere in the world which is our present residence, and doubtless the creative power, which shows itself so exhaustless in its diversified operations here, will continue to work through infinite space and infinite time on this same plan. It suits itself to the wants of man's nature— may we not say the nature of all intelligence, which must have the new as well as the old. The divine Wisdom, who has his delights with the sons of men, had an eternity in the past, "ere ever the earth was;" but He has his coming eternity when He shall make glad the city of God with fresh and ever-growing streams of knowledge. Let us not think, then, of the mansions as copies of one another, but as giving endless room to all the faculties of God's intelligent creatures in the study of his works and ways. It is to indicate this that those who stand on the sea of glass mingled with fire are spoken of as singing the new song, which has its grand parallel in God's doings in space and time: "Great and marvellous are thy works, Lord God Almighty; just and true are thy ways, Thou King of saints."

Our Lord further teaches us to connect with the heavenly world the thought of *unity*. It is "a house" of many mansions. The extent and variety of the mansions of the great future would leave us still unsatisfied, would fill us even with perplexity and fear, unless there were a centre holding them together, and bringing them close to our heart. These abodes of the future, manifold as they are, have walls around, and an over-arching roof, which make them one house, and that house a home. It will be a world of expanse for thought and action, but a world also for musing and meditation; where, as in Isaiah's vision, the wings may be spread for flight, or folded on the feet for quiet waiting, or covering the face for inward contemplation. To some this last may be the most attractive, but for all holy desires there will be a provision; many mansions, and yet a home.

There is a thought implied which to many hearts may be not less dear. The chambers of a house have their communication with one another, and the heavenly world, wide as it is, shall have a unity of fellowship. In the present world the children of God are far apart. We speak of the one family in heaven and earth, but it is of faith not of sight, seldom even of feeling. It is a multitude of pilgrims broken up into little bands which never meet or overtake each other in this world. The word that passes along their ranks is, "Here we have no continuing city: we seek one to come." The little bands themselves are separated by the emergencies of life, by inevitable death, and, what is still more painful, by misunderstandings and prejudices, by chills of heart and jealousies; and they rear their many little mansions, forgetful of the one house. The word of the Saviour promises a reversal of this long, sad history. The barriers of time and space are to be withdrawn, and all who have been and shall be the friends of God brought together for mutual knowledge and blessed converse. The family above, the unfallen and the restored, the innumerable company of angels and spirits of just men made perfect, shall be joined by the family below, and the Jordan dried up, never to overflow its bed again. How the wide dwellings spread through God's universe shall be brought together in friendship, we cannot conjecture, but in some way there shall be one great palace home, and "the Lord shall be king, and his name one." As we try to realise it, our thoughts pass along the scenes in Scripture, where heaven bends down to meet earth, and give us glimpses of this coming union; the vision of Jacob, when he saw the angels of God, and called the place God's house; the time when "God shined from Paran, and came with ten thousands of his saints, when He loved the people, and they sat down at his feet;" the scene on the mount, when the disciples would have built tabernacles that their Master and Moses and Elias might remain there and hold converse in their hearing; the sitting down with Abraham and Isaac and Jacob in the kingdom of God; the coming to Mount Zion and the heavenly Jerusalem and all the glorious dwellers whom the apostle ranges rank within rank, till he comes to the Leader and Commander of them, Jesus, the Mediator of the new covenant. To meet in one home with all the best in God's universe, to see them, listen to them, speak with them, to pass from chamber to chamber, from age to age and world to world, to learn the secrets deep buried in the past, and brood on still undisclosed depths in the future,—this will be part of the unity of the heavenly home. Peter, when delivered from prison by the angel, seems to have recognised fully what God had done for him only when he was brought into the company of his brethren; and there are poor sufferers around us confined to the sickbed and the solitude of their own thoughts, with none but God to bear them company, for whom the dreary loneliness of life shall be first broken in the enjoyment of this fellowship. "They shall be brought out of prison to praise God's name."

And yet there is a hope in the friendship of the house which comes closer to the heart. We have never seen these elder-born of the family, and we have never lost them. But there are those who have left empty places in hearts and homes, which can never be filled while life lasts. There are children newly gone, and fathers and mothers far away—some for whom the heart is sore in the busy daytime, and some who come back in visions of the night with strange and inexpressible sadness. The house Christ speaks of has rooms where He keeps his friends safe against a time of meeting. "Them that sleep in Jesus will God bring with Him;" and this makes the promise of his return a consolation to the bereaved: "I will see you again, and your heart shall rejoice, and your joy no man taketh from you." There are views of the future world for the mind of man in its activities, its pursuit of noble aims and lofty ideals,—counterparts of what in this world we call philosophy and poetry, which must have their place there if man is still to study God's plans, and rejoice in his works; but these would be cold in their height and grandeur without trustful repose for the heart in human affection; and as it is said of God in this world, "The day is thine, the night also is thine," we may believe that there too He has provided for souls their period of rest, and that there also "man shall go forth unto his work and to his labour until the evening;" to find in some way that, while the mind has its world, the heart has its home.

But something is needed to secure this, and our Lord teaches us to carry to the thought of heaven a *filial heart.* It is "the Father's" house, a paternal home. This is needed to make it a home in any sense; needed to give the heart rest either on earth or in heaven. Men who inquire into the facts and laws of the world, and find no God in it, have made themselves homeless. Men who have found human affection, but no God beneath it, have found only the shadow of a home. Thought and affection are shallow, short-lived things without Him who sets the solitary in families,—the Father of spirits. It is to teach us this that

God has made a father's love the bond of a true human household. You recollect how Joseph, when he spoke with his brethren and asked them of their welfare, could not rest until he had drawn an answer to his question, "Is your father well, the old man of whom ye spake? Is he yet alive?" And when the hope of seeing him was near, how he made ready his chariot, and went up to meet Israel his father, and fell on his neck and wept; and Israel said unto Joseph, "Now let me die, since I have seen thy face, because thou art yet alive." We may feel sure that the restored affection of his brethren, even Benjamin's, could not have filled the place in his heart had his father been no more; and the good of the land of Egypt would have been empty, and its glory gone, without his father to look on and share it with him. It is not that love like this leads us, as some would say, to think of having a Father in God; God himself, desiring to be our Father, has put this love into our heart, that it may reflect his own. It does not begin below, but is a gift which comes from above from the Father of lights. Let a soul but once awake truly to the feeling of its misery, if it is orphaned in the universe, no pitying eye looking down on its solitude, no hand to guide its wanderings or hold it up in its weakness, no infinite heart to which it can bring its own when wounded and bleeding, let it see or think it sees that the world is fatherless, and that there is no hope beyond the grave for those that are broken in their heart and grieved in their minds, and I cannot understand how that soul should not be smitten with despair. If it were possible to enter heaven and find no Father there, heaven would be the grave of hope. The soul might search its many mansions, as Mary sought Christ's grave, and when it found no God it would stand without the door weeping as before an empty sepulchre.

To cry for Him and hear no answer, would be, in the words of Richter's dream, "to listen only to the eternal storm, which no one governs; to look to the immeasurable firmament for a divine eye, and to meet a black, bottomless socket;" and then the soul might choose "strangling and death rather than life." But what will make the heavenly house a home is that it will have, not friends and brethren only, but a Father, whose presence will fill it, and make itself felt in every pulse of every heart.

If we were to think of every mansion in it having its four enclosing walls, each would have its inscription written by God's own hand. There are those who have often doubted their acceptance and forgiveness, who have walked in darkness and with difficulty stayed themselves on God, questioning whether they might not in the end be castaways; and it stands inscribed, "Thy sins which are many are forgiven thee." There are those who have felt the want of the likeness they should bear to God, and of the love of gratitude which should bestow it on them. They take home to themselves the reproach, "Their spot is not the spot of his children: is not He thy Father that hath bought thee?" For them it is written, "Ye backsliding children, I will heal your backslidings." "And they shall see his face, and his name shall be on their foreheads." There are those who have felt all through life as if God were turned to be their enemy, and were fighting against them. Their desires have been thwarted, their hearts pierced through and through with losses and crosses and cruel wounds, and failure upon failure has followed their plans. But it is written, "Whom the Lord loveth He correcteth, even as a father the son in whom he delighteth;" and under it, "All things work together for good to them that love God." And there are those who have yearnings of heart to feel God's presence close and constant, to hear Him and speak with Him, and be sure He is not, as some would say to them, a voice or a vision or a dream of their fond imagination. They have felt it at times so certain that they could say, "The Lord is the strength of my life; of whom shall I be afraid?" But clouds roll in on the assurance, and the voice seems far off or silent, as if it were among the trees of the garden; and it is toward evening, and there is doubt and fear. But it shall be "as the light of the morning, when the sun riseth, even a morning without clouds; as the tender grass springing out of the earth by clear shining after rain;" and his name shall be written as the "Father of lights, with whom is no variableness, neither shadow of turning." And he who reads it shall say, "Thou art my Father, my God, and the rock of my salvation." Here is hope and aim for stricken spirits and solitary hearts. There is a Father, there is a home. The sky is not empty, the world is not orphaned. "Doubtless Thou art our Father, our Redeemer."

Our Lord has taught us to connect heaven with the thought of *Himself*—"My" Father's house. Heaven is the house of Christ's Father. It is as when an arch is built, and last the keystone is put in which binds it all into one; or as when a palace has been raised with all its rooms and their furniture complete, but it is dark or dimly seen by lights carried from place to place. The sun arises, and by the central dome the light is poured into all the corridors and chambers, and by the windows there are prospects over hill and valley and river. The Lord Jesus Christ is the sun of this house. If we think of its mansions, and wonder where the final resting-place shall be, it is where Christ takes up his dwelling. His person is the place of heaven—"that they may be with Me where I am." If we think of its extent and variety, our imagination might be bewildered, and our soul chilled by boundless fields of knowledge, which stir the intellect and famish the heart; but where He is, knowledge becomes the wisdom of love—the daylight softened; and a heart beats in the universe which throbs to its remotest and minutest fibre; for "in Him is life, and the life is the light of men." If we think of heaven in its unity of fellowship, it is in Him that it is maintained and felt—at his throne, through his love—according to his prayer, "That they all may be one, as Thou, Father, art in Me, and I in Thee, that they also may be one in us." And if we think of a Father in heaven, it is Christ who has revealed Him. "No man hath seen God at any time; the only-begotten Son, which is in the bosom of the Father, He hath declared Him." Even in heaven, God cannot be seen by created eye; the pure in heart see Him, but with the heart. For the human eye, it is Jesus Christ, the glorified God-man, who says in heaven as on earth, "He that hath seen Me hath seen the Father." He who gave us a corporeal nature, and surrounded us with a material world, has put into us the craving wish to approach Him with our entire being, soul, body, and spirit, and He has met the wish in the Son of God. In his person are enshrined the infinite attributes of God, so that finite creatures can look on them, and apprehend them, and see the Father in the Son. Thus God becomes open to human vision, and accessible to human affection.

But beyond all this, it is Christ's Father's house because He is the way and the door to it. "No man," He himself has said, "cometh unto the Father, but by Me." I know not of any heaven for men but that which the Lord Jesus has opened up and fitted and filled, and I know of no Father for them but the God and Father of our Lord and Saviour Jesus Christ. None will ever reach it, dim as their sight has been, and broken the twilight of their groping, but it shall be found that his foot led the way, and his hand upheld their goings. Even those who needed not redemption, who were born and have remained children of the family, shall have their knowledge and happiness increased by this, that they are in Christ's Father's house. They are adopted into it, though it be by another adoption than ours; and when they worship before the throne it is for them also the throne of a Lamb as it had been slain. It is because it is Christ's Father's house that new songs have been made for it, and a new and peculiar joy created, joy among the angels for sinners that repent, joy among the saved that they have had wonderful deliverance, and joy in the heart of the Father himself—" This my son was dead, and is alive again; he was lost, and is found." It is this which gives its deepest and highest meaning to the heaven of the Gospel; it is the heaven of the Redeemer—" Where sin abounded, grace does much more abound." It is as if from the lava of a crater there should break a stream of water to heal and purify; "to give beauty for ashes and the oil of joy for mourning;" and to recover from the waste of sin a new heaven and a new earth, in which righteousness shall dwell.

And yet this truth, that the heavenly house has for its centre the throne and cross of Christ, that it is the home of the pardoned and purified, makes it needful that a closing word should be spoken to be pondered by us all. Are you on the way to it, are you preparing for it? It is surely the most reasonable of all things to believe that a man cannot dwell in peace in God's house, unless he is at peace with God himself, and that he cannot enjoy the heaven of Christ without the mind of Christ. God cannot make a man blessed by surrounding him with blessings. He cannot give him heaven, if the man will not have God himself. If, then, you are refusing God, you are refusing God's heaven; if you will not have Him in your heart, you can never look with loving confidence upon his face. All deceptive dreams, all vain illusions about what God may do, are scattered by this, that God has set heaven's door open to you, and you will not enter it; you are framing a heart and life within you which make misery sure by the most fixed of all laws, the laws of the divine nature. It is for you to ponder this now. If you will but bethink yourself, He who has made heaven ready, and who is the door to it, is now at the door of your heart, ready to enter with pardon for all the past, and divine help for all the future. Will you not receive Him? 'Lord, I am not worthy that Thou shouldest come under my roof; but I bid Thee welcome; take thy place, fill every mansion of my soul, grant me a sense of thy presence in the peace Thou givest, the peace that is thine own, and then I shall know there is a heaven reserved for me, and that I shall be kept for it by the power of God through faith unto salvation.'

XVIII.

THE EVENING PRAYER OF CHRIST'S FRIENDS.

(FOR A COMMUNION.)

"*Abide with us: for it is toward evening, and the day is far spent.*"—LUKE XXIV. 29.

ONE never wearies of reading the history of the journey to Emmaus. There are some spots in the Gospel to which our feet turn and return, almost unconsciously, as a child's feet turn homeward; and you must have observed that almost all of them are found in the houses—in the homes of man. There is that scene when Jesus passed through Jericho (Luke xix.), and looked up among the thick branches of the sycamore tree to find a contrite heart in a man that was a publican, and to show with what spirit God will dwell—"Make haste, Zaccheus, and come down, for to-day I must abide at thy house." You will remember that other, where in the house of one of the Pharisees on the Sabbath-day (Luke xv.) He spoke those parables of the lost sheep and the prodigal son, which reveal, as no other words can, the love of the Father of us all to his lost and sinful children, and the joy with which He will lighten up the eternal home for them when they are brought back to it. There is the house of Simon (Luke vii. 36), where the woman in the city that was a sinner stood "behind Him weeping, and began to wash his feet with tears, and did wipe them with the hairs of her head, and kissed his feet, and anointed them with the ointment"—where reverence and affection and contrition and gratitude, not to be shut up in any earthly language, were set free to speak for ever in the fragrance of that act which a deep spiritual instinct taught her woman's heart, and which still floats like sweet-smelling incense round the words of Christ: "Wherefore, I say unto thee, her sins, which are many, are forgiven; for she loved much." Can we forget the home of Bethany, with its hours of holy gladness and its days of solemn gloom—its times of joy, when Martha laboured and Mary listened, and it seemed as if, in the solace of such a friend, sorrow could never come; and its times of anguish, when the sight of Him called forth those bitter tears He was so soon to exchange for songs of praise? There is the sacred upper chamber where the infant Church found its cradle beneath the shadow of the cross, where its Saviour and its Lord poured over it, in its unconsciousness of danger, his divine soul in prayer, before He poured forth his blood; and where, ere yet it knew the meaning of the token, He put into its hand the memorial of his abiding love, which has come down to ours through many generations, and may pass through many still, before again it reach his own.

It would seem as if He who rejoiced in "the habitable parts of the earth, and whose delights were with the sons of men," desired when He entered the world in man's nature to gather the closest and tenderest associations of his friendship beneath the shelter of earthly roofs, and within the circle of human habitations. It helps us to look up to the infinite God as the everlasting home of the soul—"Lord, thou hast been our dwelling-place in all generations"—and to look forward to heaven as the Father's house of many mansions. It lets us understand the meaning of that ancient symbol where, when God wished to show his nearness to men, He placed his tent in the midst of theirs; and it begins the fulfilment of that grand prophecy (Rev. xxi. 3), "Behold, the tabernacle of God is with men, and He will dwell with them, and they shall be his people, and God himself shall be with them, and be their God."

It is to one of these visits to an earthly home that our thoughts are here turned. Those two disciples, with downcast eyes and hearts, had pursued their way thus far. The shades of night were closing round them, but rays of faith and hope were beginning to shine in upon their soul. "It came to pass that at evening time it was light." From the mysterious stranger who had joined their company, views of God's plan of salvation had visited their mind, which made the cross, that had been once a stumbling-block, take new form and meaning, and the death of the Lord and Master, whom they despaired of seeing any more, become the spring of new and heavenly hopes. They had reached the place of their destination, and were about to enter the house. Their unknown friend was passing on, and would have left them had they permitted Him. It is his manner so to try the hearts of men; for, though He comes unasked, He must be invited to stay. Nor did the first request, as it would seem, prevail. It needed urgency and this earnest petition, "They constrained Him, saying, Abide with us; for it is toward evening, and the day is far spent. And He went in to tarry with them."

With this evening prayer of Christ's friends before us, we shall consider, first, some of the feelings which must have been in the hearts of those who here presented it; and, second, some of the circumstances in which it may be offered by us.

I. First, then, notice some of the feelings which must have been in the hearts of those who here presented it.

The first and most natural feeling was *grateful interest in a spiritual benefactor.* They had received that light and comfort from Him which are more than cold waters to a thirsty soul; and they offer Him shelter and refreshment,— a small thing in itself, but much as the gift of a grateful heart. They did not know the stranger's home, for He had not spoken of it. He could not, for He was still that One who on earth had not where to lay his head, who came in poverty and disguise to find for his humanity a dwelling in the homes of men, and for his divine love a home within their hearts. It was a sacred instinct which led them to press a resting-place, for kindness' sake, on Him whose home was still far away.

Long before, one sitting at the door of his tent, in the heat of noon, had seen three strangers, and welcomed them to its shade and refreshment; and an inspired writer has founded on it this beautiful appeal, "Be not forgetful to entertain strangers; for thereby some have entertained angels unawares." It was a deeper feeling which drew these disciples to welcome this passer-by, and they entertained the Lord of angels himself.

When a soul has become truly alive to God, and to eternal things, there is no tie so pure and deep as that which binds it to the scenes and instruments which opened its view to the higher life. The higher the pulse of that life within it, and the stronger the throb of its heart towards its heavenly home, the more tender will be all the bonds which unite it to the place of its spiritual birth, and to the friends who helped its first feeble footsteps in the journey to the everlasting joy. It is the strong natures that cling most fondly to the memories of childhood, and that long, in the might of their manhood, for a drink of the water of the well of Bethlehem which sparkled to them in their youth. He has a poor nature, either for this world or the next, who can cast these ties lightly away. The spot is hallowed in memory where the heart was first poured out in real prayer—the closet or the congregation; the shadow beneath the fig-tree or the solitary Bethel-stone where quickening came; the Bible, through the transfigured lines of which the soul first saw the opening arms of a heavenly Father and the unfolded gate of the city of the skies. And if these views of God have come through living men, the tie of friendship begins which makes men friends for evermore. It surely had its part in that appeal of Ruth to Naomi: "Entreat me not to leave thee, or to return from following after thee: for whither thou goest I will go; and where thou lodgest, I will lodge: thy people shall be my people, and thy God my God;" in that parting cry of Elisha after the great prophet when he went up in a whirlwind to heaven, and he saw him no more: "My father, my father! the chariot of Israel and the horsemen thereof;" and certainly in that strong affection of the Galatian Christians, when the apostle bears them record that, "if it had been possible, they could have plucked out their own eyes and given them to him."

It is on these affections that the fellowship of Christian churches rests, in which the minister must receive as well as give. "For I long to see you," that same apostle says, "that I may impart unto you some spiritual gift, to the end ye may be established;" and then how finely he supplements the thought: "That is, that I may be comforted together with you by the mutual faith both of you and me." For what are we all in this world but travellers to Emmaus, speaking to one another of all these things which have happened, and weak in faith and sad of heart alike, until the great Master comes himself to lift us up.

It is when churches and families and friendships are held together by such ties as these—by helping one another in the way of God and life eternal—that they are united and strong, that they can feel there is no nightfall which has any right or power to part them, and that they must turn in at the journey's close, and dwell together in the same abiding home. One of the enjoyments of that home will be to review and renew the intercourse of the journey, and to discover how the ties were deeper and the benefits higher than our hearts at the time understood; and how these sojourning associations were preparing the way for the unending union of souls.

And Christ desires to have a personal share in these ties of grateful affection. He is the Author of spiritual light and life to all who receive it, but here He becomes also the direct instrument—He is the channel as well as the fountain—teaching us that his heart lies hidden behind every other heart that is made a source of blessing to us, and also that He wishes to attach us to Himself as " a man speaketh to his friend." We are to feel the tie to all who comfort us as they walk beside us in the way, and yet we are never to forget that it is Christ who speaks through them. So our love rises through the human to the divine, as his comes down from the divine into the human, and his own prayer is made good, "I in them, and Thou in Me, that they may be made perfect in One." The feeling of this fellowship speaks in the petition of these disciples —the beginning of a friendship on the way between soul and soul, which cannot think of being broken up at the end of the day, and which longs for the closer tie of one family and home—"Abide with us: for it is toward evening."

The next feeling which no doubt mingled in the request of the disciples was *a desire to have such conversation continued*. It was not only gratitude to the speaker, but love to the theme. The conversation had been of that which lay nearest to their heart—of Him whom they had learned to love as the highest and purest and most tender of men whom they had known or could imagine. The stranger had spoken to them of Him, and of the Scriptures, of the hope of their nation and of the world, of that great coming Redeemer who was to turn away iniquity from Jacob, and to be God's salvation to the ends of the earth. They had hoped at one time that He whom they had known as their Master, and He whom they expected from the Book of God, were to be one and the same, but fearful events had rushed in between; the black lips of an earthquake chasm had opened; and a cross of agony and shame rose on this side, while the throne and glory were beyond the impassable gulf. They could not see how Jesus of Nazareth and the Christ of the Bible could ever be the same. But He with whom they spoke had touched the very point, as if God had come down in human form to be their teacher. He had bridged a way for them across that chasm, had made a path from the cross to the throne, had caused them to feel that Jesus may be— must be—the Christ; for Christ must suffer such things before He could enter into his glory. Those only who have found and lost and found again the pearl of price, and have felt all its value, can tell the delight; those who have beheld the star of life, and been deserted by it, and have seen it re-appear to guide to Christ, understand the exceeding great joy with which they welcomed it. Alas! if these joys have lost their meaning to us, it is because we have ceased to feel the sense of what lies in such words as God, and the soul, and life eternal. These men felt it. They were nearer the fountain-head than we who live in this cold, material day, and they had a sorrow and a joy with which we seldom intermeddle. The love of their Lord and Master, his truth and tender compassion, the beauty and glory of the Scripture plan rose before them as fresh as the sun new risen over the sea, and they felt as if they could gaze on it for ever. The quiet evening hours offer the continuance of such converse, and in the hope of it they urge his stay. Nor can we think that there is much of either truth or grace in any soul where such a sign does not appear. He who has learned to look on the face of truth at all will not coldly turn from it, or let it go its way with the evening dark, without a word like "Abide with us." His cry is that of the hungering children of the family of God: "Lord, evermore give us this bread;" and his question that which finds the life-bread only with One: "Lord, to whom shall we go? Thou hast the words of eternal life."

There are some who speak of such a request as selfish. We should be willing, they say, to take from God what He is pleased to give, and cherish no wish further. It is enough to have converse with Him on the way, whether we have a home with Him or not when the evening comes. These men do not consider the nature of the blessing which God bestows when He holds converse with the soul. It is not outward gifts from his hand; it is the truth and love which are taken from his own heart; it is the gift of Himself. "*I am your God.*" If any one can carelessly turn from this, he has not seen God neither known Him. I can imagine a man dealing so with some intellectual phantasm of his own mind, wearied out with working at the problem of a universe which he can never solve, and glad to go to sleep, though even he must rise to higher desires at times, and wish to see the thread of truth unwound to its primal source. But that a man should have learned to look on the face of God as a Father, that he should have felt his heart beat with some of his divine life and burn within him at the thought of his love, and that he should be indifferent to the hope of ever seeing Him again —this is impossible. He who has had such fellowship in the thoughts of God on the way will desire to have them also in the house at nightfall. He cannot surrender them at the setting of any earthly sun, but will pray as these disciples did, " Abide with us, for it is toward evening."

The last feeling we mention in the hearts of these friends of Christ was *the presentiment of something more than they had yet seen or heard.* They had gratitude to the speaker, they had love to the theme, but they felt that there was still a mystery behind. They had learned much, but their heart told them they had not learned all. There is often a feeling in the soul which flashes to a hidden secret, and reason has to find its way slowly afterwards, step by step, like a man groping his path to a point which has been revealed to him by a glance of lightning. You have felt the look, the tone, the turn of thought in a stranger arrest you, and it called up some scene or friend—you could not tell wherefore—made some long-past passage of your life stand out before you by a subtle association you could not disentangle. As they walked beside this mysterious stranger in the closing twilight, not only the truth of Christ but his form rose before them, and seemed to walk beside them. A tone of voice or turn of thought in the speaker touched some of the marvellous cells of memory, where the past lies sleeping but never dead, and He who had his chosen place there, whom they thought gone for ever, arose and lived again, and moved by their side, as once before through the corn-fields or over the old Galilean hills. Do not our own dead often rise and keep us company so, and who can tell if not in truth? Who can say whether the thought may not be breathed from that spiritual world, the confines of which are never far away—the touch of the tip of some angel wing that ripples the surface of memory to help us to healing hopes? In this case certainly it was so; the sense of a great presence hovered near them; a great truth floated before them ere yet it disclosed itself to their eyes. They fear to ask Him of it; they shrink from whispering it to themselves; but there is a beam of light in the stranger's look which promises to lead to fuller revelation, a tone of hopeful confidence in his words that reminds them of a voice which once before spoke from the gloom. What if now, amid a severer storm and out of a denser darkness, that beloved form should step forth again, and the words be heard, "It is I; be not afraid"? Such a hope of a risen Saviour, and that this was He, unuttered even to themselves deep down in their soul, and fighting with fears as once their ship did with waves, was surely present in their hearts when they urged this request: "Abide with us: for it is toward evening."

That all these feelings were enclosed in this petition we can scarcely doubt—grateful interest in Him who had spoken comfort, a pleasure in the truth He disclosed, and a hope of higher things to be learned. They are the feelings by which we may still test ourselves, and which we should seek to bring to the table of the Lord—gratitude, faith, and hope—to set before us his person, his death, his resurrection and higher life—and to seek to realise these more closely here in this chosen home of the soul.

II. We come now to consider some of the circumstances in which this request may be offered by us.

It may be said to be suitable to *the whole earthly life of every Christian*. The Church of Christ, and every member of it in this world, is pursuing this Emmaus journey—travelling from the death of Christ on to the house where He shall give the manifestation of his resurrection. It is no fiction of fancy that draws this lesson from the narrative. What Christ did for men when He was on earth is needed by them all through time; for their wants and his ways of supplying them are still unchanged, varying in outward form but the same in essence. This makes the Gospel to those who read it aright an everlasting book—the same yesterday, to-day, and for ever—and every event in it a picture of some side of our spiritual history. Like these disciples, we have been left by our Lord and Master, and we are pressed with doubts. We have difficulties about things in the Scripture, and things out of it—events in the great world of human life, and the little circle of our own. We have difficulties about Christ and his cause—why He should be crucified so often afresh and be so slow to rise and reign, when the world is pining for Him in its sin and misery, and his friends are unceasing in their cry, "O Lord, how long?" Yet He has joined us in the way, and spoken to our hearts till they have sometimes burned within us. Through the dusk there has come some light, and through the cold of night some warmth from a Great Presence which we have felt even when we could not see it. If He has not answered all our questions nor solved all doubts, He has made us feel that there is only One who can satisfy our souls. If He has not stilled the cries of our immortal nature, He has stirred them up to lay hold of Himself, and breathed into them the conviction that He can meet them, and He alone. "Lord, to whom shall we go but unto Thee?" And in this He gives us the fore-glancing feeling that there is much which lies before—much to know, and much to possess. He cannot tell it on the way. The work, then, must be one of faith and reliance on the Word of God, and reverent listening to a voice which comes from behind a veil, and contact with a world which sense cannot see, but which a purified heart surely can.

> "A little hint to solace woe,
> A hint, a whisper breathing low,
> 'I may not speak of what I know.'"

Thus the Christian will cling to the word of God, and to Christ its great subject, not only for what they reveal, but for what they suggest. We feel that He who sustains us on the way, and drops into our soul great desires and deep presentiments, will answer them when we reach the heavenly house, and show us there things which eye hath not seen, neither hath it entered into man's heart to conceive. Our life is now hid with Christ in God, but "when He who is our life shall appear, then shall we also appear with Him in glory," and therefore we hold Him fast to the close. "Abide with us."

Next, it is suitable to those who are suffering under *some special despondency of spirit*. While all our walk through this life resembles the Emmaus journey, there are some parts of it that have a closer likeness—places of the road where, as the apostle says, "we are in heaviness through manifold temptations." Let us take one of these adapted to our present circumstances, when we are about to sit down at the Lord's table. Among so many, there are some, perhaps not a few, who have not that clear view of Christian truth, and of Christ as their Saviour, which once they enjoyed. There may be some of you who felt at one time as if you were sitting with Christ at the first communion, and listening to his words till you could say with his disciples. "Now are we sure that Thou knowest all things; by this we believe that Thou camest forth from God;" or who, like the chosen three looking on his transfiguration, were ready to say, "Master, it is good for us to be here: let us make three tabernacles." But Christ appears dead and gone from you; all the foundations of your faith and hope are shaken; and you are treading, like these two, a way of gloom with the words, 'We trusted that it had been He who should have redeemed Israel. Have we ever known Christ, or is there a Christ to know?' Such sorrow, if it be true, is the testimony of its own final success. Never, never could a God of mercy suffer such grief, for the loss of the most glorious object that ever entered the thought of man, to remain unanswered, or let such a godlike vision dawn on the horizon of humanity, to be quenched for ever in black night. There *is* a Christ, and a heart in God represented by Him, else death were better than life, and all this glorious universe an empty, troubled dream, a hideous phantasy pictured on a dissolving cloud. Yes; this sorrow for the loss of Christ is the assurance that you will find Him. If you can reason with yourselves, ask your own heart: Does not grief prove love, and will not love bring back faith? Is it true of you that, though Christ seems lost, you mourn his loss, that though He is gone, you cannot let his memory go, that you turn to the voice that speaks of Him, and grasp at every hope that promises to show you again his blessed and his gracious face? If your heart does not burn, is there even the smouldering heat of shame that it cannot? Then sure I am that He who quenches not the smoking flax will in his own time visit you. Only see that you be in the way with Him—not striving to forget the loss, or drown, or deaden it. "Yea, in the way of thy judgments, O Lord, have we *waited* for Thee: the desire of our soul is to thy name, and to the *remembrance* of Thee;" where you cannot say "to thy name"—say even "to the remembrance of Thee." Though the voice sounds strange that once was his, turn to it if it speaks of Him. Though the evening deepens, despair not of light in its darkness. It is then we need to cling to Him most, and then that He is accustomed to reveal Himself. It is his "to lighten men's darkness lest they sleep the sleep of death. If He seem to be passing by, constrain Him. "Abide with us: for it is toward evening." "I will not let Thee go until Thou bless me." O faithful heart, thou hast wrestled and overcome.

Another time suitable for presenting this request is *in approaching the evening of life*. There are some who are able to look back on times when Christ has been with them, strengthening them for duty, supporting them under trial. They have had their fears and fightings, but also their comforts and hopes. They have been enabled to bear the burden and heat of the day, and have watched through nights of trial. But a sore and strange crisis is coming on. The lengthening shadows of the evening are falling across the plain, telling that the last and deepest night of all cannot be far away. As these disciples looked into the grave of Christ, they feel that they can look into their own. It is a strange experience when a man comes first fully to realise it, that he must ere long put off this tabernacle and leave all these old familiar scenes and faces to venture out into the dark and unknown. It costs a hard struggle even for some good Christians to look the probability of death close in the face, and not to be struck with a shrinking fear of it. They are ready to lose sight of Him who has up to this time been their guide and comforter. He has helped in many and sore trials, but here is an emergency new and strange. May not his power or may not my faith fail? Then it is a time to urge this prayer, "Abide with us: for it is toward evening." "Be not Thou far from me, O Lord; for trouble is near; for there is none to help." What a comfort it is for you to think that it is presented to a Saviour who has himself already passed through death, and who comes back as to these disciples to walk beside his friends in the thickening gloom, who knows the way that we take, for He is no stranger, and is guiding us when we think we are constraining Him! Do but hold fast by Him in simple, humble faith, and He will enter the house with you. Its entrance is low; its porch is dark; but within there is large and lightsome room, and blessed company, and a world of life and movement and joy which shall make the sorrowful way you have left appear as it is—the night-time of your being. "And there shall be no night there; and they need no candle, neither light of the sun; for the Lord God giveth them light; and they shall see his face; and his name shall be in their foreheads."

Last, we remark that this request is suitable to those *who live in an age of the world such as ours.* It would be unwarrantable to say that this is the evening of our earth's history, and that we are close upon the second coming of Christ. The world has probably much to look on yet before the final end. But there are various days and nights in God's dispensations, and one of these evenings seems now creeping in upon us. There is a cold vapour of materialism spreading over the minds of many, chilling their conviction of a living God who made and superintends his world. The preaching of evangelical truth, which a generation ago was fresh and stirring, has become to numbers like a twice-told tale, partly because the life of the Church has not corresponded to its doctrine, and partly, it may be, because our preaching of the gospel has become too much a thing of orthodox tradition rather than of living experience. There are outbreaks of wickedness in the world which startle worldly men, and inroads of worldliness into the Church which make Christians despondent. I do not say these things as blaming others, but as desiring to feel that there is an atmosphere around, which has its effect upon us all, making the great eternal lights burn low and dim, and fears arise of what may be coming in the way. No man can live in an age, whether it be one of faith or mistrust, without being, to some extent, influenced by it; and mistrust is all abroad. The most venerable opinions are assailed, the firmest truths seem to shake, and those whose convictions were founded only on outside reasons know not what to think. When even men who have walked for years in the company of Christ are perplexed with difficulties and sinking in despondency, what stand can be made by those who have never really seen or known Him? There is only one duty and one source of safety for any man who wishes to have a life that rises above the most barren materialism; it is to seek a close and personal contact with the Saviour as the life of his spirit, to know Christ as the risen Son of God, who quickens dead souls. These evening shades and doubts and trembling fears, that settle down ever and again on the world's way, are permitted, to compel us to this—to urge us to seek his fellowship with a closer access, and to constrain Him to enter the house with us and reveal Himself in such living power that we, for our parts, can never doubt his truth any more. We need not fear for the gospel of Christ whatever dangers threaten it. Calvary has still its Olivet; the shades of the cross, the ascension glory; and every night of trouble in its history, a brighter day-dawn. The Church of Christ and the world with it will emerge into a better and higher time, but it is a question for all of us whether our faith can stand seasons of testing which are pressing on, and abounding iniquity when the love of many may wax cold. It is a time to urge Him to stay with us till the day break and the shadows flee away, to be more watchful to strengthen the things which remain and are ready to die, and to press this prayer, "Abide with us: for it is toward evening, and the day is far spent."

XIX.

CHRIST ABSENT AND PRESENT.

(FOR A COMMUNION.)

"*Me ye have not always.*"—JOHN XII. 8.
"*Lo, I am with you alway.*"—MATT. XXVIII. 20.

THE first of these sayings was spoken by our Lord shortly before his death, when He was among his friends in the house of Bethany; the other immediately before his ascension, when He was about to leave them. Like many of the utterances of the Bible, when we look at their surface, they seem in contradiction; but, if we follow them into their deeper meaning, they unite in harmony. Let us take them to the person of Christ, and see if He cannot reconcile them in a way which satisfies the Christian mind and heart. He has given us a memorial of Himself in the Lord's Supper, and it is like a gem with two facets; on the one is written, "Me ye have not always," and on the other, "Lo, I am with you alway."

They remind us that we have in Christ *one who is human and yet divine:* "Me ye have not always." It is as if He said to his friends, 'I have been with you for days and years, till we have learned to know one another closely and tenderly. We have shared the same privations and sorrows, partaken of the same hopes and joys. You have learned to know Me as the Son of Man, a brother who can understand you and sympathise with you, and make compassionate allowance for your fears and faintings. We must separate; for I must die, and though you have known Me after the flesh, henceforth you know Me so no more.' There is something very human and touching in this farewell, which comes at first like a hint, and afterwards becomes more plain as He draws nearer his death. "A little while, and ye shall not see Me: I go my way to Him that sent Me." And the absence of the personal Saviour from our communion reminds us always of his death and, through his death, of his true humanity. His human nature was not an appearance under which his divinity was moving and acting to gain visibility: it had everything of our nature except the sin, which does not belong to our true humanity but takes from it. When we read the account of his death, we can see that He had the shrinking from that "shadow feared of man" which we naturally feel, the recoil from the separation of body and soul which is so repulsive to us. He realised the sinking of the nature shaken to its inmost core, which that strong word *dissolution* brings before us, and which is expressed in the words of the psalm that began his own death-cry: "I am poured out like water; my strength is dried up like a potsherd, and Thou hast brought me into the dust of death." That Christ died a true human death is, then, the assurance to us that his life was a real human life. "Forasmuch as the children are partakers of flesh and blood, He also himself likewise took part of the same—in all things it behoved Him to be made like unto his brethren." His hunger and thirst and tears and weariness, his sorrow at the death of friends, and heart-sickness at the sight of sin, the clouding of his soul, the cry of his agony, "If it be possible, let this cup pass from Me," were all real, most deeply real. Let not the thought of his divinity take away from our view of Him a single fibre of his true humanity. In this memorial of his death "Behold the sign."

But his words, "Lo, I am with you alway," remind us that we have a Saviour who is also divine. How the shrinking fears of his humanity were reconciled with his true divine nature is not for us to say. There are other great chasms across which our thought cannot step, and some of them in our own history. We cannot say why our body, with the feelings and fears that belong to it, should often fall so far short of the confidence in a higher life sometimes gained by our spirit. But it is possible for us to hold fast both. So in the memory of the death of Christ we must seek to realise his divinity. The promise to be with us alway is not completed in the continuance of his words with us, or of his example, or his influence, or of his death-memorials going down from age to age. It has a deeper meaning, the promise of a presence which implies an omnipresence; so that at every communion He is divinely repeating the words, "This is my body: this is the new covenant in my blood," and bringing home to the heart which looks to Him his nearness in the spirit and the life. And, if in this communion, then always and everywhere. No sacrament should cut off the Lord Jesus Christ from communion with the rest of our life, but should remind us how He can be present with us through it all. "Lo, I am with you alway," is a promise to be constantly beside us. We fondly dream at times of our departed friends, that though unseen they may be near us, permitted to look in as witnesses, or as ministering spirits with the angels to whom they are joined. Who can tell? But here is something more helpful to us, a friend who says not 'I shall visit you,' but 'I shall be with you, with you alway,' and whose presence means that infinite power and wisdom and love are beside and around us to protect and guide and comfort to the end, true man to sympathise, and very God to save to the uttermost. And so we put our fingers in the print of the nails, and know Him to be human, and look up and embrace Him as " our Lord and our God."

These words remind us, further, that we have in Christ *one whose death as our Saviour is all-important, and not less his life*. The death of Christ is the first truth which meets us in the Lord's Supper: "Me ye have not always." He instituted it, as He himself tells us, that his death might be kept in memory; and not merely his death but the manner of it on the cross: the broken bread his body, the poured-out wine his shed blood; the memorials twice put into our hands, that in the mouth of two witnesses every word might be established.

It is impossible to account for this without believing that his death was of supreme importance. And we cannot read the Bible as a consistent book without seeing this. The Old Testament points forward to it in sacrifice and symbol through its long course; apostles point back to it—" We determined to know nothing among you save Jesus Christ and Him crucified;" and up in heaven the songs celebrate it—" Worthy is the Lamb that was slain." The incarnation of Christ, the human and divine meeting in Him, may serve other ends in God's universe, but the first end to us is that He was made lower than the angels for the suffering of death; that He by the grace of God should taste death for every man. "Me ye have not always," He says; 'I leave you to suffer for you, to die for you;' and we do not reach the full meaning of the Lord's Supper, unless we say, as we touch the memory of his death, " All we like sheep have gone astray, we have turned every one to his own way; and the Lord hath laid on Him the iniquity of us all."

But still this other word must be spoken by one who is to be a complete Saviour, " Lo, I am with you alway." It is the word of life, of life which has conquered death and sin which is the sting of death. The New Testament constantly connects the resurrection of Christ with the death of Christ, as the seal and assurance of its success, as God the Father's answer to Christ's own word, "It is finished," the sun rising on Him after the night of struggle, when He saw God face to face, and He and his were preserved. Had it not been for his risen life, the Lord's Supper would have been a memorial of defeat. We cannot see how the cross of Christ could ever have been ground for glorying, had it not been followed by an event like this. His disciples would have striven to forget and hide it; and that they did not, is token that they had a strong conviction which counterbalanced it and turned the darkness and shame of his death into something which they could proclaim with joy: "Who is he that condemneth?"—"It is Christ that died, yea rather, that is risen again." And so we may take these truths, a crucified and a risen Saviour, and bring them together into our thought of Christ. We have two monuments of them which stand side by side, the Lord's table and the Lord's day. We can follow up their history, link by link, till we fasten it to the very rock of the sepulchre; and through space and through time, as it were, put our hand on Him who was delivered for our offences and raised again for our justification.

We are also reminded that we have in Christ *one who presides over the world where we are going, and over the world in which we now are.* "Me ye have not always." The words say, 'I am going to leave you, for it is expedient for you that I go away; there is another world where I have to care for your interests, to appear for you in the presence of God, to build up and furnish the Father's house of many mansions, that when you leave the earthly house of this tabernacle you may have a building of God, an house not made with hands, eternal, in the heavens.' Sometimes we think it would be the happiest lot on earth to have with us the presence of the Lord Jesus Christ in person; but it is better for us, meanwhile, to hear these words over the memorials of his death, "Me ye have not always." They remind us that there is another and a greater world where Christ sitteth at God's right hand, and that our aim should be upward. To have our life always rising, and to carry others with us, this is the direction and bent of all true effort; and Christ goes up before, that He may lead the way and say Come. And when any Christian friends leave this world for another, though our hearts may be grieved at parting, our minds may be at rest, for He is there to welcome them, and be far more to them than we could be. Mothers who could scarcely suffer sun or wind to touch their little children may put them into his arms when He asks for them; and, when our own time comes, it gives us less to leave and more to look for, that we depart to be with Christ, which is far better.

And yet there is another word needed here also. "Lo, I am with you alway." It is the promise of a close, constant presence, not only to the first disciples, but to all who should believe on Christ through their word. He goes away to prepare the place, and then He comes to guide and guard on the journey, to be with them in the house and by the way, to welcome them at the door and to help them to find it, to make the old song of God's providence a new song of redemption: "The Lord shall preserve my going out and my coming in from this time forth, and for evermore." If we had a Saviour only in heaven we might doubt if ever we should reach heaven. How should desolate creatures bear up in their loneliness; how should worn-out travellers carry their heavy burdens;

how should fainting soldiers face strong enemies, unless the Comforter and Helper and Captain of salvation were at hand! And how should dying men and women grope their way through the great darkness unless they had his guidance! "Fear not, for I am with thee." And so we have Him there in the noon-day, here in the twilight; there amid the palms of victory, here in the heat of battle; there in the great congregation of the brethren, here with every little company on the road to it: "For to this end Christ both died and rose and revived, that He might be Lord both of the dead and the living."

When we take these words to the Lord's table, then, they tell us about his person, human and divine; about his work, dying and rising; about his dominion in heaven and in earth. Does not this meet the desire of our heart and all the wants of our life; and should it not be our endeavour to bring the thought of this friend, unseen and yet near, into our every duty and trial? When Christ was on earth He sought to teach men this; He went out of sight and came back unexpectedly, to make them feel He was not far away, though they did not see Him. He was giving lessons for the long period which has these words written on it, "Me ye have not always;" and "Lo, I am with you alway." Let us call up to memory the little ship on the Sea of Galilee. The night is dark; the sea is in storm; and the disciples are ready to perish; their Master is absent and seems to have forgotten them; and, when He appears, so strange is his look that the first sight of Him adds to their fear. But He comes to their aid, to reassure their hearts, and then to still the storm. It is to teach us that, though we think Him absent in danger, He can be near for a very present help, if not at first calming the outward tempest, yet entering the heart to reassure it. Or we may recal the family at Bethany, when the brother lay sick unto death, and Christ did not appear, and the sisters watched and counted till death at last came, and the friend who might have helped them was still absent. But He came at length, first to give them comfort and hope, and then to give them back their dead brother from the grave. And Christ means that we should learn that, though we miss Him for a while in seasons of bereavement, He is at hand in due time to give the strength of faith, which is the earnest of the resurrection. Or let us think of the last lesson He gave on the road to Emmaus, when the two disciples were walking and communing with heavy hearts, because they had lost their best friend, never to see Him again. Faith had gone from them and hope, and only love remained, holding fast by his memory and refusing to let it go. A stranger drew near, unknown to them in the dusk and in the darkness, or faintly guessed at through the veil with which He had covered Himself. And He led them on and made them feel first the truth about Himself, and then the spiritual presence, till their eyes were opened to see Him in the breaking of bread. Unseen, He had been present with them all the while, to teach his friends that when they are in doubt He will be near to uphold their faith, if their heart continues to cling to Him. These are some of the lessons which we have to learn through life, that in danger, in bereavement, in doubt, the apparently absent Saviour will be near, if we look and long for Him. He seems to have written on trying providences, "Me ye have not always;" and yet the "Lo, I am with you alway" is ready to emerge when we need it most.

This last lesson of the presence of an unseen Saviour was given in the breaking of bread. Then specially He draws near to us; let us draw near to Him, if not in strong faith, if not in bright hope, yet with true love, feeling after Him that we may find Him, though He be not far from every one of us. The unseen Saviour in the Christian life is like the unseen God in nature, hidden meanwhile in the height of the skies, but revealed in the depth of the soul. We can feel that the height and the depth must belong to one God and one Lord; that heaven and the heart are both of them his home; and that He is as great when He dwells in the heart as when He occupies his highest heaven. Jesus Christ is in this also the image of the unseen God— at God's right hand, and close beside us: "Behold, I stand at the door and knock; if any man open, I will come in." He can give the experience which was learned long ago in the house at Emmaus, that the unseen Saviour is present; and it will be the anticipation of a higher vision, which shall be a permanent one, of his person and work and large and great dominion, and of his seeming absences changed into a perpetual and blessed presence. Amen. Even so, come, Lord Jesus.

XX.

LIFE ON THE HUMAN SIDE AND THE DIVINE.

"Thou tellest my wanderings: put Thou my tears into thy bottle. are they not in thy book?"—PSALM LVI. 8.

THERE is a description of life given in the Bible which has been objected to as depressing and unreal. Life is represented, it is said, as a scene of unending struggle and sorrow; and men are made to walk under a constant shadow. There is some apparent truth in this. As existence rises above the mere animal view, it becomes serious, and often stern. If we were butterflies or birds we could flutter or sing without care; but when we realise that we have souls we come upon thoughts that are very deep, and enter on anxieties which are not easily removed. But the question to be first asked is, Has the Bible view of life truth in it, and, if so, is it not better to take it fairly into account? We may flee from disagreeable duties, go down into the sides of the ship and fall asleep, but our disregard will not prevent the storm rising, nor comfort us when we are wakened to look on it. And it may be a further question, Has the Bible no compensation for the saddening view of life which it sometimes presents? Is there any cure equal to that which it offers, when it shows us how we may connect all our life with the constant presence and loving-kindness of an Almighty Friend? Observe how both these aspects of life are intertwined and interwoven here:

"Thou tellest my wanderings: put Thou my tears into thy bottle: are they not in thy book?" We shall first, then, look at the view given us here of the *human* side of life, that we may realise how far we find it truthful; and then we shall look at the *divine* side, that we may see how human life is affected by the presence of God.

I. *The human side of life.* It is described under two forms, wanderings and tears; and the division, though brief, is very comprehensive. Life has its active part in wanderings, its passive in tears. Man's movements are the fleeings to and fro of one who is pursued by a strong enemy; and his resting-places, such as they are, may be called *Bochim*, "places of weeping." But it may be asked, Is it not an exaggeration on our part to take these words which David used of himself, and of one part of his life, when persecuted by Saul, and to apply them to human life as a whole? Would David have used these words later on in his life when its current changed? He escaped from Saul, rose to the throne of Israel, crowned his reign with victory, ended it in peace, and has left his history as an ideal one to which his nation looked back, and from which it took its brightest visions for the future. Is his later life not a contradiction to these words?

And yet some of David's sorest struggles and bitterest tears were in his later life. He had daily cares and fears which made him say, "I am this day weak, though anointed king." He had harassments from enemies round about and from rebel subjects, from sins of his family and sins of his own life, which make us sometimes think he was a happier man in the wilderness of Judah than on the throne of Jerusalem. No one of David's wanderings was so weary as when he fled from the face of Absalom, crossed the brook Kidron, and ascended the Mount of Olives weeping as he went; and no tears were so bitter as when "he went up to the chamber over the gate and wept; and as he went thus he said, O my son Absalom, would God I had died for thee, O Absalom, my son, my son!" Or, if we come to other and still deeper troubles, what wandering so dismal as when he sinned his great transgression, and what tears like those wrung from his soul in the fifty-first psalm, "Deliver me from blood-guiltiness, O God, thou God of my salvation!"

Still it may be said, What reason can there be in taking David's life, and making it a copy of all human lives? Has not God given us in the world sunshine as well as cloud, has He not scattered manifold pleasures through it, and should we not thankfully acknowledge this? It is very true, and we must beware of taking any part of the Bible, and pressing it so far as to make it contradict both itself and our experience. Now, there are two things which God in his kindness has sent to the relief of men in the journey of life. There are the natural blessings that are, in a measure, close to all, visiting them often whether they will or not; and there are the helps and hopes which come from a felt relation to Himself. The first may be called the blessings of his hand, the second of his heart. We shall have to speak of the second afterwards, and so we turn meanwhile for a little to the sunshine let in upon life in the way of nature. The cloud would be too dark for poor humanity, unless God had given it a silver lining, and it is neither good for us, nor grateful to Him, to overlook this. We may begin with the strange, mysterious pleasure God has put into life itself—to live, to breathe, to look on things and have an interest in them, to move, to walk among them—these are roots that go down into the world and hold men on to it by an indescribable attachment. Long agony may loosen these roots, or strong attraction upward may fix them in other soil, but it is one of the kind things in the world, that God has given man a liking to life itself. There are many things, besides, which come to us more consciously. There are the pleasant sights and sounds of nature round us, the flowers and birds of which our Saviour spoke on the Mount of Blessings, the beautiful sunlight, the gentle "rain coming to the evil and the good," "filling men's hearts"—notice the word *hearts*, for this can be said only of men—"with food and gladness." There are the exercises of the thought and the fancy, which take us away, with no guilty forgetfulness, from the over-heavy burden of sore troubles. We have been placed in such a wonderful residence, with marvellous floor and ceiling, hieroglyphics and illumination beneath and above, which science seeks to read for us, and poetry to transfigure in far-off memories and great possibilities. There is the benediction of work, of honest, earnest work, whether it be of hand or head. Let us thank God for work, if we are able for it in any way. How it wards off temptation, and beguiles sorrowful thoughts, and soothes, if it cannot heal, sore wounds! "In all labour there is profit." There are the kindly affections of the human heart, the love of home and kindred, a father and mother's tenderness, brotherly and sisterly affection, the solace of friendship, the happiness of doing any good. There is no one perhaps who has all of these, but no one is shut out from the opportunity of some, and it needs only the open heart to have more come in than the sight at first perceives. You look, it may be, into a dark, cheerless room, but when the eye expands amid its dulness, there are objects there which can make it full of interest to some lonely inmate. So there are angels in the world of nature which come down in the night-time, if we will listen, to sing "peace to men of good-will."

We seem far enough away now from wandering and tears, and yet they return upon us. We might call the Bible to witness, not as an inspired book, but as a record of human life. Here is Jacob, "Few and evil have the days of the years of my life been,"—and Moses, "All our days are passed away in thy wrath"—and Job, "Man that is born of a woman is of few days, and full of trouble"—and Isaiah, "We all do fade as a leaf"—and the Moralist King, "Vanity of vanities; all is vanity." There is the testimony of the men of the New Testament, that life is a fight of afflictions; and there is the greatest life of all, "The man of sorrows." We might take the common witness of the world. It was a saying of the ancients that "for every joy granted to man, there are two sorrows, one before and one behind." There is a lurking fear of the serpent under the flowers, which prompts the song, "Let us eat and drink, for to-morrow we die." "Even in laughter the heart is sorrowful." There must be something more in all this than traditional sentiment.

But we would rather address ourselves to the experience of life, of those at least who have made some acquaintance with it. Have you not felt this description of life true in its changefulness? How few of us are in the homes of our youth! Or, if near them, how far have we wandered in associations! Changes have taken place around and within which make us almost forget what we were. "Our fathers, where are they?" Old scenes, friends, affections, hopes dead and gone, or changed and far away, till we see them like cloud-land, or like things in dreams. We may have the new and dear, but where is the old so well-beloved? Does it not come on us with a sense of wandering and tears? Or think of life in its constant struggle. A man may have a narrow round, he may sit in his place day after day, but he may have long paths of anxiety and toil to traverse within. No Alpine climber has such panting heights before him, or such threatening depths to look into, as some men in the journey of life And, worst of all, they never gain the summit of rest The old burden, the old battle in some new form! Rest is the cry of their heart—if we could only reach some spot of perfect rest; but necessity without, or impulse within, forces them to begin again. And close to this there is the imperfection of life. It never reaches a fixed goal, never gains a faultless and secure prize. Is this not wandering? So far as men seek only natural good, they do not gain it in their own estimation. It does not fill the heart, or it fails to give the pledge of permanence. You that have found in family affection that which of earthly things gives most repose need not be told this. You have had your tears already, and they bring to you this sense of wandering. My child, my wife, my husband, my brother is not, and I, whither shall I go? Or if you have not felt this you can fear it, and the fear sends a chill to your heart. No, with such things behind and before, there cannot be perfect repose. "It is not your rest, it is polluted." And herein we find the secret of the imperfection. Impurity is lurking everywhere in the world, poisoning the springs, withering the flowers, darkening the light; and all because it is in ourselves. Well for those who have found it in the conviction that they have wandered from God, and can recover rest only when they return to Him—that tears cannot have hope of ceasing till sorrow leads to the Divine Friend. "Blessed are they that mourn; for they shall be comforted." And after all these thoughts about life, some of us may feel how the human view of it suggests its growing fatigue.

There is at first an elasticity which makes wandering please for its own sake. The spirits are light, the morning young, and all is new. But as day advances hopes are checked, difficulties thicken, and strength declines. The man walks on, not from pleasure, but from necessity. He ceases to expect more than he has seen, and nothing can bring any great change except death. Then, if ever, men begin to feel how little there is in life itself, apart from something deeper and higher. They reach a commanding table-land where they can look all round and estimate the world. What aimless wanderings, frequently what bitter tears, not wiped away but cold and stiffened on the cheek! The compensations God mercifully granted have had their day, and what have they left? Have they been a mere pastime, instead of leading us to Him who can give the wanderings of life a true and happy end, and can shine in with his light at eventide? For life may be compared to the ascent of some hill in our native land. At first, the man has by his foot the pleasant wayside flowers, and the clear stream as it hurries from cascade to pool. Then he nerves himself for the steep breast, and forces his path amid rock and bush till he gains the summit, brown and barren with hill-tops girdling him round. And such, many say, is the whole of life. But the air may brace the spirit to a higher tone, the sky may be clearer, the stars when they come out more bright and tranquil, and ere nightfall he may have his visions of other lands, "sweet fields beyond the swelling flood, all dressed in living green," such as Moses had from Nebo, and when he sang in the 90th Psalm that "according to the days wherein he had been afflicted, God would make him glad." Life changes its character when we can say, "Thou tellest my wanderings: put Thou my tears into thy bottle: are they not in thy book?"

II. We come to *the divine side of life.* This belongs only to the man who can feel, know, and be regulated by it, as the pole-star shines for those who take it for their guide. What, then, does the view of God secure for the man who looks to Him? It secures for his life *a divine measure.* "Thou tellest my wanderings." That is, not merely Thou speakest of them, but Thou takest the tale and number of them. There is nothing so absolutely fixed and sure as the science of numbers. Some ancient philosophers held that it is the secret of the structure of the universe; and Plato has said that in making the world "God mathematises." But, on the other hand, there is nothing so like the sport of circumstance as the shape of life dependent on the will of others and on our own. Yet here, in its wanderings, a believing man may be comforted by knowing that God has made his life the subject of a numbered order. We ask Him to teach us to count our days, and He replies by counting them for us. They look often as restless as a bird's flutterings, as unregarded as the fallen leaves, but they are reckoned up by God, and there shall not be too many for the wanderer's strength, or too few so as to fall short of the promised rest. "Thou tellest my wanderings." Who can say how many weary exiles, and persecuted remnants in mountains and deserts, have been cheered by this word, and have seen it like a guiding-star in the sky, or rather like the eye of God looking down and making the night to be light about them? And it is a word still ready for the help of all who need it. If there be any one who has come to feel how deeply he has sinned against God and his own soul, who has gone astray in dark and slippery ways open to the view of the world, or seen only by the Searcher of hearts, until in his backslidings he seems lost in despair; yet, if his heart will truly look up to

God, and if he will set his face homeward, there is One who can tell all his wanderings to forgive them, and to answer his prayer, "Turn Thou me and I shall be turned, for Thou art the Lord our God." Or if there be some one shut up in gloomy thoughts, as if all things and all men were against him, bewildered and alone, ignorant of the next step for duty or deliverance, there is a way open upward which has availed many: "When my spirit was overwhelmed within me, then Thou knewest my path. Bring my soul out of prison." Or if there be those who feel that, with all their endeavour, their life seems planless and aimless, unlooked-for events thwarting their efforts, disappointing their hopes, and making the world a place of shifting exile—here is something fixed by which they may steady themselves under a wise Teacher and Guardian: "He led him about, He instructed him; He kept him as the apple of his eye." There are people who meanwhile have no changes, whose strength is firm, and they are not in trouble as other men. They can think lightly of these comforts; but there must be some guidance in the world for "the home-sick who wish to find home," and the time for it may come to us all.

Let us bless God, then, that, whether we be wanderers in sin or doubt or self-tormenting thoughts, there is a Guide who, if we ask Him, will lead us on to the closing words of this psalm: "For Thou hast delivered my soul from death; wilt not Thou deliver my feet from falling, that I may walk before God in the light of the living?"

This view of God secures *a divine sympathy* in life: "Put Thou my tears into thy bottle." However skilful the guide might be, he would not meet our case unless he had a heart. There are rough defiles and thorny brakes through which the road leads—there is no help for it: these things make it the road; but what concerns us most is the manner of the Guide. It is not so much the way by which He leads as the way according to which He leads, taking frailty into account, and providing resting-places and refreshments as they are needed. What an exquisite tenderness there is in the description of his guidance of the people through the wilderness, notwithstanding all their provocations: "Many a time turned He his anger away—for He remembered that they were flesh; a wind that passeth away, and cometh not again." But the sympathy here is not so much for those who are in movement as for those who are brought to a stand. There are times when we cannot walk, cannot work, when we can only suffer. "He sitteth alone, and keepeth silence, because he hath borne it upon him." Our Saviour felt this to be the hardest part. While He was in the active path of duty, it was a gladsome thing to Him—"My meat is *to do* the will of Him that sent Me." But when He had to *suffer* it, the cup was bitter: "If it be possible, let this cup pass from Me." Though his case was very different from ours, we too feel how much more easy it is to do the hardest work than to sit and endure. Then most of all we feel the need of sympathy; and yet then it is sometimes most difficult to find it. Some kind friends who will assist us in toil, and succour us in danger, have a dislike to be near us in suffering, and they have no patience with tears. But God has patience with tears: "Put Thou my tears into thy bottle." It is not necessary to enter in any minute way into the figure; the general meaning of it is clear. This, first of all, is taught us, that God is close beside a sufferer in the time of sore trial; so near that He can mark and catch the tears. I do not think we could have understood this at all but for the thought of the Son of God coming down and sitting with the weary by the wayside and in the houses of grief, and weeping Himself at the grave. There is a way of looking at all this as if it were an impossible dream, but if we think of Him who made us with human hearts as having a heart in Himself, then that the Lord Jesus should enter the world to bring that heart nearer us is not so strange, —it seems natural. But the language here implies that the tears are not only marked and sympathised with, they are preserved. They enter into God's memory, and become prayers: "Hold not thy peace at my tears." It is true that, like other prayers, they may not be answered at once. We often wonder that it should be said, "Like as a father pitieth his children, so the Lord pitieth them that fear Him," and yet that He should let them suffer so much and so long. So long! He seems to be hiding their tears, and so He is; but, meanwhile, He sends hidden strength and comfort. "He gives them tears to drink in great measure," but, like their wanderings, it is in measure. And the language implies, moreover, that the tears shall be brought forth again. It is for this they are marked and preserved. The tears of God's people are like "nature's tear-drops," as they have been called, lying all night long on the branches; but, when the light comes at last, nothing reflects God's sunrise so clearly, or seems so much to rejoice in it, as the drops of dew from the womb of the morning. Whether they be natural tears, as those of Mary and Martha for their dead brother, or contrite tears, like those of the woman in Simon's house, or tears of sorrow about the state of the world and the mysteries of God's providence, as of him who wept much because no man was found worthy to open and to read the book, they shall be found to have been all kept and recorded and finally answered.

This view of God secures *a divine meaning* in life—"Are they not in thy book?" It is natural to understand this of both the wanderings and the tears. They are written down, and this gives us an additional thought about them. When a man puts matter into a book he seeks to give it an intelligent and consistent meaning. He collects his facts, joins them one to another, and compacts them into a continuous whole. It is possible, then, if a man puts all his wanderings and tears into the hand of God, that they may be seen at last to end in a plan—man freely contributing his part, and God suggesting and guiding. Even now, when we look back from some points of the road, we can trace the beginning of this. Things which at the time looked accidental have determined the course of our existence in its most important interests, and events we feared have turned out to be our greatest blessings. Another hand than our own supplied the material, and we had to choose, or rather were helped in our choice by that same hand. If we have chosen Godward, and taken the higher road, we begin to see a growing plan of kindness which gives us the conviction that when the book of life is completed all that is dark and doubtful will be explained. There are different "books of God" spoken of in the Bible. There is the book of our natural life, in which "all our members were written;" and there is "the Lamb's book of life" for them that enter the holy city. There is the "book of the wars of the Lord," as we may call that which contains the deeds of those who have wrought righteousness, and waxed valiant in fight; and the "book of remembrance," for the converse of them that feared the Lord in evil times. But surely not the least interesting will be this, which holds the wanderings and tears of God's people, when the divine side of them is fully revealed. We may think of it as a history, and then its theme will be, "They wandered in the wilderness in a solitary way; they found no city to dwell in. And He led them forth by the right way, that they might go to a city of habitation." We may think of it as a high argument, and then its basis is, "And we know that all things work together for good to them that love God." Or we may think of it as some transcendent poem, and then the strain will be, "Nay, in all these things we are more than conquerors through Him that loved us." And, if God writes his book of lives, it is not that He may let it moulder into nothingness, or lie idly past. He works and writes for readers. He has stone tablets for the history of his meanest creatures, records preserved on their tombs, as is befitting those that have an existence only in time; but for his sons and daughters He must have a more complete and living history, and means by which those who are most deeply concerned in it shall peruse it. We cannot but think that this shall be one of the occupations of eternity, to read the meaning of the past in the possessions of the future, and this not for each one interested in himself alone, but for each interested in all. Then the words of the Lord shall have a perfect fulfilment, "What thou knowest not now, thou shalt know hereafter." Every wandering and every tear shall have over-against it, as its counterpart, some lesson, some blessing. We may apply to them the saying of the prophet, "Seek ye out of the book of the Lord and read. No one of these shall fail, none shall want its mate." What wondering curiosity, what high and holy expectancy may this not excite in us, that we shall have such a book to read, if God in his wonderful mercy bring us first to read our names in that other book—the book of life! And what dignity and deep, composed joy should it give to our sojourn in the world, changing our wanderings even already into a heavenward walk, and brightening our tears into divine hopes!

Having looked at these two sides of life, we cannot

part with them without a few thoughts which may give them a still closer practical bearing. If there are those who object to the Bible view of the world in its shadows, let us ask, Does it not offer a glorious counter-vailing light? Would you take the short and superficial side that belongs to time, and exclude what is grandest and most divine? If a man will consider with himself, and have the courage to look within, he has depths which go down below the senses, below the mere intelligence, into the heart, the conscience, the spirit; and no view can be true which does not take account of these. It is from these depths, with all the solemnity and struggle which belong to them, that the heights arise. This is the true universe. No profound searching of the soul into itself? Then no hill of God above. "Out of the depths have I cried unto Thee, O Lord." It is still as of old—evening and then morning were the first day.

But how shall we find our way upward?—how pass from the natural to the divine life? Do you not seem to feel that while David was speaking there was also another sufferer, even He who has said, "It is written in the psalms concerning Me"? Wherever there has been a soul struggling toward God, it has been Christ's life that was in it. He is the "root" as well as "the offspring of David," and his spirit was moving beneath, inspiring desires which were going forward, as He himself was, to his visible coming as the Son of God, the Saviour of men. He came and had his wanderings and tears for them and for us all; and in the volume of the book it was written of Him that He delighted in God's will for our salvation. Neither is there salvation in any other. In whatever night or twilight men have been feeling after God, it will be found that He was not far from every one of them. And now, would you have it in the open language of God's word?—"I am crucified with Christ: nevertheless I live; yet not I, but Christ liveth in me; and the life which I now live in the flesh I live by the faith of the Son of God, who loved me, and gave Himself for me." This is the transition from the natural to the divine—such a hand laid on Christ as gives us his life even unto the death for us, and then his life springing up through death within us.

And would you know how it may advance in growing consciousness? We feel as if we could learn it from the way in which the soul of the speaker here has been rising to fuller confidence in God. First it is a simple faith—"Thou tellest my wanderings,"—my sins to bring me to thy grace, my pilgrimage to bring me to thy glory. And then faith ascends in prayer, that God would take all life's trials and hide them and the sufferer in Himself—"Put Thou my tears into thy bottle." And, last of all, prayer becomes the communion of friend with friend,—"Are they not in thy book?" If you have your foot on the first step of this ladder, let it be your endeavour to rise from faith through prayer and fellowship into the higher life, where the human is not lost, but purified and blessed in the divine. If this step has not been taken, remember that, though for a time the deeper side of life may be denied or slighted, it will assert itself whether men will or not. Sin, trial, death, are realities, and those who refuse the divine help should bethink themselves how they are to face these issues unaided and alone.

XXI.

TROUBLE AT THE THOUGHT OF GOD.

"*I remembered God, and was troubled.*"—PSALM LXXVII. 3.

THIS psalm gives the experience of a man in deep perplexity. When we read it we are ready to think that men have not now the same power of feeling on spiritual subjects. With the progress of knowledge the soul's sensibility would seem to have been blunted: so deeply earnest, so profoundly miserable were these men till they gained the great object of life, and saw the face of God in righteousness. And yet surely such men have been found all through time, with a burning fire in them, kindled by the power of the world to come, and counting all things of little moment till they could stand right with God. Such men were Paul and Augustine, and the great Reformers, and Pascal, and Bunyan, and Haliburton, and Payson, and M'Cheyne, and many more, widely different, as we have sought to name them, in church and intellect, but enclosing in their nature the one divine spark that will return to Him who gave it. It is well for us to learn how we ought to feel, by coming into contact with them, with

"All that chivalry of fire,
The soldier-saints who, row on row,
Burn upward each to his point of bliss.
Since, the end of life being manifest,
They burned their way thro' the world to this."

To these men belonged the writer of this psalm. No wonder that with such a seeker the psalm has a close so different from the troubled opening. It is with the commencement, however, that we are now concerned, and especially with the difficulty which some feel in the search after God. This man felt it. Surrounded by many and sore adversities, he turned to what men are taught to consider the great source of all comfort, the thought of God; and here is his remarkable experience—"I remembered God, and was troubled." We cannot conceal from ourselves that this is an experience repeated in the case of many. The thought of God does not give them that comfort which they desire, or which they feel it ought to give. It may be very useful for us to consider such a subject—"*Trouble not removed by the thought of God.*" In doing so we shall not confine ourselves to the phase of the subject in the heart of this speaker, but take a wider view, so as to meet, through God's help, a larger range of difficulty. There are two points of view under which we wish to present the subject—the strangeness of such an experience, and some of the reasons that may account for it.

1. THE STRANGENESS OF SUCH AN EXPERIENCE—that a man should remember God and yet be troubled.

For consider that such an experience is *against all that is made known to us of the nature of God*. We do not now speak of the nature of God as made known in his works, for here we believe there might be room for very great trouble to the most reflective mind; the question of sin is so perplexing, and the voice of Nature is so discordant. On the whole, perhaps, a thoughtful man would be swayed to the view of God that gives comfort. The very reflection—I am a sinner, and yet I am spared by a God of justice—may suggest to us the idea of mercy in God, and of his long-suffering kindness having a gracious purpose.

And yet it is so difficult to say how much of this reasoning comes from the reflected light of God's Word that we cannot tell how far it would go if left to itself, or rather we can say that left to itself it has done very little.

We speak of the strangeness of the case where God, as we believe, has spoken and made his own nature known. From the very first that revelation has had one purpose, and could have only one—to present God in such a light that his sinful creatures should come and find rest in Him. For God to preserve them in this world, and then to speak so as to drive them away or keep them away from Himself, is utterly inconceivable. And so from the very beginning, and all through, the revelation has been one of mercy. They read it falsely who read it otherwise. Its first light is not a flash from a thunder-cloud but a beam from the sun—the darkness of man's sin pierced by the ray of God's promise. If there are thunderings and threatenings and judgments that follow, they are all in mercy's hand, not to keep back the sinner but to keep back the sin. As the revelation proceeds, this view of God becomes always more clear till it opens fully in the cross of Christ, and shows us mercy not prevailing over justice but taking it into friendship, that it may prevail over transgression and make a way for the guilty to the heart of God. Here is its complete expression—"God was in Christ, reconciling the world unto Himself, not imputing their trespasses unto them. For He hath made Him to be sin for us, who knew no sin." It is free, infinite mercy, not obscuring any part of his character, but taking it all into its keeping, and offering Him as a reconciled and reconciling God to every child of the human race. If in the Gospel there are still warnings and threatenings and terrible views of the evil of sin, let it be remembered that the end for which it entered the world was not to present these, but to present that which saves from them. Many think the Bible hard because it speaks so of sin and the sinner's doom. But let it be borne in mind that the Gospel finds the disease in our world; it does not make it. The only new thing it brings is the cure, and it describes the disease and shows the danger, that the cure may be made welcome. Its great word, like that of its Lord and God, is—"I am come not to destroy men's lives, but to save them." This, becoming ever more distinct, is the view given of the nature of God in his revealed Word,—a view surely fitted to dispel fear and to inspire full and unalterable confidence. Is it not, then, strange that there should be men who, with this Word before them, can remember God and be troubled?

It becomes strange when we reflect not only on the nature of God but on *his promises*. We need to have these before us to see the case more strikingly. They are so universal, so free, so full, that they seem fitted to meet every want and satisfy every yearning of the human soul. They are not human inferences from God's nature, but divine assurances direct from Himself, as if a monarch should pluck the jewels from his diadem and put them into the hands of his subjects, who are also his friends, making every gem a pledge of some rare gift even rarer than itself, each one having written on it, "Ask and ye shall receive, that your joy may be full." Has any one the trouble of guilt, then what can be desired after this? —"Look unto Me and be ye saved, all the ends of the earth;" "Him that cometh unto Me I will in no wise cast out;" "The blood of Jesus Christ, God's Son, cleanseth us from all sin." Is it the trouble of a fallen and depraved nature?—"I will heal your backslidings, I will love you freely." Is it some heavy cross that crushes to the very earth?—"Commit thy burden to the Lord, and He shall sustain thee." Is it some great void, clear or undefined, some deep and weary longing that cannot articulate, but can only cry?—"My God shall supply all your need according to his riches in glory by Christ Jesus." What of the sad changes and desolations of time, when Jesus Christ promises to be "the same yesterday, to-day, and for ever," and when his eternal love shall bring all that we lose of the pure and true back like the engulfed waters from the bitter sea to be poured again into a fountain-head that shall never dry! What of death when we have the word, "I am the Resurrection and the Life"! Such promises offer us the possession not only of divine gifts, but of God himself; "whereby are given unto us," says the apostle, "exceeding great and precious promises; that by these ye might be partakers of the divine nature" (2 Pet. i. 4). That the heart of a man who hears these words and believes that they come from the lips of God should be troubled at remembering Him, must seem very strange.

It must appear strange, further, when we consider that trouble at the thought of God is declared to be *against the experience of all sincere seekers.* God's own declaration is, "I never said to any of the seed of Jacob"—to any of those who wrestled as he did in the dark with God—"Seek ye my face in vain." There is a history of cases reaching all through the Bible, and the burden of them is—"This poor man cried, and the Lord heard him, and saved him out of all his troubles." And outside the Bible, in the history of the Church, and near ourselves in our own experience, we have read of and seen numberless men who in the most terrible extremity of loss and agony and death, when nothing else could comfort, have "looked to God and been lightened." The appeal of all ages has been, "O Thou that hearest prayer, unto Thee shall all flesh come." It is but what we might expect when we approach God with the wants of the soul. We may ask from Him any earthly good—outward comfort, health, the life of our dearest friends, and in order to our soul's highest welfare we may be denied; but if we seek truly the soul's good it must be impossible to meet a refusal from the Father of spirits. We feel that it would absolve a man in the great day of judgment if he could say, 'I earnestly sought God's face, but it was turned away from me; I remembered Him and found only trouble.' We must believe that no such voice can ever be raised, for the responsibility of the soul's loss can never rest on God; and so much the more strange does it seem that there should be an exception here, and that it should be repeated by men who complain that they seek God, and do not find Him.

We shall make this last remark, as showing the strangeness of it, that such an experience is *against all that we can reasonably believe of the nature of the soul of man.* If one thing be true about man's soul it is this, that out of God no full, satisfying end can be found for it. The soul is greater than the whole world, and the greater cannot be blessed of the less. We should not have wondered if a man had said, 'I thought of life and its fleeting joys, of time and its emptiness, of earthly possessions and fame and knowledge and all the pleasant things of life—how brief they are, and how in one day they perish. I looked abroad on worldly friendships, and saw how fickle they were, how a man is wounded in the house of his friends, how death lays desolate homes and hearts; and the bitterness of death flowed in upon my own soul.' But that a man should turn with his soul to God, to God for whom that soul was made, else it is objectless, to Him who can satisfy it and who alone can, to the light of all intelligence, the life and joy of all holy spirits, and that he should say, "I remembered God, and was troubled"—this must seem passing strange. Some account can surely be given of it that may help to clear the character of God, and put us in the way of finding Him, if we have been seeking fruitlessly.

II. We shall consider, then, SOME OF THE REASONS THAT MAY BE GIVEN FOR SUCH AN EXPERIENCE AS THIS.

The first reason we mention is that *many men do not make God the object of sufficient thought.* They think of Him now and then in a general way, when the fact of his existence is forced upon them by the discourse of others, or when they are compelled to confront the idea of Him in some crisis of life, in a moment of conviction, or in an hour of trial. But the thought flashes across like lightning in the night, as unwelcome and almost as rapid : God is there, charged with the possibility or the probability of some dreaded calamity or painful restraint, and they are glad to put the thought away. They do with it as with their dead—"bury it out of their sight." Can anything be conceived that shows more clearly the alienation of the natural heart from God ? and does it not prove the Bible view of human nature to be the true one ? This is the religion or irreligion of immense numbers, and of not a few who call themselves Christians ; they "do not like to retain God in their knowledge." They feel as if they could be comfortable only when they banish Him out of mind, and enjoy his world without being troubled with Himself. Their courage or their consciousness will not let them come to the dreadful atheistic negative, "There is no God ;" but they will not aim resolutely at the only other consistent alternative, 'There is a God, and I know Him to be my friend;' and so they hang in wretched suspense, remembering God only to be troubled. But if He is to be known He must be sought, and sought with earnest effort. There is nothing in his world worth finding that does not require anxious seeking. Is He alone unworthy of it, or are you so independent of Him? "Consider this, ye that forget God."

Another reason why many are troubled at the thought of God is that *they are seeking Him with a wrong view of the way of access.* There is a class of men who are anxious in the search after God, but choose a mistaken road. I do believe with all my heart that, if they are honest seekers, they will find God at last; but they may cause themselves long pain; they may walk under a cloud all their life, and perhaps only see the face of God clearly in a better world. It is surprising how many Christians have this trouble, in some form, at the thought of God. And yet it is not surprising, for if we are to find we must not only seek the right end, but seek in the right way. The most frequent mistake of all is that men think they cannot look God in the face without trouble, unless they have something of their own in their hand, some portion of good works or good thoughts, some outward reformation or inward repentance. They do not perceive, or at least they do not feel, the all-sufficiency of Christ as a Saviour, and the freeness with which they may take hold of Him and all that He is and has, at once as their own. They are constantly putting the question, "What shall we do that we might work the works of God?" and here is the answer, so old, yet needing always to be repeated, "This is the work of God, that ye believe on Him whom He hath sent" (John vi. 29). There is something so great and God-like, so utterly unlike the manner of men, in pardon and peace and eternal life being offered without a single condition on our part, that it is hard to realise it. Hence the many false forms of Christianity that are constantly springing up, and that put outward ceremonies and works, or inward purifications and states of mind, in the foreground ere we can reach Christ. Now, it is the whole effort of the Bible to put Christ first and before all. The Father brings Him forward with the words, "This is my beloved Son; hear ye Him." He steps forth with the invitation, '"Come unto Me, all ye that labour and are heavy laden, and I will give you rest." Rest begins and ends with Me.' The Holy Spirit has this great work, "to take of the things that are Christ's and show them unto us." The ancient sacrifices and ceremonies point to Him with empty hands, in the words of John the Baptist, "Behold the Lamb of God, which taketh away the sin of the world!" Saved men on earth declare, "Not by works of righteousness which we have done, but according to his mercy He saved us;" and glorified saints in heaven sing, "Unto Him that loved us, and washed us from our sins in his own blood." It is the testimony of all things in heaven and earth to the infinite and sole sufficiency of Jesus Christ as the Redeemer of sinful men; and if men will try some other way of paying the broken law save with this gold of the covenant, or if they mingle their own dross in any degree with it, what can they expect but trouble? Our own eye is sometimes quick enough to see the miserable flaws and defects in all that is ours, and, if it does not, God is greater than our hearts, and will show us to ourselves by some lightning-flash that makes us cry, "Behold I am vile!"

Strangely enough, we all say we believe this, and yet trouble remains. It is because there is so wide a difference between saying we believe, or believing in a vague, general way, and feeling all the meaning and power that lie in a great truth. Many a man has the field in which the treasure lies hid, and knows it to be there, and traverses it often; but his eye has a glimpse of it only when God's sunlight strikes on the precious ore. If we have not found the comfort of possession, let us pray Him more earnestly to reveal his Son in us; let us pause and stoop in deep humility of spirit and emptiness of self, till we can grasp but one golden word, and find a reconciled God in it. "Therefore, being justified by faith, we have peace with God, through our Lord Jesus Christ; for God commendeth his love toward us, in that while we were yet sinners Christ died for us" (Rom. v. 1, 8). If there be work before receiving Christ, the only work is to feel the void, to present the emptiness, and then into this the water of life rushes to supply all our need; and if you bring this need, and bring it now, you will find that trouble flees, as you turn from thoughts of self-preparation to Christ's prepared fulness, and to God's arms that are waiting to receive you in Him.

A third reason why some are troubled at the thought of God is, that *they are seeking Him with some reserved thought of sin*. There is a class of men who have a sense of the importance of salvation, and a certain desire to obtain it, but lurking in the life there is some darling and unholy object, some friendship with evil, some forbidden pleasure, open or secret, which they will not resign. How many a Herod would hear John gladly, were not Herodias there to paralyse his will; and many an Agrippa is almost persuaded to be a Christian if he could come down to the bonds of the Gospel, which in some form still gall men; and many a young man approaches Christ respectfully, with the word "good Master" on his lips and the great prize of eternal life in his eye, but the world's love in some form is there to draw him back. They go away sorrowful, for the conscience rises up to reproach the heart, and the heart itself in silent hours counts its poor gain, and feels its loss. And whether a man has turned his back on Christ, or professes to be his friend, he can never think of God without trouble, if he is cleaving to conscious sin. True peace can never dwell in the same heart with impurity.

You may think this inconsistent with what we have said of Christ saving the most sinful without any condition; but contradiction there is none. Nothing can be more true than that the Gospel offers pardon unbought to every sinner, but it is equally true that it cannot save a man who resolves to continue in sin; because the Gospel is more than pardon, it is life—and then only can it be peace. It says with its author, "Neither do I condemn thee;" but it adds, "go and sin no more." We say, 'Open your hand to receive the free gift of God,' but how can you receive it if every finger closes down on some sinful indulgence? And, if you open it far enough to let the Gospel enter among your sins, the sins must die or the Gospel cannot live. Do you complain of this? Complain that it will not save you from sin and let you live a sinner! That Christ will not quietly hold fellowship in your heart with Belial! And you, you wish to write Christ's name over the door, and will have not only men but God read the inscription, "The Lord is there;" and yet you will keep the world and the devil in the house and wonder that you should have trouble! You sprinkle the lintel with the blood, and yet sit still in the darkness and bondage of Egypt, and complain that you have not the light and freedom of the land of promise! I pray that such may have trouble and trouble evermore till they find a peace that will stand the test not only of their own consciences but of the eye of God. A false God or a perverted religion might compound and say, "Peace, peace," where there can be none, but "there is no peace, saith my God, to the wicked." If there were no trouble, it would be worse. It might be token that God had left you alone; and trouble is there because He is still striving with you lest you sink into the slumber of delusion that makes a fatal opiate of the very Gospel of Christ. Come to a free unconditional salvation, but remember that deliverance from sin is the very essence of the cure, and that without this you cannot enjoy it neither see it—that, as the banishment of clouds is the work of the sun and the means of seeing his face, so the removal of sin is Christ's great work, and the way by which from a purified sky He lifts on you the light of his countenance and sends you peace; for, as every new ray from Him quenches the unholy and impure, and kindles the heavenly and divine, it proclaims at the same time a grace that is free and broad and unbought as the sunlight —" Blessed are the pure in heart, for they shall see God."

We mention as a fourth and last reason, why some think of God with trouble, that *they have a mistaken view of God's manner of dealing with us in this world.* We wish to speak here of a class more advanced than any we have yet adverted to, comprising many sincere and enlightened Christians. They have thought very earnestly about God; they have a clear view of the way of acceptance through Christ; they are very desirous to be delivered from all that is opposed to the divine will; and yet they have trouble in thinking about God. There are so many things in the world most dark and dismal which He permits—so much of difficulty in the Bible which they feel He could have made more clear—such troubles in our life, in what we may call our true life, our spiritual life, which we long to have ended, and which still go on. What volcanic outbursts of human iniquity, what slow progress of the only thing that can cure it, how our way is hedged in with thorns, even when it seems the way of duty, how our prayers, do as we will, scarcely rise above the level of our lips and appear to bring no answer! It is impossible to enumerate all those troubles, for every Christian has his own, but the strange thing regarding them is that the remembrance of God comes to add to them. The most earnest and thoughtful natures often feel this most. They are pained, as when the character of a beloved friend is concerned whom they dare not question but cannot understand. God has the power to end this sore struggle, to put down sin and doubt, and bring in the blessed reign of righteousness and peace for which our hearts are sighing; and why then does He not act? Why at least does He not speak? If He would only utter his will more distinctly, show them the end and tell them what to do, how gladly would they spring to their feet and press through fire and water to fulfil it! I know that this passes through many hearts when they think of God, and troubles them by night and day. It was the perplexity of Asaph when he wrote this psalm; it was the pang in Job's heart worse than the loss of all his substance or the reproaches of his friends; it was the stumblingblock of Jeremiah, "Righteous art Thou, O Lord, when I plead with Thee; yet let me talk with Thee of thy judgments: wherefore doth the way of the wicked prosper?" It was foretold by Christ, "Because iniquity shall abound, the love of many shall wax cold;" and, still more wonderful, it finds its echo from the souls under the altar, "How long, O Lord, holy and true?" (Rev. vi. 10.)

Does it not seem very strange that in a revelation of the will of God there should not only be no attempts to solve these questions, but that this revelation should be so filled with the expressions of them? When we consult these inspired men, instead of answering us they say, 'We have felt these very doubts.' And yet they do give us the answer by showing us in what way they found peace. It was not by the intellectual solution of their doubts about God's procedure, but by the repose of the soul on God himself and its fuller life in Him. It was thus that Asaph gained it and ended this psalm in calm repose. So Job had his murmurings quieted: "I have heard of Thee by the hearing of the ear, but now mine eye seeth Thee; wherefore I abhor myself, and repent in dust and ashes." The souls beneath the altar have white robes given to them, and are bidden "rest for a little season." In heaven itself repose is gained not by seeing all God's way, but by the assurance of acceptance and life with God. This makes the Bible a grander and more solemn book than man would have made it, not a text-book of speculative theories, but a history of souls that have found their rest in God, with Him in the centre who made it possible for them to find it, and who himself leads the way through struggle and shadow up to the clear face of God. This fits best into the system of our world, which, disordered by sin, is a world of struggle and trial, the hard portal to new and regenerated life, a world where the great lessons are not those of knowledge, but reverence and humility and trust in God.

These questions of God's ways are still for our study, for nothing that belongs to Him can be indifferent to us, and earnest souls will thirst for light on all that concerns Him. But we shall not wait for the answer before we embrace Him; we embrace Him first that we may find rest, and from that centre pursue our search, or calmly wait till God disclose it. The Gospel proposes God in Christ to the soul that feels its sin and want and misery, and invites it to make full trial of Him in every emergency of life and death. It assures us that we shall find Him able to keep that which we commit to his trust. Myriads have found it so, and left their seal to his truth; and you that have tried it know that in proportion as you have trusted you have found Him faithful. It is in the experience of this divine life that doubts melt away or can be held in quiet expectancy of a solution, and that we approach gradually to the calm of those that rest beneath the altar. He who has learned to trust his soul with God, and felt it safe in his hand, can trust Him with all else. I would not forget that this, too, demands often a sore struggle both in the beginning of our spiritual life and in many of its onward stages. The darkness that gathers on the face of the world rolls in at times upon the individual soul, and all is wrapt in gloom. Then comes the time for that grand utterance of the prophet that has held up many a sinking heart, "Who is among you that feareth the Lord, that obeyeth the voice of his servant, that walketh in darkness, and hath no light? let him trust in the name of the Lord, and stay upon his God" (Isa. L. 10). The soul is capable of this sublime act of faith—this faith that comes not of despair but from the deepest instinct of the spirit of man inspired and guided by the Spirit of God—capable of trusting God where all in God himself seems dark. Have you felt it? are you feeling it? be sure that never was such trust betrayed. As sure as the gloom of the cross yielded to the light of resurrection, as day succeeds night, as the ordinances of heaven fail not, so sure will God have his present strength for you, and his coming song. The thought of God that for a while brings trouble shall be made the source of hope, the pledge that all with you and with his universe shall be ordered to a happy end, and even here amid the trouble and struggle of earth He can put into the mouth some notes of the praise of heaven: "I will sing unto the Lord as long as I live : I will sing praise to my God while I have my being. My meditation of Him shall be sweet. I will be glad in the Lord."

XXII.

THINGS PASSING AND THINGS PERMANENT.

"And this word, Yet once more, signifieth the removing of those things that are shaken, as of things that are made, that those things which cannot be shaken may remain."—
HEB. XII. 27.

THE voice which in times past shook the earth was the voice of Jesus Christ, as one may see by comparing verses 24-26 immediately preceding. This proves the transcendent dignity of Christ, which it is an object of this epistle to show. The time when his voice shook the earth was at the giving of the law from Mount Sinai. The mountain trembled, and Moses said, " I exceedingly fear and quake." But the same great Lord has said, " Yet once more, and I shake not the earth only, but also heaven." This He said in the prophet Haggai (ii. 6), " For thus saith the Lord of Hosts ; Yet once, it is a little while, and I will shake the heavens, and the earth, and the sea, and the dry land ; and I will shake all nations, and the desire of all nations shall come." The giving of the law shook the earth, the giving of the Gospel is to shake earth and heaven. The concussion begins when Christ comes ; it is going on now ; and it will continue till the world receives its last shock, and falls asunder.

This is not a very common view of the Gospel history, but it has its side of truth. The Gospel cannot build up and make strong without shaking down. In the midst of the broken and perishing things of this world there are others that are immoveable and eternal, and the object of this process is to prove that they can stand the test. The things that are shaken are "things that are made." They are created things, and therefore they can be and must be changed. But the things that are not made cannot be shaken. They are things that belong to God's own nature, his truth and righteousness and love, which are unassailable and eternal, and give eternal power and life wherever they enter and become part of a creature. It is a very great thing for us to feel assured of this in the midst of the perpetual breaking down of everything around us. Well for us to know that outside in the world, and within our own souls, there are stable realities, and to see them, and to have them rising up and becoming stronger under the shock of every earthquake.

We shall, first, illustrate this law of things, and, secondly, show some of the benefits that result from it.

I. In illustrating the law, we may begin with the more general and come to the personal.

The Jewish dispensation was shaken, but the great realities enclosed in it remain. The coming of Christ in the flesh was the signal for the overthrow of that venerable and magnificent system. When He uttered the word "It is finished," the earth shook as did Sinai, and the rocks opened, and the veil of the temple was rent in twain. For a little while the effect was not visible, but soon the Roman armies came, the temple was burned with fire, the daily sacrifice taken away, the priesthood abolished, the most expressive and beautiful ritual that ever existed, the only true ritual that ever did exist, was annulled, and the Jewish people ceased to be the Church of the living God. That shaking broke to pieces a divinely-instituted system and the wreck of it can be seen in a nation still scattered over the face of the whole world.

x

But there were things intended to remain. The daily sacrifice was taken away, but the great sacrifice of Christ abides to the world's close. There is no longer an earthly high-priest, but the Lord Jesus is entered in within the veil to appear in the presence of God for us. The temple is destroyed, but its floor widens out into the universal world, so that wherever a praying knee bends to God, or a true heart seeks Him, He is to be found. The Jewish nation has ceased to be the peculiar people of God, but there is a spiritual Israel, all of them priests to offer sacrifices continually, in lives holy and acceptable through Jesus Christ. The Jews of that age thought that all of the divine and true was perishing, but when the crash has passed and the dust of the collision cleared away we can see the real temple of God, rising as it ever must do calmly and majestically from the ruins of the old. The New Testament Church emerges like a spirit clothed in a new and ethereal body fitted for a greater time.

The forms of human society are shaken, but the principles that regulate it remain. This was true before the coming of Christ, and it seems as if the commotion in the world had been increased by his appearance. Christianity intensifies social struggles by pouring new light upon human rights and duties. The oppressed learn what belongs to them, and the oppressor does not yield without a conflict. This is the meaning of Christ's own word, "I am not come to send peace, but a sword." Since He came, the great Roman empire has been shattered to fragments. The kingdoms of modern Europe that rose out of it have changed their dynasties and limits and institutions countless times. Again and again the part of the world called Christian has altered its face, as if a deluge had swept it. The terrible wars that accompanied the Reformation, and the tremendous struggles of the French Revolution, are illustrations. Some look on these things with unmitigated dislike, and others with unalloyed terror. They tremble at the thought of ancient systems falling, lest universal anarchy should be at the door.

But there are great principles of right and freedom that assert themselves amid all changes. When God ordained that man should live in society, He placed these principles in his nature, and, though they may be buried for a while, they inevitably work themselves clear of the confusion, and rise up into a better shape, fitted for higher progress. They have two indispensable elements, law on the one side, and liberty on the other, and there is a constant struggle to bring these two into greater harmony, but neither of them can finally perish. Let us have confidence in the fact that God has made man for society; let us have faith in the experience of all past history; above all, let us have trust in the word of Christ, that the things which cannot be shaken shall remain. Every chaos has its harmonising voice, "Let there be light;" every flood its ark and its rainbow. Amid the tumults of nations and the guessing plans of politicians, a Christian man need never lose hope, for he has his foot on a kingdom that cannot be moved; and the communities of this world are being shaken and broken that they may be built up again, with more in them of that kingdom which is truth and righteousness, and which at last shall be peace.

Outward systems of religion are shaken, but the great truths of the Church of Christ remain. By outward systems of religion we mean the organisations that men form, with a particular human name and locality and administration; by the Church of Christ we mean the spiritual children of God, called together by his grace out of every country, and built on the foundation of the apostles and prophets, Jesus Christ being the chief corner-stone. We do not mean to undervalue outward church organisations. It is a very narrow way of thinking, under the guise of being broad, that would do so. God has made Christians for them as He has made man for society; He has put the principles that lead to outward association into the believing heart; He has laid down the great lineaments of such organisations in his word; and He has made it our duty to bring them as far as possible into conformity with the laws He has laid down. But the Christian nature is still more narrow that would shut itself up in any one of these, unable to look abroad on the large brotherhood outside, and to feel that there is a great, deep foundation that reaches beyond the base of our walls. These churches of men have been shaken, and must be again. Where is the church of Jerusalem founded by apostles, the church of Antioch where the name of Christian rose, the seven churches of Asia watched by the last and most loving of the disciples? The church of Rome, once so pure, planted by apostolic zeal, watered by the blood of martyrs, has been degraded by superstition, until she has rejected what apostles held most precious, and inflicted more martyrdoms than she endured. The churches of the Reformation have many of them denied that living word which was their sword of victory, and renounced or forgotten the justifying grace of Christ, which was the bread of life to famishing generations. What conflicts and changes there are in the churches of our own day! Sometimes a relapse to antiquated rudiments and outworn, empty forms, sometimes a downward rush to the most barren rationalism and denial of a present God and an ever-living Christ! There are some who, when they see such monstrous shapes coming from the churches that call themselves Christian, fall into utter scepticism, put the question which Pilate put in the presence of Christ,

"What is truth?" and turn away without waiting for the answer from Him. Others of timid nature fear that religion is about to vanish from the face of the world, and that we shall be left on a sea of doubt without a haven to seek, or a star to steer by.

But amid all these commotions of opinion there are things which God has settled, and which cannot be shaken. There are, first of all, the principles which He has implanted deep in human nature, the need of God himself, the yearning for something that goes beyond time and above earth, the cry of conscience when it feels the pang of guilt, of the heart when it sees at times the perfect and ideal and longs for it, and when it knows that both the vision and the aspiration are divine, the soul's affections in bitter bereavement that cannot stay in the sepulchres of their dead without despair, and that hope of immortality which has risen above the wreck of all passing faiths to put on new and higher shapes. Those are, in some form, as wide and constant as human nature, and they have this peculiarity, that as the lower wants are satisfied they rise more distinctly into view. They may seem to be buried for a while, but it is always to re-appear. No system of infidelity can ever reason them away, much less can it meet their requirements; and these wants, which cannot be dealt with save by acknowledgment, lie at the root of all religion. They are furrowed in the soil of human nature by God's hand for his own seed—foundation-trenches that are deepened by every earthquake, and refuse to be filled save by a divine structure. And then, with these wants, there are the truths of the word of God which meet them—God stepping forward in his Son our Saviour to pardon, to heal, to help and to hold up to view an immortal inheritance—God the Father for us, God the Son with us, God the Spirit in us—

one God over all, our God, blessed for ever. The great wants of man's soul cannot be changed any more than the necessities of his physical nature, and the great truths of the Bible that satisfy them can no more be shaken than the ordinances of heaven that furnish man with bread and light and life. Churches may rise and fall, and human creeds may seem to lose their hold of men's convictions and change their shape and drop away like worn-out garments, but the eternal verities of God abide, the seamless robe of Christ cannot be torn by any enemies, and the true spiritual Church united to its Head remains one, secure and unassailable. It is a blessed thing to have the conviction of this in the midst of religious convulsions, to feel that these cannot touch our faith and hope; and they are the best Christians who, while they seek the good of their own particular church, constantly expect the end of conflicts in a larger brotherhood and in the One Name which the mouth of the Lord shall name.

The temporal circumstances of men are shaken, but the great possessions of the soul remain. There are few who pass through life without experiencing many changes in it. The calamities that overwhelmed the early years of Joseph and Job and David are not exceptional, and the calm sunset that shone on them is not always granted. Perhaps there never was a time when there were greater struggle and anxiety about the surroundings of life, and more rapid falls from affluence to privation. When the nations of men are shaken, every home and every heart now vibrates. What changes, too, in the relationships of life! Those who were encircled with families like a flock have to walk almost alone to the grave. Death is shaking our friendships as the autumn winds do the trees, and leaves fall thicker at every gust. Increasingly we feel that our affections can have no fixed home under any roof below the skies. All our possessions are in things of earth, and we hold them by a clay-tenure. Disease and pining sickness fall upon men till at their best estate they are seen to be vanity. In any case, age comes sure and not slow, till the keepers of the house tremble and the strong men bow themselves and the earthly house of this tabernacle is shaken to dissolution. Perhaps the saddest change of all is that which takes place in our feelings. How different the dreams of the opening of life from the realisations of its close! What broken hopes, what frustrated aims, what a poor handful of ears for the rich sheaves we saw before us! So God shakes our lives till all seems gone, things of possession and things of promise.

And yet, the while, the soul may have within its grasp things that cannot be touched, that youthful expectations once thought little of, but that now grow into bright and great realities. It may have faith rising to God and laying hold of the treasure that nothing can endanger or diminish. It may have hope going down like an anchor and keeping the heart stable in every storm. It may have love within and around, dwelling on the things of God and giving, in communion with Him, a peace in trouble that is above all earthly good. If these have become part of the soul they may be clouded, but they are never lost. When we lose hold of them Christ holds them fast for us, and brings them out like stars over drifting sky-rack, and brightens them as night deepens. We have seen the aged Christian, from whose memory the very names and faces of his children were blotted out, looking with an undimmed eye on the face of Christ, weak and wandering in all things else, but clear and consistent on eternal truths, and dwelling on them with the freshness of youthful affection. There is surely something sublime in a man standing with his feet firm on the unseen rock of eternity, when the waves are reaching unto his soul—whole and unbroken in his noblest nature and in the shipwreck of all the powers that bind him to time. If men would think, it is proof of the divinity of the Gospel, and of the almighty hand of God that can put something into the heart which cannot be shaken, when all things else give way.

The material frame of man is shaken, but the immortal spirit remains.—We have adverted to the commencement of this in disease and old age, and it certainly goes on till the earthly house is dissolved. Our life is removed from us like "a shepherd's tent," where pole after pole is taken down and you cannot tell where it stood. The tenant is gone and the tenement, and the place that knew them knows them no more.

But there is, notwithstanding, something indestructible in man, and few have sunk so deep in materialism as to have lost all feeling of it, even in a natural way. Where the divine life enters, it brings with it not only the promise but the pledge and foretaste of the immortal life. The light of faith already spoken of, shining when all else that looks out at the windows is darkened, is one of its foretokens. Augustine said of his mother, Monica, that the crevices of the falling tabernacle only let the celestial light shine in more clearly.

"The soul's dark cottage shattered and decayed
 Lets in new light through chinks that time has made."

And when death gives the last shock to the frame the work is completed. The soul is that light in Gideon's pitcher which shines out most clearly when the earthen vessel that held it is broken. The soul, we have every reason to believe, retains in the separate state its inherent powers of thought and feeling, and in due time it will draw up the body to a blessed assimilation with it, and make it a fitter organ for doing God's work. When we see around us with pain, or feel with shrinking, the signs of this decay that is to end in dissolution, we should strive to fix our thoughts on the other and permanent side. Though the outward man perishes, the inward man may be renewed day by day. There may be a growing life within, corresponding to the growing death without, and the one may be conditioned and, through the grace of Christ, carried on through the other. The law of decay may be promoting the law of life; and death, which is the completion of the first, is the full assertion of the second, —the entrance of divine life into its true and proper sphere. It cannot be otherwise. If in every change in God's world we perceive a permanent residuum, a soul of things left, that goes on to live in a higher way, what are we to say of this spiritual and divine life that has in it more than all these other things, for it has in its personality the conscious love and likeness of God? This surely, that while they continue in their manner and sphere it must also have its own in which it survives,—a life of conscious love and likeness to the Father of spirits.

Last of all, we observe, as an illustration of this law, that *the whole system of nature is shaken, but the new creation remains.* The time is coming when, as there is an hour of death to each individual, there shall be also to the framework of this part of God's universe. Its own construction testifies to this. We can see that it had a beginning, that it has a development, and this points to a close, as the growth and ripening of the fruit indicate its fall.

They are as much opposed to reason as to Scripture who say, " Where is the promise of his coming?" They may see it written, not only in the living pages of God's Book, but in the dead tablets of stone beneath our feet, and in the fiery scroll of suns and planets. The chronometer of the world is not made to go on for ever. It is wound up for its time and proclaims its own hour of doom. The voice that shook Sinai, that rent the rocks on Calvary, that is swaying by its powerful breath all the movements of our earth, shall be heard over land and sea, and all nature shall shake at its word.

But that last great earthquake is not, any more than those that went before it, to end in destruction. We, according to his promise, look for " a new heavens and a new earth, wherein dwelleth righteousness." The fire is a destroying fire to the evil, but also a purifying and transmuting fire, as when the mixed ore is cast into the furnace, and comes out at last a vessel of noble fashion and brilliancy, fit for the Master's use. That which we can trace in all past eras, rising still to a better and a brighter, must reach its brightest and its best if there be truth in earth or heaven. The passing things in the universe must lead to something permanent, for time no more than space can have a sea without a shore. That new material creation shall be suited to the nature of man's glorified, material frame, as that frame is suited to his perfected spirit. It must be free from all the elements of disorder and decay that press upon us here —a soil that never opens for a grave, a sky that never darkens with a cloud; to describe which God's word fails, because it can only use figures drawn from things that are passing, and speak to finite minds enclosed within these limits. I do not know if there is anything that can give us a higher idea of that great end than this, that it is *the end*—the close to which all the events and processes around us are conducting—the one permanent, imperishable result of the history of the universe. Everything that our eyes look upon, however grand or glorious, is a "thing temporal," a passing thing, only a covering for the invisible and the eternal, and its movement, its shaking, its decay is but the heaving of the unseen and enduring world beneath and behind it, that is struggling to come into fitter form and fuller life. It is the eternal God conducting his world on through these changes to an eternal issue—for " I know," the wise man says, " that whatsoever God doeth, it shall be for ever." He, as befits Him, can work only for the permanent, and when it is gained it shall be worthy of his nature, and of all this long and terrible history that fills our minds with such awe, and our hearts with such pain. When the curtain is gone, and the enduring result appears, He, with his everlasting work, may be addressed as in that noble hymn of the ancient church: " They shall perish, but Thou shalt endure; yea, all of them shall wax old like a garment; as a vesture shalt Thou change them, and they shall be changed: but Thou art the same, and thy years shall have no end. The children of thy servants shall continue, and their seed shall be established before Thee."

II. We now come to indicate, for we can do little more, some of the benefits that result from this law. Could not God, it may be asked, have made a permanent world at first, without requiring us to pass through this process of change deepening so often to ruin? After all, this may be asking why God has seen fit to make this world under the condition of time, for, wherever time enters, change, as far as we can see, must accompany it. It may be that finite minds can learn, or at least begin their learning, only under some such forms of change as we see around us— processes of birth and growth and death and revival, taking place under our eyes, arresting our attention, and stimulating our study. It is a book where God is turning the pages to every generation, and giving it something new, an advancing development that bids men look back and forward. The world as we here see it is a becoming—a process where constant change is imprinted on all. There is a school of philosophy, from the earliest period down to our time, which has affirmed that this is all—that it is a BECOMING without a BEING, a course without an end, a covering curtain with nothing behind. Now the Maker of the world has all the while, to those who will seek it, given access to the unchanging in the midst of change. In the spiritual nature of man there is the possibility of this, and the apostle has told us that God has never left Himself without a witness to it in things around. Wherever a soul can come into contact with God there is the touch of the permanent, and as truth and purity and goodness are loved there is the assurance of it. A man may look on the changing surface of things and deny the eternal, as a man at sea may deny the existence of land; but it is all beneath and around him, and it is only on the fixed that the passing things can lie. Let us cast out our fathoming line into the depths of the soul, and we shall find it there, and feel that it passes away beneath us on to the great shore of the eternal world and of God. It has seemed fit to God's wisdom to put us through such a course of learning, where change should be so prominent, and yet the permanent never far off to those who will feel after it till they find it; and if we could understand all things we might see that the proportion in which the two are mingled is best suited to our present condition.

We come, however, to something more practical when we remark that this is a world into which moral disorder has entered, and that the painful changes that touch us are the consequence of it—the consequence of it, and yet an aid to the cure of it. Without sin there might still have been mutation, but it would have wanted the sting and the shadow. We have lost through our fall the true perception of spiritual and eternal realities, and we must be made to see them through painful contrasts. The pleasures, the affections, the hopes of earth perish, that the relations of the soul to God, its faith, its hope, its love may stand up stronger and clearer. The furnace is heated often seven-fold, that these three, like the holy children, may walk through it with One like unto the Son of Man, and when they come forth without the smell of fire on them we shall learn the power of their God, and trust Him in all the soul's future life.

It is by this process, too, that we not only see the greatness of these permanent things, but learn to cleave to them as our portion. This at least is the purpose, and if God's Spirit stirs the heart when his providence shakes the outward life this will be the result. When we see this world's wealth shaking, it is that we may seek the enduring riches; this world's friendships,—the Friend closer than a brother; this world's health,—the welfare of our souls; this world's solid frame,—the city which hath foundations. All things are made to tremble in the hand of man, that he may hear them saying, "Arise, this is not your rest!" —that divine and imperishable things may be felt to be indispensable, and through all eternity more dear; that the soul may strengthen its grasp of them, and plant its foot with firmer confidence on the Rock: "My foot standeth in an even place."

Still further, things that are shaken preserve those things that are to remain, until their suitable time of manifestation. They are wrapped round them, and fall away when men are ready for their reception. The ancient church could not have comprehended the spiritual truths of the Gospel, and these were enfolded in a system that spoke to their senses. God gives us earthly comforts and hopes, till He gives something better in their stead. A young Christian could not be reconciled to many things which the more advanced cheerfully accept. In our present state we could not bear the view of another world, and the veil is kept between, till our souls are attempered. Meanwhile, the seed of the incorruptible is here now—the seed of the everlasting inheritance in these frail hearts, of the glorious body in these dying frames, of the new creation in the world we look on. The things that perish encase them, as winter's snow covers the seed, as the husk the flower. When all is ready, the sun will come and the snow will melt, the husk will fall, the flower will blossom to the summer day, and we shall see that the things which perish have also their place in the plan of God. They are the veil between grace and glory, very needful, and only to be done away when that which is perfect shall have come, and we are ready to take possession of it.

What a joy to be assured in the midst of changes that sweep over all things round us, and roll in their waters on our souls, that there is something fixed and eternal! When everything that our hearts have rested on of the earthly, the deepest and dearest to our human spirits, shakes to dissolution, there is a deeper basement to which we can go down where all is immoveable, and which will give back whatever has the divine in it. This is the essence of true existence—the union of the soul with God. No permanence elsewhere; everlasting permanence here; and every change that takes place, when this union is formed, is but to give to this life with God more depth of assurance.

> . . . "All that is, at all,
> Lasts ever, past recall;
> Earth changes, but thy soul and God stand sure:
> What entered into thee,
> *That* was, is, and shall be:
> Time's wheel runs back or stops: Potter and clay endure."

What comfort to know that all the changes of earthly things are regulated by the voice of Christ! They may come at times as with the blast of a tempest, but they are measured with an infinite wisdom, so as to gain their end. They will touch nothing of the soul's true treasures; and, though they hide them for a while, it is to give them back again in a better and more enduring form. As He walks on these waves, his voice may be heard by those who listen, "It is I, be not afraid." He will still them as He stills our hearts, and bring us in safety to the desired haven.

It is Christ who shakes all things, but He stands unshaken. Amid tottering commonwealths and conflicting creeds and shifting scenes and dying friends and fainting hearts, He abides ever, and He shakes all besides that we may cling more closely to Himself alone. "To whom can we go but to Thee?" and as we come we shall find a peace and strength that are the pledge of the eternal life laid up in Him—"Jesus Christ, the same yesterday, and to-day, and for ever."

XXIII.

THE BETTER RESURRECTION.

"Others were tortured, not accepting deliverance; that they might obtain a better resurrection."—HEB. XI. 35.

THE eleventh chapter of the Epistle to the Hebrews is the roll-book of a noble army. Human history records the triumphs of knowledge and courage and energy; the divine history records the triumphs of faith—that great power which rises from earth to God, and passes from time into eternity. One of the brightest pages of this divine history is found in the Old Testament. The writer of this book looks to it, as a man might look up to the sky in a clear night when it is alive with stars, and he sees it all bright and blazoned over with the names and deeds of those who have done valiantly through their trust in the living God. He begins to count them one by one, and then they crowd upon him so thick and thronged that they cannot be reckoned up in order. They gather into clusters and constellations, like the seven stars and Orion, "clouds of witnesses," set there on high for spectators as examples.

Among these are found two groups mentioned in this verse—"Women received their dead raised to life again: and others were tortured, not accepting deliverance; that they might obtain a better resurrection." There is a comparison here to which we wish to turn your attention, but, before looking at it, we shall try briefly to show the meaning of the words.

This inspired writer teaches us that these ancient saints were believers in a resurrection to eternal life. It is strange that this should ever be doubted. It seems clear they were, when we think of the very instinct of the spiritual life—of such expressions as those of David: "I shall be satisfied when I awake with thy likeness"—or of the language of Martha and Mary when they were still standing on Old Testament ground: "I know that he shall rise again in the resurrection at the last day." Their faith could not have the certainty and clearness which ours should have; but that they did look forward to a life to come there can be no question. They gave the best evidence of their faith, for they submitted to the most cruel tortures and to death, that they might obtain a better resurrection. But what are we to understand by a *better* resurrection? If we look to the first clause of the verse we shall see—"Women received their dead raised to life again." This was one kind of resurrection, a restoration to the life of this world, and to achieve it was a great triumph of faith. But there is another and superior resurrection—to the life of the eternal world—and the faith which carries men to this is of a nobler kind, because it is more difficult. The meaning will be more clearly seen if we render the words so as to bring out this comparison—"Women received their dead again by resurrection; and others, that they might obtain a better resurrection, were tortured, not accepting deliverance."

The women who thus received their dead are recorded in the Old Testament. There was the woman of Sarepta, in Sidon (1 Kings xvii. 17), whose child was raised by Elijah; and there was the Shunammite woman (2 Kings iv. 18), who had her child restored by Elisha. But there must have occurred also to the mind of the writer those women whose history is given in the New Testament—the widow of Nain and the sisters of Bethany—and therefore, in speaking of this subject, we shall keep them also in memory. Those who were tortured, not accepting deliverance, may have been such men as Isaiah, who is said to have come to a violent death by persecution, and the martyrs to the true Jewish faith in the time of Antiochus. In the New Testament there were men like John the Baptist and James and Stephen, who, when they could not retain life with a good conscience, freely surrendered it.

There are then two spheres of faith—that of those whose dead were brought back to a resurrection in this life, and that of those who pressed on for truth's sake to a better resurrection in the heavenly life. The first of these has given place to the second, in the midst of which we live; and we shall consider these three things—the better resurrection—the higher faith required for it—and the means by which this higher faith may become our own.

I. We have to consider THE BETTER RESURRECTION.

Imagine to yourselves an event you must in all likelihood meet, or which many of you may already have passed through, when some object of your dearest affection has been torn from you by death. There is the utter blank of desolation—the light of the eyes in which you could read tenderness and truth, quenched—the heart that beat to you as no other on earth, motionless—no ear to listen to you, though you had the most bitter griefs to tell—no counsel or comfort, where you could always find it, however sore bestead. And if there came, in that day of darkness, One who gave you back your dead to be with you, to listen to your history of grief—of this very grief—to take your hand in his again, and make you feel he was yours as before—more than before—what could you ask, what could you think of, better than this? It happened once at Bethany: a woman received her dead raised to life again, and a poet has attempted to describe it :—

> "Her eyes are homes of silent prayer;
> Nor other thought her mind admits
> But, he was dead, and there he sits,
> And He that brought him back is there."

But Scripture is silent, and leaves the joy unspoken of as too great. And yet if we could for a little rise above feeling, and appeal to reason—the reason which comes of faith—we might see that there is a better resurrection.

For think of the *place* of it. However quiet and happy the home might be to which the earthly life was brought back, it was part of a world which was smitten with the curse. Cares and fears and dangers and griefs were always ready to invade it. Bethany, with its tranquil retreat, was near Jerusalem, with its stormy passions, and it felt their terrible throb. I think sometimes of the joy that was in it when Lazarus was brought back, and then of the consternation which entered it on the day of Calvary, when the great Friend was taken away. Or I think of the scenes that followed Christ's death, when Olivet was the marching-ground of Roman armies, and the temple perished in flames and blood. Better for Lazarus and Mary and Martha if they were not there to look on it, but had reached that higher home, where "desolation and destruction and the famine and the sword" cannot come. And, if we think of the body as the place to which the soul is brought back, it is a home that has also the curse resting on it, subject to pain and disease, which often make death to be chosen rather than life—to long torturing agonies, and to those strange depressions which cloud the soul, so that to those who look out at the windows everything is darkened.

It is otherwise with the place of the better resurrection. It can be most fitly described in the language of God's own Book:—"There shall in no wise enter into it anything that defileth, neither whatsoever worketh abomination or maketh a lie. And there shall be no more curse —and there shall be no night there; and they need no candle, neither light of the sun; for the Lord God giveth them light, and they shall reign for ever and ever." And the body which here depresses the soul shall be framed to lift it up, to give it perception and vigour, insight and wing, made like unto Christ's glorious body; for "the earthly house of this tabernacle shall be dissolved, and they shall have a building of God, an house not made with hands, eternal, in the heavens."

Then think, by way of comparison, of the *company* in the place. In the case of all those who were raised again to life in this world, we find that they were restored to the family circle—the child of the Shunammite and the daughter of Jairus, the son of the widow of Nain and the brother of Martha and Mary. There was an anxiety, if I may so speak, to surround them with their nearest friends when they opened their eyes again, that the first faces they looked on might be those of kindred—of father, mother, brother, sister. It was a merciful arrangement, to break the strange transition, to soothe the agitated, wondering spirit. But there was surely something more in it than this. It was, I think, also predictive. For if these resurrections, as a whole, were intended to help men to the faith of a power stronger than death, they were also intended to lead us to something of the manner of the life beyond. Do they not shadow out this truth, that God will begin our life again among those we have known and loved, and cause us to open our eyes in the bosom of what we shall feel to be a family and a home, with faces round us that are dear and familiar, and voices, whose tones we know, ready to reassure us? If it were not so —if the spirit had to awake all solitary, and pursue its way cut off from its past of life and love, we could not call it the better resurrection. Even in heaven, "the echoes and the empty tread would sound like voices from the dead." Bethany would have something of the blissful in the joyful reunion of souls, which heaven itself could not show; and therefore we must believe that there also God will "set the solitary in families," and that in some way broken household ties will be re-knit "in the day that the Lord bindeth up the breach of his people, and healeth the stroke of their wound."

Only, there will be something better in it. In this world our dearest friends become at times more dear to us. Some glow in them, or in us, suffuses the soul, and we feel that they are more ours, and we can be more theirs—times when we see deeper into each other's nature and melt into one spirit—those times, above all, when we know that we are touching one another in the thought and life of God. Now, in that heavenly world, we shall have the best at their best. The feeling of sad distrust which sometimes comes over us, as if the truest human friendship had an element of selfishness in it, shall pass away. What we gain here, at intervals, in some chosen crisis of our life,—the meeting of souls in one, and profound, untroubled trust in the sense of it,—shall then be a fixed condition. This must be part of the meaning of that word, "They shall see eye to eye, when the Lord shall bring again Zion." Nor do I need to remind you how that company shall be enlarged—what a grand and glorious compass it shall take in, indicated in the saying of the apostle, "Ye are come unto the city of the living God, the heavenly Jerusalem, and to an innumerable company of angels, to the general assembly and church of the firstborn which are written in heaven." So that, while the heart has its centre in a home, it shall not grow narrow nor stagnate there, but move out on wide wing, and make its friendships among all the families of the redeemed. So deep and true in its love, and yet so comprehensive—a Father's house with many mansions—shall be the state of the better resurrection.

Think then of the *essence* of this eternal life. Its essence consists in its entire freedom from sin. The presence of sin in our nature is at the root of every other evil, and deliverance from suffering in heaven is connected with perfect deliverance from sin. "The inhabitant shall not say, I am sick: the people that dwell therein shall be forgiven their iniquity." Doubt about God and distrust of Him are the most painful of all things to any one who feels what the soul's life ought to be—a perfect repose in God's love, that there may be freedom and happiness in his service. This world to most Christians is a fitful struggle to attain a portion of this. When Moses said, "I beseech Thee, show me thy glory," he was answered that he could not see God's face, but that his name would be made to pass before him, as "the Lord God merciful and gracious." It is still the utmost we can hope for here, and we do not always enjoy it. But of the resurrection-state it is said, "They shall see his face; and his name shall be in their foreheads." That must be a happy condition when all of them shall feel the blessedness of the man whose iniquity is forgiven, and the subject which often causes anxious thought, 'Can I look to God as my friend and Father?' shall be settled for perpetuity—no doubt, nor shadow of a doubt upon it—

but quietness and assurance for ever. And when there shall not only be no guilt on the conscience, but no sin in the heart, no lurking sympathy with it, but every fibre of the root of poison extracted, and the tree of life shall find its counterpart in the perfect fruit of every redeemed soul! How blessed must that state be when there shall be no envy, nor uncharitableness to any one, nothing of humiliation or shame for having done or cherished what is impure and base, nothing of the feeling of lurking evil within, which makes us wishful, if it were possible, to hide our hearts from the sight of God! This is an ideal which it never entered into man's heart to conceive, which the gospel alone has taught us, and which we feel to be worthy of God and of our spiritual nature. It is the prize of the better resurrection, for when the apostle speaks of pressing forward to the high calling of God in Christ, he connects it with this, "If by any means I might attain unto the resurrection of the dead" (Phil. iii. 11).

But we have to think also of the *security* of this state. These resurrections of earth were a return to a world of change and death. Were it not for the great ends to be served, it seems a hard thing to oblige one who had fought a good fight and gained the victory to enter the lists again. After the joy of reunion would come the thought, But we have to part once more, and all the anxiety of sick-beds, the tears of farewells, the bitterness of death, must be renewed. The shadow has been retarded on the dial-plate, not removed—who shall be mourned next, when there is no great Deliverer to bid death restore his prey? Once to be raised to this world is twice to die. But the children of the heavenly resurrection "die no more; death hath no more dominion over them." The shadow is all behind, the light before, and the light shall no more go down. We can imagine, in some degree, the thrill of rapture at Bethany, when these women received their dead raised to life again, and the joy of the moment swallowed up, for a little, the fear of the future. But to be able to contemplate the future steadily and see every cloud gone, to know that the last fight is over for all who welcome one another on that blessed threshold, to have the power to turn to death and say, "O thou enemy, destructions are come to a perpetual end,"—who shall help us to imagine this?

There is one thing more without which the thought of this better resurrection would be incomplete—the *presence* to which it introduces. The best of these other resurrections brought their subjects into the earthly presence of the Son of God; but this, into his heavenly fellowship. At times we look back with longing desire to the intercourse which some of our fellow-men had with the great Saviour and friend of sinners,—to the Galilean hills and the house of Bethany and the upper chamber of Jerusalem. We cannot escape this. His presence was so near and human and homelike. And yet they did not enjoy it as we think. There was the veil of their imperfect vision, and of his humiliation, between. It is the light from his resurrection which lets us see so much more in Him, and which stirs up these desires. And in the better resurrection this will be completed. Christ will not be farther from his friends in his exaltation, but nearer them. For as the human nature in Him was intended to bring the Divine more close to us, so, the more we see the Divine in Him, the closer shall we feel the human. The more of God we feel in humanity, the more there is of true humanity to touch us. And it seems as if, after He rose, his friends felt a deeper power in his words, a more tender and tremulous sympathy in his nature. Think of Mary's cry of rapture when He spoke to her by his open grave—of the burning heart of the two as they walked to Emmaus—of the joy of the disciples when they saw the Lord,—and let us be very sure that this, and far more than this, is felt by those who have entered his presence, not only beyond His death, but beyond their own.

It is true their resurrection is not yet complete in itself, but it is, as they are, complete in Him. His hand is on their grave, his peace is in their heart. He bids them rest for a little season, and they wait in calm and happy expectancy, with an unalloyed and satisfying foretaste, for they have already felt that to depart and to be with Christ is far better.

II. We come now, in the second place, to THE HIGHER FAITH REQUIRED FOR THIS RESURRECTION. It needed very great confidence in the living God to believe that He could reanimate the dead frame which the soul had quitted for a few hours or days; but to face entire decay and mouldering dust, and to believe that those who sleep in it shall yet awake and sing, this requires a frame of soul still nobler. Let us mention some of its features, that we may aim at them.

It needs more of what I may call the *patience* of faith. The faith of the sisters of Bethany demanded one great effort, and the battle was gained. But ours cannot be so compressed. We have to bury our dead out of our sight, to wait the weary days and years, and "feel God's heaven so distant." Poor children of sorrow, you know what it is to be cheered by the first rush of comfort when you think of their happy change, and then to have the coldness of hope deferred creep over you, to realise the long and lonely way you have to walk before you meet them again. "Till the heavens be no more, they shall not awake, nor be raised out of their sleep." This needs patience. We must endure the scorn of unbelievers, the talk of unchanging earthly laws rolled like the great stone to the door of the sepulchre, and must listen to the taunts of those who rejoice most when they think they hear the iron gates of a materialistic universe grate in upon the grave as an eternal prison. We have to struggle with the murmurs of our own hearts, that it is hard in God to put us to so long and so sore an encounter. If we had but one grand heroic effort, we sometimes say, we could nerve ourselves for it, but this harassing warfare, day after day, with fightings without and fears within, is more than we can bear. And yet, you see, there are those who have endured it all—of whom the voice from heaven has said, "Here is the patience and the faith of the saints."

It needs also more of what we may call the *sanctified imagination* of faith. The circle of these earthly resurrections was very narrow and very simple compared with that which we expect. Their faith had only to bring back their dead to the old accustomed house, the well-known seat, the familiar haunts. Ours has to win out a footing for itself from the void and formless infinite, where the scenes and inhabitants and states of mind are so different that our friends seem to have passed away beyond our knowledge. Our thought falls back, like a bird whose wings find the air too thin. 'If we could only see them for one little minute,' we say, 'as they are, we should walk on, so satisfied and calm in heart, till we meet them again. But the very light in which they live makes their state so dark to us.' Yet there are those who have risen above this also. There is an imagination of faith, not unbridled nor unscriptural, which has formed for itself a true and real world beyond death, which gives substance to things hoped for, and thereby helps to the evidence of things not seen. The Bible has encouraged it by its figures—"the tree of life," "the river of life," "the city of gold," "the Father's house of many mansions,"—and imagination has no nobler work than to enter among these visions, and brood and muse till they become a palpable and real world: and till those who are not, because God has taken them, are seen walking there. "Now," says the most vivid of such true dreamers, "just as the gates were opened to let in the men, I looked in after them, and behold, the city shone like the sun; the streets also were paved with gold, and in them walked many men, with crowns on their heads, palms in their hands, and golden harps to sing praises withal. Which when I had seen, I wished myself among them."

This better resurrection needs more of the *spiritual insight* of faith. The faith of those who received their dead back to the present life had a visible Helper with wonder-working power standing before them. God was pleased to vouchsafe them such aid because they required it. Their faith could take but short steps, and his hand was put out to uphold its infant goings. Our faith has not such aid. It has a harder, but a nobler work. It must seek to live as seeing Him who is invisible. It must rest for its ultimate foundation, not on any outward sign, not even on any uttered word as spoken to the ear, but on the nature of God himself, and the life He infuses into the soul—on that basis which Christ has given it, "God is not the God of the dead, but of the living." Christ himself must be known to us in his ever-living, spiritual power. "I am"—not "I promise"—but "*I am* the Resurrection and the Life;" and then it follows, "He that hath the Son hath life." This is harder, we say, but it is nobler. There are men who have risen to it, to whom the unseen Christ has been as sure a reality as the sunlight, and who have gained through Him a more glorious vision than sunbeams ever disclosed. "They saw the King in his beauty, and the land that is very far off."

III. We shall consider now, briefly, some of THE WAYS IN WHICH WE MAY STRENGTHEN OURSELVES IN THIS HIGHER FAITH.

It is necessary that we should limit our view here, and therefore we shall take only some of the thoughts immediately connected with our text.

The first thought is one addressed to *your reason.* We read here of men who were tortured, not accepting deliverance, that they might obtain a better resurrection. They surrendered all that life holds dear, and life itself, from loyalty to the God of truth. Not only is the Bible full of this, but the course of history. The noble army of the martyrs is seen in every age, marching on, by scaffold and through fire, into the unseen. I do not appeal to them now to confirm the truth of any one doctrine, but to prove this, which lies at the root of all doctrine, that the soul of man can love truth more than life. If you will think of it reasonably, it will give you a conviction that in man there is a principle above what can be given by dead matter, and that the system of the universe must be framed in some way to meet this fact. Can you imagine that their self-devotion was founded on delusion, and that God has made his world so that the noblest and divinest deeds in its history have a perpetual falsehood at their heart? Then the temporisers and hypocrites would be the wise men, and the faithful unto death would be the self-deluded fools. Even if a man were to say, "There is no God," would not a universe that grew up to moral perception by the strength of a lie—that cheated true men in order to build up truth,—would not such a universe be a self-contradiction, and a thing of deserved contempt? It would falsify our holiest instincts, and be at everlasting war with the soul's deepest voice. And, therefore, as we believe in the honest structure of the universe, we believe in God, and, believing in God, we must hold that these men were advancing through death to a great reality. You may see kindling on their faces the reflection of an eternal sunrise, the light of the better resurrection.

The next thought we draw from the context is one addressed to *your heart*. "Women received their dead raised to life again." Observe the expression, "Women —*their* dead." That side of human nature which has the deepest affection is clinging to *its* dead, claiming an abiding right of possession in them, and aiding faith to draw its lost treasure back to its arms. And it is a striking truth that in all the resurrections of which we read there was not only strong faith, but deep love—the love of woman. When Christ raised the daughter of Jairus, he took in with Him the father and the mother of the damsel. When He saw the widow of Nain weeping, He had compassion on her, and said unto her, "Weep not;" and He said unto the young man, "Arise," and delivered him to his mother. When He saw Mary weeping, and the Jews weeping which came with her, He was moved to perform his greatest work, and cried with a loud voice, "Lazarus, come forth!" And Christ himself was no exception. There were tears of women heard outside his grave; and He listened and yielded to their love as well as to their faith: and they too received their dead raised to life again—the ground and the pledge of every other resurrection to life eternal. Let us not think that these things are without a meaning. God intended that our deepest heart affections should be the helpers of our highest hopes, and the instinctive guarantees of a life to come.

When the Shunammite woman came to the prophet to tell him of her dead son, she said, "Did I desire a son of my lord? did I not say, Do not deceive me?" As if she had said, 'Now that he has been given and taken away, I *am* deceived; my heart has been drawn out only to be mocked!' And if it were so that God had bestowed on us these yearning affections, and then taken away their objects for ever, He would be torturing us hopelessly by that which He has put into us of the most tender and pure. We have a right to reason that He would either have made our love less deep and lasting, or that there must be a final home in which its longings shall be realised. Every pure affection points us towards a city in the skies; every happy Christian home is a pledge of it; every bereaved heart is a divine reason for it. A ground this why you should make your family ties so loyal and sacred that they shall keep your dead still yours, and bind you irrevocably to a life to come.

The last way we mention of confirming ourselves in this faith is addressed to the *spirit*. It is gained by the exercise of that spiritual insight to which we have already referred, leading the way to a spiritual life. The object of this sight, and the source of this life, is described by the sacred writer in words that follow—"Looking unto Jesus the author and finisher of our faith; who for the joy that was set before Him endured the cross, despising the shame, and is set down at the right hand of the throne of God." Reasoning about immortality may lead us so far, and the instinct of the heart may lead us further; but I know of no certainty save what grows from union with the dying and risen and living Son of God. Some men may speak of this as mystical, and regard us as visionaries; but they are words of truth and soberness, and have been tested in the calm, constant life, and happy, hopeful death, of thousands upon thousands of our fellow-men. It is not only possible to some, but open and offered to all, to become so conscious of God's sustaining grace, in duty and in trial, to be so joined in fellowship to an unseen but real presence, that we shall feel we have a life formed in us which can never die. There is a spring of immortality not only welling out from the throne of God, but ready to rise up in every heart that will admit Him who is the true God and eternal life. It is this faith entering into the soul as a vital principle which formed those ancient martyrs, who counted it all joy to face suffering and shame, and to meet death, when the God of truth summoned them. They are sleeping, wide apart, in the catacombs of Rome, and the Greyfriars of Edinburgh; and it was no vague guess, no nebulous haze of sentiment, that made them fill those graves; but because Christ's own life in them had made them partakers of the powers of the world to come. It has been asked by some who hang garlands on their sepulchres, 'Who would be martyrs now-a-days?' and they add 'that the bitterness of the question lies in its truth.' Those who make such a statement might surely ask themselves whether the principles held by them can possibly be the same on which these heroic souls of old lived and died; and they might further ask themselves whether the principles can be true which are confessedly unable to nerve men against the last extremity of duty and of trial. I thank God, and I am sure you can thank Him with me, that we have known men who would have been martyrs, and that we know them yet—men who have proved their allegiance to truth so fearlessly against reproach and loss—who have faced the "arrowy sleet and hail" of the bitterest calamities so calmly and nobly, day by day, as to make us feel with the surest conviction that they would have walked to the scaffold or the stake.

This is not a thing to promise for ourselves, but no man shall stop me of this boasting on behalf of men and women I have known. We may not be able on our own part to realise God's grace as so powerful in us that we could meet, here and now, the martyr's death. But one thing we can seek to do: We can let Christ's life rise in us as a life of humble obedience to the will of God. We can say in the sorest trial, 'I would not have it otherwise when it is He who puts the cup into my hand; I would not choose to live if He has seen the time fit for me to die.' And, even if we cannot yet advance to this, we can let our life be a following of God's will day by day; we can learn what it is daily to die to sin and self, being made conformable unto the death of Christ. And then, when the crisis comes, we shall be ready for it. The martyr's spirit descends on him when the fire is kindled, and the Christian's willingness to depart comes when his Master calls. There is the same grace for both, and the same triumph. "Thanks be to God who giveth us the victory through our Lord Jesus Christ!"

XXIV.

THE COMPLAINT FOR FRUSTRATED AIMS.

" Then I said, I have laboured in vain, I have spent my strength for nought, and in vain : yet surely my judgment is with the Lord, and my work with my God."—ISAIAH XLIX. 4.

THE final and perfect reference of these words is to our Lord Jesus Christ. The best proof of this is that the passage is applied to Him by the apostle Paul and by Barnabas (Acts xiii. 47); and, if any will not accept this authority, we have no further reason at present to give. These interpreters at the fountain-head tell us that Christ is the great speaker here,—He who comes as " a light to the Gentiles, as God's salvation unto the end of the earth." All the highest utterances of the Old Testament go forward till they find their complete fulfilment through the voice of the eternal and incarnate Word of God.

But they are in general, if not always, the utterances of living men like ourselves, and are real parts of human nature and history. These prophetic sayings go to Christ, not outside of and separate from man's struggle, but in and through it. As all true Christians are living over again, in an imperfect way, the details of Christ's own experience, so were all true godly men, before his coming, feeling their way into it, being guided by Christ's Spirit and having the throb of his life, which is the life of God, already palpitating in their bosoms. This is what makes the Old Testament a divinely permanent book: it contains the record of the felt weaknesses and wants, aspirations and hopes of the spiritual nature, stirred up by God himself, and taught to stretch out their longing arms to Him who is the Desire of all nations. It is God in the beginning of his new and higher creation, who is moving over the face of the waters, preparing for the time when He shall speak the word "Let there be light," and cause the day-spring from on high to visit his world. But the waters over which He moves are the great deeps of human hearts, that swell and utter their voice and lift up their hands on high while He passes over them. We never close rightly such far-reaching desires until they attain their end in the world's Redeemer, but neither do we begin them naturally unless we trace in them something of our common human feelings seeking their satisfaction and completion in Him. It is thus that we shall consider these words.

They bring before us a feeling that belongs to the human heart in all places and times—*the complaint of man for frustrated aims.* It is not easy to say in what distinct form it is present to the mind of the original speaker here. Sometimes he appears to express the feeling as his own personal experience—a man among his fellow-men—and sometimes he seems to personify the nation to which he belongs. Probably both are struggling together in his heart. The people of his race were selected by God for a great purpose—to hold up his name and knowledge pure and unsullied in the midst of the world's defections. But the purpose is, for the while, an apparent failure. The world has corrupted those who should have purified it, and God's judgment has fallen on their unfaithfulness till they are scattered among the heathen and ready to perish. It seems as if Israel's history were labour in vain. For himself, the prophet thought that he had been chosen to bring back his people to the way of truth and righteousness. God's word shaped itself like a sharp two-edged sword in his mouth, till he felt as if it must be irresistible, and that he was hidden like an arrow in the hand of an unerring marksman, to smite home to heart and conscience and bring down their pride into the obedience of truth. But the sword had found no entrance in the joints of the harness, and the shaft had glanced aside, pointless if not broken. The people have erred, the prophet has failed, and he speaks both for himself and for the best part of the nation, the true Israel of the Covenant,—"Then I said, I have laboured in vain, I have spent my strength for nought, and in vain."

I. The first thing we ask you to consider here is, *sorrow for the failure of labour*. In thinking of this we may go down to a still lower stage than that from which these words sprang in the heart of this man of God. The complaint is made by many who have never sympathised with his high aim or shared in his divine work. It is the cry that has passed on from generation to generation throughout the history of the world—the heavy sigh of toiling, yearning, unsatisfied humanity, "I have laboured in vain." Who has been always exempt from it, high or low? Who does not feel it, sooner or later, when he pauses for a time in the midst of the world's struggle and looks round to estimate his real gain? When we think of what life might be and the poor thing we have made of it; of the wonderful instrument put into the hand of the weakest of us, in being possessed of a soul capable of such development and influence, and that we have so idled with it, and dwarfed and debased it; when we recal perhaps the great visions which once glimmered before us of what might be accomplished by earnest effort, and then the miserable result, "the petty done, the undone vast,"—these words may well express our feeling.

Take the first of the two great objects that call man to labour—the gratification of self. Most men commence their work with this, and too many never pass beyond it. They make their personal pleasure in some form the centre of all their efforts. The desire of their heart may be sensual or airy—the spider may weave a web dusky and dense or threaded like silver—but it is still the same if self sits in the midst. The object may be animal gratification, the lowest and most evanescent of all the things that a man can pursue, or the acquisition of wealth and power, or fame and fashion, or knowledge and affection, the highest things next to the divine which a man can covet. It is not necessary to deny that these objects have their attractions, that many of them in their place have their own value; but it is well to consider how often men are brought to confess that they have spent their strength vainly in the pursuit of them. We may learn at least to moderate our ardour and to give them their proper place. How few prizes are drawn for the many blanks! The power and wealth have always gone to the minority, and must continue to do so;—no possible way of avoiding this. But that minority does not find in the prizes the pleasure which onlookers fancy. To think of this may be a consolation to some envious men, but to most of us, I trust, it is very sad. When some one spoke to Napoleon of his Italian campaign, and asked if that marvellous part of his career did not give him exquisite pleasure, he replied: "It did not give me one moment of peace. Life was only incessant strife and solicitude. The inevitable battle of the morrow might annihilate all memory of the victory of to-day." We cannot doubt that this witness was true. We may call to mind the saying of poor Keats when dying:

"I have written my name in water;" nor would it probably have comforted him much more at that time to think he had engraved it in marble. Even affection and sympathy,—how often are they not reciprocated, or returned with ingratitude, or felt to be not of the deep kind the heart had yearned for! All these things are frequent deductions from the prizes of life which men covet, and, even though they were gained to the full, there is one thing they all want— continuance. When a man is brought to look at the best of them and compare them with what his nature needs in its depth and breadth and length, he must say, "I have laboured in vain."

We have said that there are two great objects that urge man to labour; the first is self, the second is God and the good of his world. We may be thankful that many, even of those who are labouring for personal objects, mingle with their work a pure, disinterested kindness, and that there are some men in whom self seems entirely forgotten, who are consumed as by a burning passion to spend themselves in the effort to make God's earth better and his creatures happier than they found them. The speaker here was one of them, and it seems strange that he, too, is visited by a sense of failure. And yet it is not so strange. The higher a man's idea of what the condition of the world should be —of what a reign of righteousness and happiness there might be if God had his due place—the more likely is he to be depressed at times by the view of things around him, and the slow way in which all our effort is bringing us to the goal. Do we not feel as if the Gospel of the blessed God itself were doubtfully struggling to prove itself a success? Evils are cured so imperceptibly, if they are cured at all; they leave in one form, to return in another; and sometimes, instead of the demon we cast out, seven others worse than the first take its place. When we think of all that Christianity promised in the first flush of its spring—of all the glorious things which it hides in the germ—and when we compare the miserable ears, blasted with the east wind, with the rich harvest of a ransomed and regenerated humanity which we hoped for, it seems to us very often like labour in vain. All of you who have set to work earnestly to do good in your own sphere must have met with like disappointments, especially if you have commenced your work with high enthusiasm. How many teachers with their scholars, parents with their children, men with their fellow-men, and Christians with professed fellow-Christians, have laboured to educate and elevate and reclaim, and have felt the dead dulness of no result, no echo to their earnest appeals, or echoes that misrepresent and mock them! The seed you sow never perhaps springs, or if it does, it has the tares with it; or, it is so different from what you expected that it seems itself the tares. We have all such hours when disappointments crowd in upon us, and we feel as if we had spent our strength for nought and in vain.

II. Let us consider next some of the *temptations* to which this sorrow for the failure of labour is subject.

We may take first, again, that class of men who have set before them in life some personal object, and have been disappointed in it. Some of you have not succeeded as you would wish in the world's battlefield. You have not gained the position or the comfort or the reputation to which you think your merits and your efforts entitle you. Your affections have not been satisfied, and you have a sense of loneliness and want of sympathy. The great temptation in such cases is for men to brood over and magnify their disappointment. There are many who, because they have not gained some favourite object, hasten to the conclusion that life has no more any good for them. They embrace failure with a sort of morbid pleasure, and idolise grief. This is of all things the most barren, and their apathy becomes more selfish than their activity. Under the show of being weaned from the world, it has the very essence of worldliness. It is ready to turn over, not merely into despair about themselves, but into peevishness with all around them, envy at better success than their own, and discontentment with the arrangements of God's providence. The light-hearted cheerfulness that chases new objects still to be disappointed is better in the light of this life, and no worse in the light of another, than the moody spirit which frets at disappointment without learning any true lesson from it.

Then as to those who have a higher aim in life than any mere personal one—who are truly seeking the glory of God and the good of their fellow-men—they have also their temptations under failure. We are so ready to judge of the plan of the world by our own little share in it, and to think all the war is lost when our small detachment suffers a check. We have taken up some cause, of the excellence of which we are thoroughly convinced, but its chariot-wheels drag heavily or roll backward. We have set our hearts on reclaiming some fallen fellow-creature, and, notwithstanding all our efforts, there is no token of amendment, or our hopes are lifted up only to be cast down with a more bitter sense of defeat. Our sacrifices of means and time turn out to have been misapplied, and our kindness heartlessly abused. Such cases are occurring daily, and it is not to be wondered at that they make the hands of earnest workers hang down. It is not for gratitude they work, but it is very hard to go on labouring when it turns to no account. They have their confidence in human nature and even in divine truth greatly shaken; they feel as if evil in the world were an overwhelmingly gigantic enemy which it is hopeless to attack. It comes every day with its boastful challenge and its brazen armour, and God seems to stand aloof in indifference, till we are tempted to do the same and to put up the prayer, not in faith but in fretfulness—"Arise, O God, plead thine own cause." We have tried and failed, and shall try no more. Let God himself look to it. There is much of the apathy of indolence among Christian men; but we must all feel that there is much also of this apathy of disappointment, and that, even where it does not stop our hands, it lies like a stone upon our hearts, and prevents us going forward with that joyful vigour which is the fore-token of victory.

III. We shall now consider, in the third place, the *resource* we have in the midst of this sorrow for failure. It is in these words: "Yet surely my judgment is with the Lord, and my work with my God."

There are two things this speaker fixes upon, and they are a powerful stay if we can bring them as clearly and confidently to God as he did. "My judgment is with the Lord." I can appeal to his decision for the character of my motive. It was, so far as I knew it, pure and true.— "My work is with my God." I can cast on his decision the result of my labour. I have put it into his keeping, and I leave it there. I place myself with the aim of my life, both as to *how* I have pursued it, and *what* shall come of it, in the hand of the Searcher of hearts, and the Disposer of all things. "Judge me, O God, and plead my cause."

Now, I do not say that any mere man can do this with a perfect assurance that all is right with him, and that He who searches the hearts, and tries the reins, can absolve him as faultless; but I do say that there are men who, by the grace of God, can appeal to God himself for the sincerity of their aim, and that this is the steadfast pole-star of our life's voyage, which we should constantly contemplate—God's face upon our heart, and God's hand upon our effort—" My judgment is with the Lord, and my work with my God."

Let us see how it should influence both the classes we have been considering. Those men who have been seeking some personal object in life, and have failed in it, may learn much here. You have been striving for a position which is still far out of your reach—for some acknowledgment of your merits which is denied you—for comfort in the home life and the affections, which is never likely to visit you in this world. Let us take it for granted that there was nothing sinful in your aim, and that you did not wish for any good, inconsistent with the rights and the happiness of your fellow-creatures. It seems very hard to you that you should be denied what many of them enjoy, and you can scarcely help comparing your lot with theirs, with a sense of bitterness, at least of regret. Their brightness deepens your shadow. Your life seems a maimed and broken life, your home a cold and comfortless one, set over against theirs; and this world is to you, in a measure, a lost world. Now here is a more excellent way of it. Instead of putting your life beside theirs, refer yourself to God's judgment. Say, I have done all my honest endeavour to secure a place in the world, and I am here in this lower room notwithstanding. It is God's will then—my work is with God.

If you can put the case truly before the Judge and Controller of life, you may find something in your life to correct, and something also that will give comfort. May it not be that you have been making the aim of your life too narrow, even as it concerns your own welfare? You have been thinking perhaps, of worldly position and acknowledgment, more than of the building up of your character in what is true and pure and godlike—more of your outward than of your inward and real life. These failures may be to teach you to begin again, and to aim at a wider basement and a higher top-stone—to take into your edifice the soul's interests, and to let its front look Godward and heavenward. And you have been making, perhaps, the aim of your life too narrow as it concerns your fellow-men. You have made self too exclusive, and have been looking on your own things, but not also on the things of others. On a conscientious review, you may feel that you are to take their interests with you, if you are to have God's approval. "Except ye bring your brethren with you, ye shall not see my face." And if you come, after all the failures of life, in this submissive spirit to God for his judgment, He will give you not only means of correction but comfort. Though you may have lost what you once reckoned the good of life, there is another and higher good still open to you, not merely hereafter but here. God can teach you how to build on the ruins of former hopes—nay, He can show you how you may take the very stones of them that have fallen and lie scattered around, and may joint them into a new and more beautiful and enduring structure. "The city shall be builded upon its own heap and the palace remain after the manner thereof," and the faults and failures of the past shall give a strength and chastened beauty to your new and nobler life. You may never in this world have the keen thrill of joy your heart once panted for, but a conscious and deep peace will recompense its absence,—more satisfying and more abiding. Let no one who grieves over frustrated aims of personal happiness despair, if he is only willing to take his marred life and miserable handful of results and put them at God's disposal. When He instructs, it is said of Him that "He giveth to all men liberally and upbraideth not" (James i. 5) —never reproaches us with our narrow and foolish past; nay, sustains us against our own self-reproaches, and at last takes them away, when we see how our very failures are overruled to bring us to a higher place and fill us with a truer wisdom.

But there is a resource here, also, for that nobler style of men, who have laboured for the cause of God and their fellow-creatures, and have failed to find the success they sought. It may seem strange at first sight that there should be such failures—that a man should set himself to the best of all works with true and warm enthusiasm, and meet with defeat and disappointment. Yet there are some things which make it not so strange, if we will but reflect. Are we sure that our motives are always as high as we ourselves fancy, and may not failure be meant to send us back to sift and purify them? Our very despondency may arise from our having looked too much to success and too little to duty. We are poor soldiers if we make our fealty to our banner depend so much upon its glittering in the sunshine of victory. God must have standard-bearers who are ready to make a shroud of their colours, and how can they be known but in hours of defeat? In these disappointments He proves whether we are fit to keep our ranks in the noble army where martyrs lead on, and to fill up that which is behind of the afflictions of Christ, the Captain of our salvation. And though our motives are pure, is our work always wise? Do we choose our objects and our ways of gaining them with thoughtful discrimination; and are Christians to expect that carelessness and rashness will succeed, simply because of good intentions? He who sent out his followers on the greatest of all errands commanded them to be "harmless as doves," but also "wise as serpents." And even though all our benevolences were perfectly wise and pure, is it reasonable to expect certain or, as we should rather choose to term it, direct success? Success would then be the immediate test of rightness, and whoever failed would be at once thereby condemned. This would be to erect in this world the judgment-seat of God, and to destroy its purpose as a field of training for faith and trustful obedience. It would be to forget, moreover, that the higher the end to be gained, the more difficult and intricate the path to it. Man's conquest over the simplest material laws lies to his hand; his victory over her hidden uses, her subtle magnetic powers, demands laborious days and sleepless nights, and many a turning back from false pathways. To do good to men's bodies is a comparatively easy thing—to train their intellect more difficult; it is harder still to reform, even outwardly, their moral nature —and most arduous of all to reach and renew the springs of their spiritual life. "This kind goeth not out but by prayer and fasting." We need not be surprised if we have to work and wait and think and study, for the grandest of all results. It is a proof of wisdom to attempt to win souls, and it needs wisdom to succeed in the attempt. But the prize is worth the trial, and will repay all expenditure. "He that winneth souls is wise."

After all, however, the great resource we have is to fall back on this appeal, "My judgment is with the Lord, and my work with my God." If we can sincerely put our fruitless endeavour before the all-seeing eye, we shall have our final recognition all the same. Man judges by success, God by simplicity of heart; and many an unnoticed effort and inarticulate prayer that never seemed to touch the conflict shall share in the full triumph of the victory. "As his part is that goeth down to the battle, so shall his part be that tarrieth by the stuff: they shall part alike." "Kings of armies did flee apace: and she that tarried at home divided the spoil." There is no greater praise in all the Word of God, nor will be in the final award, than "She hath done what she could." But more than this, the result in God's world shall not be wanting. "Our work is with God." If we have done our part, let us be very sure that in some way He will do his, not as we expect perhaps, nor within our present vision, but in due time, and when we can watch it following us while we rest from our labours.

"No work begun shall ever pause for death."

If we cannot go now with our talents and say, "Behold, I have gained beside them five talents more," yet if we have not hidden our trust in the earth, if we have in any way put it out to the exchangers—put it, in the way of doing good, out of our sight and away from our hand— at his coming He will receive his own with usury. Much seed is germinating underground in silent hearts, green blades lie hidden beneath the cold indifference of spring snows; but when the Spirit's gentle breezes call, and God's sunshine of love invites, the seeming lost will be found, and dead things live, and far-off prodigals come back to hearts that despaired of their return. Ministers and teachers looking sorrowfully round to see so little promise, the mother weeping for a thoughtless son, the anxious wife praying in secret for a careless husband, the man who struggles as in deep waters to hold up his drowning fellow's head—will find in the day when the Lord of Hosts takes away the veil spread over all nations, and the Father of us all welcomes back his wandering children and wipes away the tears from off all faces, that not a work of faith, or labour of love, or prayer, or sigh of intercession, but did its part in helping some sinner in his way to the eternal home. Wherefore, "In the morning sow thy seed, and in the evening withhold not thine hand; for thou knowest not whether shall prosper, either this or that, or whether they both shall be alike good."

It would be unnatural to close this discourse on seemingly frustrated aims in life without recurring, however briefly, to Him with whom we commenced. These words of sorrow for failure, and of continued faith in God, went forward through many human hearts, until they were taken up and perfectly fulfilled in Him who bare our sorrows, and who is the author and finisher of our faith. God was pleased that He who came as the Son of Man, our brother, should have this also as one of his trials—to labour in vain. He came to his own, and his own received Him not; He stretched out his hands all the day to a gainsaying and rebellious people; He encountered dead indifference, fierce opposition, reproach, and calumny; He was betrayed and deserted; was lifted up on a cross in the midst of that Jerusalem over which He had wept in vain, died a malefactor's death, and was buried in a stranger's grave. Those of you who have failed to find position or comfort, fame or sympathy in the world may have One who can bear his share with you here, who chose this place in life, which you call loss, that He might be nearer you, and show you that life has greater things than all you have coveted. Those of you who complain that you have laboured for your fellow-men and God with small return, have One here who gave up infinitely higher things, and met from men a more cruel award. Is it not token of God's compassion that, into a world of loss and disappointment, of bruised hearts and shattered hopes, He sent his own Son to be the sharer of them?—their sharer, that He might show men how to bear them. He had his hours of depression as we have—true, real, deep—explain it as we will; but He put his motive before the eye of God, and left the result unto

Him. "He did not fail, neither was He discouraged." Through the clouds of depression He had star-like glimpses of the travail of his soul—the fruits of his toil that made Him say, "I thank Thee, O Father"—and that helped Him to press on till He uttered from his cross, "It is finished"—that grand prophetic word which assures us that every life which has sought to do the will of God is a complete and perfect life, whenever and however it may close. That word, "It is finished," repeats this saying which came up from his Spirit long before—" My judgment is with the Lord, and my work with my God." And all the highest good that has visited our earth for eighteen hundred years has come from that life and death of seemingly frustrated aims; all the harvests that angels will reap for heaven have sprung from the furrows by which He went forth weeping, bearing precious seed. The highest success in the universe of God has come from the deepest outward failure, to assure us that if we calmly move forward, setting our trust in the Lord and doing good, failure there can be none. One may sow and another reap; but he that soweth and he that reapeth shall rejoice together, and gather fruit unto life eternal.

Only, let all be done under the cover and trusting in the strength of Him who alone "works all our works in us." Let the sinful past come under this shadow to find forgiveness; the narrow and selfish life, to find a new and lofty aim; and all our fears and griefs and disappointments, to find comfort and hope in Him who entered the world to redeem it from fall and loss, and to make every true life succeed at last, even where it seemed to fail. "Therefore, my beloved brethren, be ye steadfast, unmoveable, always abounding in the work of the Lord, forasmuch as ye know that your labour is not in vain in the Lord."

PRINTED BY T. AND A. CONSTABLE, PRINTERS TO HER MAJESTY,
AT THE EDINBURGH UNIVERSITY PRESS.

www.ingramcontent.com/pod-product-compliance
Lightning Source LLC
Chambersburg PA
CBHW030402230426
43664CB00007BB/714